Jaguar Mks 1 and 2, S-Type and 420

OTHER TITLES IN THE CROWOOD AUTOCLASSICS SERIES

ALFA ROMEO 916 GTV AND SPIDER Robert Foskett

ALFA ROMEO SPIDER John Tipler

ASTON MARTIN DB4, DB5 & DB6 Jonathan Wood

ASTON MARTIN DB7 Andrew Noakes

ASTON MARTIN V8 William Presland

AUDI QUATTRO Laurence Meredith

AUSTIN HEALEY Graham Robson

BMW 5 SERIES James Taylor

BMW M3 James Taylor

BMW M5 James Taylor

BMW CLASSIC COUPÉS James Taylor

CITROËN DS SERIES John Pressnell

FERRARI 308, 328 AND 348 Robert Foskett

FORD CONSUL, ZEPHYR AND ZODIAC Graham Robson

FORD ESCORT RS Graham Robson

FROGEYE SPRITE John Baggott

JAGUAR E-TYPE Jonathan Wood

JAGUAR XK8 Graham Robson

JENSEN INTERCEPTOR John Tipler

JOWETT JAVELIN AND JUPITER Geoff McAuley & Edmund Nankivell

LAMBORGHINI COUNTACH Peter Dron

LAND ROVER DEFENDER, 90 AND 110 RANGE James Taylor

LOTUS ELAN Matthew Vale

MGA David G. Styles

MGB Brian Laban

MGF AND TF David Knowles

MG T-SERIES Graham Robson

MAZDA MX-5 Antony Ingram

MERCEDES-BENZ CARS OF THE 1990s James Taylor

MERCEDES-BENZ 'FINTAIL' MODELS Brian Long

MERCEDES-BENZ S-CLASS James Taylor

MERCEDES-BENZ W124 James Taylor

MERCEDES SL SERIES Andrew Noakes

MERCEDES W113 Myles Kornblatt

MORGAN 4/4 Michael Palmer

MORGAN THREE-WHEELER Peter Miller

PEUGEOT 205 Adam Sloman

PORSCHE 924, 928, 944 AND 968 Glen Smale

PORSCHE CARRERA – THE AIR-COOLED ERA Johnny Tipler

RELIANT THREE-WHEELERS John Wilson-Hall

RILEY RM John Price-Williams

ROVER 75 AND MG ZT James Taylor

ROVER P4 James Taylor

ROVER P5 & P5B James Taylor

SAAB 99 & 900 Lance Cole

SUBARU IMPREZA WRX AND WRX STI James Taylor

SUNBEAM ALPINE AND TIGER Graham Robson

TOYOTA MR2 Nigel Burton

TRIUMPH SPITFIRE & GT6 Richard Dredge

TRIUMPH TR7 David Knowles

VOLKSWAGEN GOLF GTI James Richardson

VOLVO P1800 David G. Styles

Jaguar Mks 1 and 2, S-Type and 420

James Taylor

THE CROWOOD PRESS

First published in 2016 by
The Crowood Press Ltd
Ramsbury, Marlborough
Wiltshire SN8 2HR

www.crowood.com

© James Taylor 2016

All rights reserved. No part of this publication may be reproduced or transmitted in any form or by any means, electronic or mechanical, including photocopy, recording, or any information storage and retrieval system, without permission in writing from the publishers.

British Library Cataloguing-in-Publication Data
A catalogue record for this book is available from the British Library.

ISBN 978 1 78500 112 3

Typeset by Jean Cussons Typesetting, Diss, Norfolk

Printed and bound in India by Replika Press Pvt Ltd

CONTENTS

	Introduction and Acknowledgements	6
	Timeline	7
CHAPTER 1	JAGUAR BEFORE THE COMPACTS	8
CHAPTER 2	DESIGN AND DEVELOPMENT OF THE JAGUAR MK 1	20
CHAPTER 3	JAGUAR MK 1 (1955–1959)	29
CHAPTER 4	DEVELOPING THE JAGUAR MK 2	51
CHAPTER 5	JAGUAR MK 2 (1959–1967)	56
CHAPTER 6	JAGUAR 240 AND 340 (1967–1969)	82
CHAPTER 7	DAIMLER V8 (1962–1969)	95
CHAPTER 8	DEVELOPING THE JAGUAR S-TYPE	109
CHAPTER 9	JAGUAR S-TYPE (1963–1968)	116
CHAPTER 10	DEVELOPING THE JAGUAR 420 AND DAIMLER SOVEREIGN	135
CHAPTER 11	JAGUAR 420 AND DAIMLER SOVEREIGN (1966–1969)	141
CHAPTER 12	SPECIAL VARIANTS OF THE MK 2, S-TYPE AND 420	157
CHAPTER 13	THE LEGACY OF THE COMPACT JAGUARS	170
	Index	175

INTRODUCTION AND ACKNOWLEDGEMENTS

This book combines the essence of two earlier books I wrote for Crowood – *Jaguar Mk 1 & 2, The Complete Story* and *Jaguar S-type and 420, The Complete Story*. It made complete sense to me to combine the stories of all four compact Jaguar saloons into a single book because all were developed from a single original design and all remained quite closely related. However, times have changed since I wrote those original books in the mid-1990s and more information has become available about some aspects of the compact Jaguar story. So this book contains some material that is old, and quite a lot that was not in the original volumes.

Some of the research I did all those years ago on the development of the original 2.4-litre Jaguar was originally published in *Jaguar World* magazine, and I am still grateful for that opportunity. Back in the mid-1990s, I was also privileged to interview Cyril Crouch, who had been Jaguar's assistant chief and later chief body engineer when the cars were being developed.

That was then, and I am pleased to acknowledge the more recent help of several people in bringing this present volume together. Karam Ram at the Jaguar Heritage Trust helped out with vital photographs from the factory archives, Simon Clay took a number of the photographs of all four generations of compact Jaguar, and Magic Car Pics provided the photographs I could not find elsewhere. The Kent Police Museum provided some fascinating photographs, and I am particularly grateful to Paddy Carpenter of the Police Vehicle Enthusiasts' Club for giving me access to the club's collective knowledge and photographic archives.

James Taylor
Oxfordshire
April 2015

TIMELINE

1955 (October)	2.4-litre model announced
1957 (February)	3.4-litre model announced
1957 (November)	2.4-litre Automatic becomes available
1959 (September)	Mk 2 models available with 2.4-litre, 3.4-litre and 3.8-litre engines
1962 (October)	Daimler 2.5-litre V8 announced, based on Jaguar Mk 2
1963 (October)	S-type announced, with 3.4-litre and 3.8-litre engines
1966 (August)	420 and Daimler Sovereign announced as further developments of S-type range
1967 (September)	240, 340 and Daimler V8-250 announced
1968 (June)	Last 3.8-litre S-type built
1968 (August)	Last 3.4-litre S-type built
1968 (September)	Last 340 and 420 models built
1969 (April)	Last 240 models built
1969 (July)	Last Daimler Sovereign built
1969 (August)	Last compact saloon of all built – a Daimler V8-250

CHAPTER ONE

JAGUAR BEFORE THE COMPACTS

When Jaguar introduced their new compact saloons in 1955, the company was enjoying an unprecedented wave of success. Most important in that success had been the US market, where the marque had been able to exploit the post-war fascination for European cars that would also make the fortunes of MG, Triumph and others.

To a considerable extent, that success helped to shape the basic parameters of the new compact saloons. Despite the radically new (for Jaguar) engineering that went into them, they had to conform to public expectations of the Jaguar marque. And those public expectations were inordinately high in 1955.

Jaguar's range for the year that preceded the compacts' introduction consisted of two basic models. One was the Mk VIIM saloon and the other was the XK120 sports car, available in either open or closed forms. The Mk VIIM was a large luxury saloon, offering spacious accommodation with a traditionally British wood and leather interior, while the XK120 was a stylish and charismatic two-seater. In many respects, they were as different as chalk and cheese and yet they had three very important factors in common: pricing, performance and good looks. It was these three charac-

The 1948 XK120 sports model was an oustanding success for Jaguar and was the first production car to have the company's own XK engine. The curvaceous shape was superb, as this photograph shows, and the wheel spats are a very modern touch.

teristics that defined the Jaguar marque for the motoring public of 1955.

It had always been Jaguar's policy to keep prices as low as possible, both in order to undercut competitors and to promote an image of value for money. In this, the Mk VIIM and XK120 were fully representative of the Jaguar tradition. The Mk VIIM was essentially a 'poor man's Bentley', and in 1954 its basic retail price, inclusive of taxes, was £1,616. The cheapest Bentley then available cost around three times as much. As for the XK120, which was similarly priced, its most obvious rivals came from the likes of Ferrari and Aston Martin, and all of them were vastly more expensive than the Jaguar.

High performance was also a Jaguar trademark, and the company had furthered its image in that field with a spectacular series of successes in international motor sport during the early 1950s. First had come the C-type sports racers (strictly known as XK120C models), which had won the Le

Looking positively benign as an older man in the 1950s, William Lyons (who would be knighted in 1956) still had a keen eye for a good shape.

JAGUAR BEFORE THE COMPACTS

Mans 24-Hours road race in 1951 and again in 1953. Then in 1954 had come the D-type, which won at Le Mans in the early summer of 1955. But perhaps the most important aspect of these and other sporting victories, as far as Jaguar customers were concerned, was that the sports racers depended on race-tuned derivatives of the same engine that powered both the Mk VIIM saloons and the XK120 sports cars.

That engine – the XK twin overhead camshaft 6-cylinder – had first appeared in 1948 and would not finally go out of production until more than forty years later. In road-going 3.4-litre form, it endowed the big Mk VIIM saloon with a top speed of 103mph (165km/h) while the XK120 laid claim to 120mph (193km/h) or more. For the early 1950s, this kind of performance was the stuff of which dreams were made: the average family saloon of the time struggled to reach 70mph (112km/h).

Both the XK120 and the Mk VIIM (announced as a Mk VII in 1950 and newly updated in 1954) were strikingly styled cars. Bulky though it undoubtedly was, the saloon looked elegant thanks to its graceful curves and sweeping wing-lines. It had a special sort of presence that was lacking in other saloons of its day, and when parked alongside the rather upright Bentleys and Armstrong Siddeleys of the early 1950s, it appeared low and streamlined. By contrast, it looked upright and traditional next to contemporary American machinery, but that very conservatism (a distinctly British characteristic) distinguished it from the crowd and endeared it to discerning Americans.

As for the XK120, its long and low lines – reminiscent of the sleek pre-war BMW sports cars – stood out in any company. Once again, graceful curves and sweeping wing-lines were the distinguishing features, and the Jaguar could hold its head up in the company of any fashionable Italian exotics from the styling houses of Pininfarina, Vignale, Touring or Zagato. Across the Atlantic, the only additional competition for the XK120 came from the Chevrolet Corvette, which at this stage did not have the attractive lines for which the marque would later become known.

JAGUAR'S ORIGINS

Styling more than any other factor was essential to Jaguar's roots. Back in the early 1920s, William Walmsley had moved his small motorcycle sidecar business from Stockport to Blackpool where he had met and entered into partnership

William Lyons was a keen motorcyclist in his youth. This photograph shows him in the 1920s astride a Harley-Davidson registered in his native town of Blackpool.

with the younger William Lyons. Walmsley's sidecars were notable for their elegant design, and the enthusiastic Lyons, who had served an apprenticeship with Crossley Motors in Manchester before joining the sales staff of a Sunbeam dealership in Blackpool, developed his eye for a good line from Walmsley's example. In 1922 they jointly formed the Swallow Sidecar Company, and their business was so successful that they were able as early as 1927 to branch out into making car bodies.

These car bodies had styling that was as distinctive and elegant as the sidecars, but Swallow stuck to a policy of offering bodies for relatively cheap cars. So, while many coachbuilders preferred to work on the grand luxury chassis whenever they could, Swallow instead provided special coachwork for possibly the most mundane chassis of them all, the little Austin Seven. This made their cars attractive

9

JAGUAR BEFORE THE COMPACTS

ABOVE: **The Swallow sidecars had a distinctive elegance about them and soon gained a good reputation.**

LEFT: **The next stage was a move into car bodywork. This 1929 advertisement is for the Austin Swallow – based on a cheap everyday chassis but adding an element of style not otherwise available.**

BELOW: **There were closed bodies by Swallow, too. This is a 1931 example, again on an Austin chassis, and shows the two-tone paintwork and V-screen typical of the breed.** SANDRA FAUCONNIER/WIKIMEDIA COMMONS

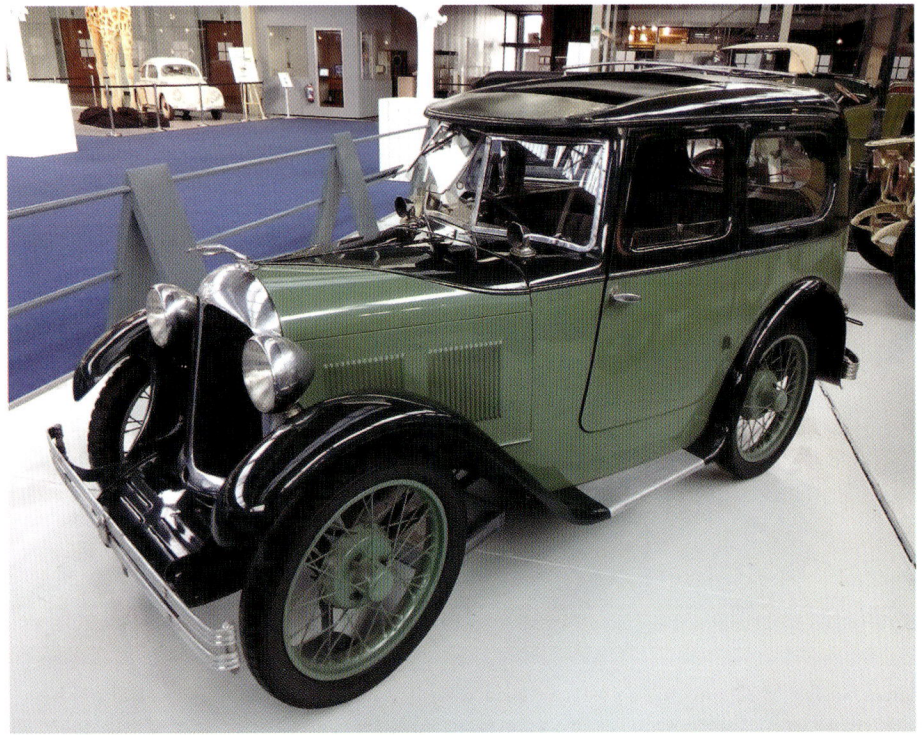

to the customer who could not afford an expensive luxury car but nevertheless wanted something that stood out from the crowd of everyday models. The origins of the market positioning that Jaguar cars would later adopt probably lay in this early experience.

One important factor in Swallow's success was pricing, and by adopting quite sophisticated production processes the company was able to minimize the cost of making its bodies. So it was that, when the growth of their business forced them to seek larger premises, Walmsley and Lyons looked carefully at how best to use this new opportunity to minimize costs further. One overhead they had been unable to control was the

JAGUAR BEFORE THE COMPACTS

cost of transporting chassis to Blackpool from the Midlands heart of the motor industry; and they had already recognized that it was easier to recruit skilled staff in the Midlands than in Blackpool. The solution was therefore obvious: Swallow would move to the Midlands. And so the company moved to premises at Holbrook Lane, in Coventry's Foleshill district, in the autumn of 1928.

Expansion continued. Lyons introduced further new production methods and before Christmas 1928 had pushed the rate of production up from twelve car bodies a week to fifty. The sidecar activities meanwhile continued. In 1929, Swallow took a stand at the Olympia Motor Show, and that year they also began to work on a wider range of chassis, including Fiat, Swift and – most notably – Standard. From early 1931 there were Swallow bodies for the Wolseley Hornet with its pioneering 'small six' engine, too. In all cases, their combination of attractive lines and striking paintwork completely transformed the perpendicular look of the originals, and created cars that were genuinely different from others available in Britain. Mechanically, however, they were unmodified. The next logical step was for Swallow to start building cars that were mechanically as well as bodily different from anything that could be bought elsewhere, and in 1931 they took that step.

FIRST SS MODELS

The new models that Swallow announced in October 1931 are often described as the company's first complete cars, although to call them that is really overstating the case. Standard, content with the special bodies Swallow had been offering on their chassis since 1929, had agreed to supply Swallow with their 16hp (2-litre) and 20hp (2.5-litre) 6-cylinder engines, fitted at the Standard works into a special chassis designed to meet Swallow's requirements. The key to this chassis was that it was much lower than those normally fitted to saloons of the period, which enabled Swallow to clothe it with rakish new sporting bodywork.

It was William Lyons, always the front man at Swallow, who had secured Standard's agreement, and it was he who had persuaded them to allow the new car to be badged as an SS. Those letters probably stood for Standard Swallow, but their real significance was that Swallow now had a marque of their own. The SS1, as the 6-cylinder car was called, went on sale in 1932, and was then accompanied by a much smaller new model based on the Standard Little Nine chassis with its 4-cylinder 1-litre engine. Even though this was more in the vein of Swallow's earlier rebodying efforts, it was also badged as an SS – in fact as an SS2 – and this development

The second-series SS1 coupé introduced for 1933 had much better-balanced lines than the earlier model of the same name. Those are of course dummy hood irons; rear-seat passengers could not see much out of the car!

■ JAGUAR BEFORE THE COMPACTS

made fairly clear what Swallow's next move was likely to be.

The company name had already changed twice, the original Swallow Sidecar Company becoming the Swallow Sidecar and Coachbuilding Company in 1926 and then the Swallow Coachbuilding Company a year later. From October 1930 it had become a limited company and now it was only a matter of time before the name changed yet again to reflect the nature of the new business. In 1933 Lyons and Walmsley set up a new company with the name of SS Cars Ltd and at the end of July 1934 they purchased Swallow.

From then on, Lyons' primary objective was to establish the company as a credible builder of complete cars. Styling remained important and the later SS models were offered with a variety of attractive bodies. Road performance to match that styling was also important. SS improved the lukewarm performance of the early SS2 models as soon as they were able by fitting larger and more powerful new engines provided by Standard. A gradual process of redesign made the SS1 and SS2 much better cars all round and by 1935 SS had become established as a small-volume maker of stylish sporting cars costing rather less than their exotic looks suggested.

WATERSHED – THE SS JAGUARS

By this stage, high performance had become a very important ingredient in Lyons' vision of SS Cars. As Standard had nothing in the offing that was likely to fit his future requirements, he turned to tuning expert Harry Weslake and asked him to develop the big Standard engine for more power. Weslake's solution was to redesign the top end of the engine with a new cylinder head and overhead valves in place of side valves. Lyons somehow managed to persuade Standard to manufacture this revised engine exclusively for SS Cars.

However, Lyons wanted more. The new engine needed to go with a new body, and for the new body it would be neces-

The SS Jaguars were based on Standard running-gear, but had low-slung and stylish bodywork. This 1935 example was photographed at the Salon Privé event at Syon Park in 2014.

JAGUAR BEFORE THE COMPACTS

Stunningly attractive, this was the first of the SS Jaguar saloons. This example dates from 1937.

sary to design a new chassis. The bodywork was something he was more than capable of tackling himself, but there was no one at the Foleshill works who had any experience of designing chassis. This was why SS Cars took on their first proper engineer in April 1935. William Heynes, who joined the company from Humber, was later to become a central figure in the Jaguar story.

The new car was ready in October 1935. Seeking to give it a new name, Lyons had settled for Jaguar, after the First World War Armstrong Siddeley aero engine that had interested him many years earlier. And so the new SS Jaguars went on sale for 1936, a range of sleek sports saloons and open four-seat tourers. In addition, there was a new short-wheelbase two-seat sports model called the SS90 – an important model historically because it was the first proper sports car from the company. The saloons could be obtained with either 1.5-litre or 2.5-litre engines, the smaller one actually having a capacity of 1608cc and being a production Standard side-valve 4-cylinder, while the larger engine had 2664cc and the Weslake overhead valve arrangement. The open cars, meanwhile, came only with the larger engine. Although both SS1 and SS2 models remained available alongside the newcomers, their production would soon end.

Towards the end of 1935, William Walmsley left SS Cars and joined a caravan manufacturer in Coventry. The split appears to have been amicable and probably resulted from

The optional leaping Jaguar mascot is in evidence on this 1938 SS Jaguar saloon, photographed by the auction house Historics at one of their sales. The discreet indicator light visible in the wheel arch was not an original feature.

13

JAGUAR BEFORE THE COMPACTS

Introduced in 1938, the SS100 had the 3½-litre engine in a lightweight structure and could reach 104mph (167km/h).

Walmsley's desire to avoid the complications and stresses of running a large company such as SS Cars seemed set to become. With his departure, SS cars was floated as a public company and thereafter was obliged to have its own board of directors who met at regular intervals. However, the board meetings of SS Cars Ltd were more of a legal formality than anything else: in reality, Lyons now took over the running of the company.

The SS Jaguars were further improved for the 1937 model season but the major changes came that autumn when the 1938 models were announced. For a start, the traditional coachbuilt bodies with their wooden frames had been replaced by all-steel bodyshells of similar appearance, which were both lighter and cheaper to manufacture. These had been joined by a new wooden-framed drophead coupé body which added to the SS marque's upper-crust pretensions. The 1.5-litre engine, too, had been reworked and now sported overhead valves, giving the engine much more performance than the old side-valve engine.

In addition, there was a sleek new sports tourer called the SS100, available with either the 2.5-litre engine or a new 3.5-litre type, which could also be had in the saloons and drophead coupés. Although this was in fact yet another development of the Standard 6-cylinder, and was once again made exclusively for SS Cars by Standard, it was still the closest the Foleshill company had yet come to an engine they might call their own.

WARTIME

By the time war broke out in 1939, the SS Jaguars had already established a formidable reputation. At home, they had been eagerly adopted by the sporting fraternity and there was even an SS Car Club for enthusiastic owners. Looking back rather wistfully in 1944, Montague Tombs of *The Autocar* magazine described the SS cars of the late 1930s as 'capable of providing an outstanding performance on the road, and offering exceptional value'. Yet the SS Jaguars were by no means common: by the time the Foleshill factory ceased car manufacture and focused on the production of military materiel in 1940, just 14,383 had been built in five seasons. Of the earlier SS1 and SS2 models, there had been no more than 6,029 examples.

When the war came, SS Cars Ltd was poised on the brink of further expansion. Production had increased enormously to meet the rising demand during 1938–39, and 1939 had seen a record output of 5,320 cars. Most popular of all was the steel-bodied 1.5-litre saloon, which accounted for over 60 per cent of that total. During 1939, William Lyons had bought Motor Panels, one of SS Cars' suppliers of body parts. His intention had been that SS Cars should be able to manufacture their own bodies entirely in-house, which would have minimized costs and given the company greater flexibility in the manufacture of their bodies.

However, the expansion never took place. Like every other motor manufacturer, SS Cars was obliged to respond to the needs of the armed services. The Foleshill plant started to turn out aircraft parts, took on aircraft repair work, and in 1944 designed and built some experimental lightweight miniature jeeps intended to be carried in transport aircraft and parachuted into action. Meanwhile, the Swallow Sidecar Company – which still existed as an SS subsidiary – took care of the entire requirements of the Army, Royal Navy and Royal Air Force for motorcycle sidecars.

There was, therefore, little time to spare for thinking about new car designs or improving the standing of the

JAGUAR BEFORE THE COMPACTS

company – although Lyons and those close to him were far from inactive on the matter of future designs. In fact, the war proved a major setback for SS Cars, and Lyons was obliged to sell Motor Panels shortly after hostilities ended for the simple reason that SS could not afford to keep it on and expand as they had planned six years earlier. The Swallow Sidecar subsidiary was also sold off in 1945 in order to raise capital.

In the meantime, Standard had announced that they did not wish to resume production of special engines on behalf of SS Cars when the war was over. Fortunately for the smaller company, they were quite prepared to sell the tooling for the 2.5-litre and 3.5-litre 6-cylinder engines, and at an advantageous price. Lyons seized this opportunity with both hands and by the middle of 1945 the redundant Standard tooling had been installed at SS Cars' Foleshill plant to give the company its very own engine at last. Tooling for the 1.5-litre engines remained with Standard, and that engine soon reappeared in cars from the Triumph marque that Standard had bought as the war drew to a close.

There was one final change at Foleshill before car production resumed over the summer of 1945. The initials SS had taken on negative associations during the war years, as they had been used by Nazi Germany's notorious frontline combat troops. Clearly, with sour memories of SS brutality lingering in the minds of British citizens, any company bearing those initials was likely to be shunned. So at an extraordinary general meeting in March 1945, William Lyons had his company's name changed to Jaguar Cars. It was the logical choice and a happy one.

JAGUAR IN THE LATE 1940s

The British economy had been shattered by the immense cost of the war and the government of the day saw as its clear priority putting that economy back on a sound footing. This could only be achieved by a combination of austerity measures to limit consumption at home and an emphasis on foreign trade to earn revenue abroad.

The car makers, in consequence, were encouraged to build cars primarily for export, and the government ensured that they would comply by rationing sheet steel and allocating it in quantity only to those companies that could show a good export performance. For Jaguar, the need to export was an entirely new concept; although a few cars had been exported in the late 1930s, the company had been able to sell all it could produce on the home market and had therefore never gone to the trouble and expense of setting up overseas distribution networks. But now, it had to.

The first post-war Jaguars were visually very similar to their pre-war counterparts. This elegant left-hand-drive Mk IV tourer was photographed for auctioneers H & H when it passed through their hands. Again, discreet indicators have been added for safety – in this case, just inboard of the bumper ends.

JAGUAR BEFORE THE COMPACTS

Like the majority of other British car manufacturers, Jaguar started production after the war with cars that were essentially little changed from those they had been making when production had been halted in 1940. Standard had agreed to resume supplies of the 1.5-litre engine for the time being (although post-war versions differed from pre-war types), and so a full range of three engines was available. The first bodies were all saloons, however; drophead coupé bodies did not become available again until December 1947, and then only with the 6-cylinder engines – and the SS100 open tourer was never revived.

It was typical of Britain's insularity, even in the second half of the 1940s, that Jaguar should have thought only in terms of right-hand-drive cars for export. The company had never built left-hand-drive cars before the war and it seems to have resisted the idea as long as possible. However, new and promising markets like the USA were only prepared to put up with right-hand-drive cars as a novelty for a limited period. Jaguar exports to the USA started in January 1947 and by August that year the company had been forced to capitulate and start making left-hand-drive models.

Developing the XK Engine

Jaguar had no intention of continuing with its pre-war 1.5-litre, 2.5-litre and 3.5-litre models for much longer. With his original plans for Jaguar's expansion in the early 1940s in ruins, Lyons had nonetheless begun during the war years to think of the new car that would eventually take over from the SS Jaguar range. Most importantly, he wanted his new saloon to be a genuine 100mph (160km/h) car – a 1939 3.5-litre saloon was capable of about 92mph (148km/h) – and that meant he would need a new engine. For maximum power, he thought it should have the twin overhead camshaft configuration that at the time was the preserve of racing machines and some exotic road cars. However, it was widely believed to be too complicated to produce economically and too difficult for the average garage mechanic to service and maintain.

So it was that Lyons began to discuss with his engineers ways of achieving what he wanted. The design target was 160bhp, which had been achieved for brief periods with a highly tuned 3.5-litre engine in an SS100 in 1939, and the discussions mostly took place while Lyons and others were on fire-watching duties at night in the Foleshill factory. Chief among those involved were Bill Heynes, SS Cars' first engineer; Wally Hassan, head of research and development and formerly with Bentley and ERA; and newcomer Claude Baily, who had joined SS Cars from Morris on the outbreak of war. Independent specialist Harry Weslake would later be consulted about the design of the cylinder head and combustion chambers.

A batch of Mk V saloons destined for foreign markets. Exports became vital to Jaguar in the late 1940s.

JAGUAR BEFORE THE COMPACTS

The work started in earnest during 1943 and the first experimental engines were 4-cylinder types. In due course a satisfactory design was developed and Jaguar built a 6-cylinder prototype. In the form eventually adopted for production, this displaced 3442cc and put out exactly the 160bhp that had been Lyons' design target. It took on the name of the XK type.

Lyons decided not to put the new engine into his existing models but rather to make it the centrepiece of an all-new saloon with new chassis, suspension and body as well as the new engine. Work on the new body design quickly demonstrated that it would need large pressings that Jaguar could not make itself now that Motor Panels had been sold. So Lyons turned to Pressed Steel, who were happy to accept the contract but needed a year to tool up for the new saloon body.

Meanwhile, Jaguar needed to do something about the current range of cars, because even the seller's market of the late 1940s could not be expected to tolerate pre-war designs indefinitely. By 1947 many other manufacturers had come up with new designs and these were making the Jaguars look increasingly old-fashioned. To bridge the gap and keep interest in the marque alive until the new saloon could enter production, Lyons therefore decided to develop the existing saloons further – and to show off his new XK engine in a striking-looking sports car that would attract sales in the newly opening US market.

The XK120 was initially given a wooden-framed body with aluminium alloy panels, but high demand forced Jaguar to switch to a steel body that could be volume-produced.

Mk V Saloon and XK120 Sports Car

For the new saloon, Lyons had the chassis stiffened and equipped with a torsion-bar independent front suspension in place of the old leaf-spring type. He drew up a new body, broadly similar to that on the existing cars but markedly

With a keen eye for the publicity to be gained from record runs, Jaguar took the XK120 to the new Belgian motor-road at Jabbeke, where a long straight section provided the ideal venue for speed runs. Pictured in 1949, the white car was only mildly modified. In 1953, Jaguar's chief test engineer Norman Dewis sat under a streamlined 'bubble', the headlamps had been streamlined and the bumpers had been removed – he broke the production car record with an astonishing 172.4mph (277km/h).

17

■ JAGUAR BEFORE THE COMPACTS

The XK120 made a name for itself in rallies as well. Most successful of all was NUB 120, with a string of victories in the early 1950s for Ian Appleyard, which is today preserved by the Jaguar Heritage Trust.

more modern in appearance, and he made sure that this body could be built in the traditional way at Foleshill. The result was a much heavier car than those it replaced, and that was one reason why the new Mk V Jaguar (as it was called) came only with the 6-cylinder 2.5-litre and 3.5-litre engines. One other reason for the absence of a 1.5-litre version must also have been that Lyons no longer wished to depend on Standard for one of his engines.

The Mk V Jaguar was announced in October 1948 at Britain's first post-war London Motor Show. Available in both saloon and drophead coupé forms, it was an elegant if unspectacular car, of which most examples went abroad to help Britain's export drive. Lyons knew he had bought time until his new 100mph (160km/h) saloon could enter production, but he probably had little idea just how important Jaguar's second new model at the 1948 Motor Show was going to be. That car was called the XK120.

In the Jaguar scheme of things, the XK120 was a belated replacement for the pre-war SS100. It was not really intended for long-term production, and had a wooden-framed body with aluminium panels that could only be made by hand in the traditional way. When it became a huge sales success, the body had to be redesigned as an all-steel structure for volume manufacture in early 1950.

The XK120 had a shortened version of the new Mk V saloon chassis, clothed with sleek and streamlined two-seat bodywork styled as usual by Lyons and clearly drawing some inspiration from the pre-war BMW 328 Mille Miglia roadsters. That alone was attractive enough to have guaranteed its sales success, but in addition the car became the showcase for the new 3.4-litre 6-cylinder XK engine. In the light sports-car body, this gave extraordinary performance for the time, and the XK120 went on to become a major export success. By the time it was succeeded by the rather better developed but generally similar XK140 in 1954, more than 12,000 examples had been built.

MK VII – THE 100MPH SALOON

The Mk V soldiered on for two more years before Jaguar's new saloon was ready to be launched, but all those who saw the new car at the 1950 London Motor Show agreed that it was worth the wait. The car's flowing lines echoed those of the XK120; the 3.4-litre XK engine offered a top speed of more than 100mph (160km/h); and somehow, Jaguar had managed to keep the basic price below £1,000 – the figure above which cars attracted a higher rate of purchase tax. Jaguar had called it the Mk VII, deliberately skipping a number after the Mk V because the contemporary Bentley saloon was known as the Mk VI.

The car's pricing was hugely attractive, but it was of largely academic interest to British car buyers because the Mk VII was intended initially for export only. In pursuit of that aim, Jaguar whisked the London Motor Show car across to New York as soon as the show ended. There, the

JAGUAR BEFORE THE COMPACTS

car was accorded a reception perhaps even more rapturous than the one it had received in London. Within three days, Jaguar had taken orders for no fewer than 500 cars in the USA. Following the success of the XK120 sports car, Jaguar had now definitively broken into the transatlantic market, which would soon become their largest single source of income.

Demand for the Mk VII and the XK120 built up so quickly that Jaguar's Foleshill premises were bursting at the seams by 1951. They were very fortunate that year to be able to purchase a redundant Daimler plant at Browns Lane, near Coventry, and to move their entire manufacturing operation there. It was a good thing they did, for demand would continue to expand, driven by the US market.

It was US demand that led to the introduction in 1953 of an optional automatic gearbox for the Mk VII Jaguar. Next came an overdrive, more popular in Europe where Autobahn, Autostrada and the new Belgian motor-roads offered opportunities for long-distance, high-speed cruising. Then in the autumn of 1954, at the same time as the XK140 replaced the XK120, came the substantially revised Mk VIIM with a more powerful engine, new bumpers and a host of minor but valuable improvements. And all the time, Jaguar's reputation was growing as fast as its production volumes. Before the introduction of the XK120 and Mk VII, Jaguar's annual production figures had hovered at a little over 4,000; by 1954, with both models selling strongly in the USA and sales on the increase in the home market now that restrictions had eased, the annual totals were regularly hovering around the 10,000 mark.

This improvement in Jaguar's fortunes had far-reaching effects, for without it the company would not have been able to finance the design, development and introduction of a new range of saloon cars, which increased the number of its basic product ranges to three. Those cars were the compact Jaguars, which entered production in 1955.

The XK engine had been designed primarily to power Jaguar's new large saloon car, and this was it – the Mk VII of 1950. Though the car was large and heavy, its lines were graceful and the 3.4-litre engine made it capable of over 100mph (160km/h).

19

CHAPTER TWO

DESIGN AND DEVELOPMENT OF THE JAGUAR MK I

Many of Jaguar's engineering records from the 1950s still survive, but sadly there is very little relating to the design and development of the compact saloons. After all this time, the most likely explanation is that the crucial documents were tossed into a skip during the iconoclastic days of Jaguar's ownership by British Leyland. So the story of how Jaguar's engineers created these iconic saloons has to be pieced together from the few pieces of the jigsaw that remain available.

THE NEED FOR A NEW JAGUAR

It is often assumed that Jaguar missed their smaller-engined saloons after the demise of the 1.5-litre and 2.5-litre models in 1949. The big Mk VII cars with their 3.4-litre engines were selling into the very top end of the traditional Jaguar saloon market, and the would-be Jaguar owner who could not afford a car of that calibre was therefore obliged to buy from another manufacturer. However, a weakness of this argument is that it suggests Jaguar sales were suffering in the absence of these smaller-engined saloons. In fact, the very reverse was true.

Jaguar sales had done nothing but increase since the last of the smaller-engined cars had been built. The final examples of the 1.5-litre had been built in 1949, when Jaguar had made 4,190 cars. During the 1950 model year that followed, when only the 2.5-litre and 3.5-litre engines were available in the Mk V saloons, production shot up to 7,206 cars. Even more revealing is that the best-selling Jaguar of all in 1949 and 1950 was the 3.5-litre Mk V saloon; it sold more than three times as many as the XK120 sports models and around four times as many as its 2.5-litre sibling. All this makes abundantly clear that it was the big-engined saloons that Jaguar buyers wanted and that the smaller-engined cars were not being missed. It was, above all, the performance available from the big-engined cars that made them so popular.

So why did William Lyons decide that Jaguar should develop a third range of cars? There seem to have been two reasons. First, Lyons wanted to give Jaguar a more solid market base than was possible with his company's existing two-model strategy. Second, the company was expanding rapidly in the 1950s and it was important to build on that expansion in the most appropriate way for Jaguar's future.

Jaguar was certainly doing well as the 1950s opened. Sales were up to such an extent that the company was forced to move to larger premises in Browns Lane simply so that it had enough space to match production to demand. However, it must have been very clear to Lyons that Jaguar's success was potentially fragile. After 1950, it was totally reliant on two models – the Mk VII luxury saloon and the XK120 sports car. Both of these sold in specialist areas of the car market, and both of those market sectors were likely to be volatile.

Recent experience had shown that when the economy was in the doldrums, the first sectors of the car market to suffer were precisely those in which Jaguar was operating. There was also the problem that the company was depending more and more on export markets, and events in the early 1950s showed that overseas markets could be closed almost overnight if governments decided to protect their economies by imposing trade bans or high taxation on imports. Jaguar could not risk remaining in this position for long: the company needed a model that would sell in the less volatile middle sector of the market, and one which would sell strongly at home so that it was less dependent on exports.

Such a car would help protect Jaguar's interests against

the uncertainties of the world economy, and it would also help the company to continue its expansion if the economic situation remained stable. The new Browns Lane premises were large, and it must have been obvious that Jaguar would never fill them completely with assembly lines for the Mk VII saloons and XK120 sports cars. To get the most out of their new investment, therefore, they needed a car that could be made in larger volumes than either of these. If it was successful, it would move Jaguar from the ranks of the specialist manufacturers into the ranks of the volume car makers, which would guarantee the company a more stable future. However, it would be important that a new volume-production Jaguar should not debase any of the qualities on which the marque had built its reputation. This consideration had a profound effect on the eventual design of Jaguar's third range of cars.

It is difficult to sort out the sequence of surviving Jaguar 2.4 mock-up photographs, but this one was certainly early. The flip-front plan is in evidence here (note the curved shut-line just behind the wheel arch), along with slim bumpers painted in the body colour. The major details are already in place, though.

This photograph shows the other side of the same mock-up, this time with some wheels in place to give a fuller effect. The wheel trim is a production Jaguar type, but with a section apparently painted in the body colour, as on the Mk V models. Perhaps that was what came to hand most easily when a hubcap was needed!

This is the same mock-up again (note the odd headlamps), but this time with different A-pillar shapes being tried and also, it appears, with a more conventional bonnet. Shut-lines are in evidence on both sides, although one side differs from the other. There is also a raised centre section.

This rear view of the 2.4-litre mock-up shows distinct Mk VII features – and there is something very 1930s about the shape of that rear window.

DESIGN AND DEVELOPMENT OF THE JAGUAR MK 1

WHAT SORT OF CAR?

Quite clearly, Jaguar's new third model range had to be aimed at a different set of customers from those who bought the Mk VII and the XK120. It might have been tempting to create another sporting model, but the sports car market would always be subject to the fluctuations of the economy. When times were hard, people would stop buying sports cars and turn to practical saloons capable of transporting the family. So to protect the company against the effects of such hard times in the future, it must have been clear from the start that the new third model range would have to be a saloon.

However, it could not be an ordinary family saloon because it would be impossible to build a car with Jaguar characteristics at a price that would suit that market. So it would have to be priced to sell midway between the better family saloons and the cheaper luxury saloons. This was territory occupied by makes such as Armstrong Siddeley, Riley and Rover; and of these, only Riley offered a blend of luxury and sporting qualities similar to those associated with Jaguars. As Riley gradually lost their grip on the market after 1950, it must have been obvious to William Lyons that Jaguar would face very little competition indeed for a new saloon in that area of the market.

So the overriding consideration in creating the new Jaguar was very probably price. Starting with an on-sale price guide, Lyons and his team must have worked out a maximum production cost after deducting an appropriate percentage for their dealers' and Jaguar's own profit margins. It would have been a complicated set of calculations, affected also by the numbers that Jaguar thought they could sell and by the length of time they thought they could keep the car in production. Even a ten-year production life would have been longer than any previous SS or Jaguar car had enjoyed, so this was to some extent virgin territory. A lengthy production life would also mean that the car had to incorporate the very latest engineering, so that advances made by other makers would not make it look old-fashioned long before the projected end of its production life.

It was probably some time in 1952 when work began on the new Jaguar, which was given the code name Utah within the engineering department. By then, the company had moved into the Browns Lane plant and was able to take a more considered look at the future. But most importantly for dating purposes, records still exist of the earliest work that was done on creating a new engine for the car, and that work was done during 1952.

POWERTRAIN

The average engine size in the sector of the car market where Jaguar hoped to sell their new car was rather less than 2.5 litres. In 1952, the Armstrong Siddeley engine was a 2.3-litre, Rover had a 2.1-litre, and Riley had the largest engine at 2.5 litres. Power outputs averaged a little over 80bhp, with the Riley being by far the most powerful at 100bhp. So Jaguar clearly needed an engine of around 2.5 litres with rather more than 100bhp.

Experimental Engines

The most obvious way of achieving this was to make a short-stroke edition of the existing 6-cylinder XK engine by fitting the 3.4-litre block with a new crankshaft and connecting rods. In order to get as close to 2.5 litres as possible, engine number X102 was built with a 77mm stroke and the existing 83mm bore size, giving a swept volume of 2499.69cc. It first ran on the test bed at Browns Lane on 25 August 1952, and ended its test cycle some sixteen months later on 11 December 1953.

What the Jaguar engineers called the '2½-litre 6-cylinder engine' was not yet satisfactory. So over the summer of 1953, two further experimental engines went on test. One of them was a refinement of the first 2½-litre XK 6-cylinder; the other was a 4-cylinder XK derivative with a capacity of just under 2 litres.

Jaguar had originally planned a 4-cylinder version of the XK engine as early as 1948, when the plan had been to introduce a less powerful and less expensive XK100 version of the XK120 sports car. That plan fell by the wayside when sales of the XK120 took off so spectacularly, but the idea of a 4-cylinder XK engine did not go away, and this was what the engineers resurrected for the engine they called EXP1-1 in 1953.

Records show that the engine was first tested on 14 July 1953. EXP1-1's 4 cylinders had the familiar 83mm bore size of the XK engine, with a 91mm stroke to give 1970cc. Running a high 12:1 compression ratio, it initially breathed through two SU HS6 carburettors, which were changed later in the test programme for twin Webers. However, that programme was relatively short, and the last entry in the engine's test log is dated 10 November 1953. Whether EXP1-1 proved unsatisfactory for some reason is unclear. Although there is little doubt that it would have met the requirement for

100bhp or more with ease, that long stroke in an engine with just 4 cylinders might have made it rougher than the Jaguar engineers wanted. Perhaps it was rejected because the new version of the 2½-litre 6-cylinder was simply proving superior.

This new engine had gone on test some six weeks after the 4-cylinder, and its first test entry was logged on 26 August 1953. Numbered EXP2, it had a slightly shorter stroke than the earlier 2½-litre experimental engine, to give a swept volume of 2483cc. Whether it still had a 3.4-litre block or the shallower block eventually adopted for the production engines is not clear. However, it seems likely that the new block had been specified along with the shorter stroke.

At this stage, the first 2499cc engine, X102, was also still on test, but the new engine appears to have proved its worth early on. On 14 October, after less than two months on the test bench, it was joined by a second 2483cc engine, this one numbered EXP3. Less than a month later, tests of the 4-cylinder engine stopped, and just over a month after that, tests on the long-stroke 2½-litre engine came to an end. The 2483cc engine had clearly won the day, and by the end of 1953 Jaguar had no doubt settled on this version of the XK engine as the power unit for their new compact saloon.

One further experimental engine of the early 1950s deserves mention. This was EXP9, described as a '2½-litre, light-alloy block'. Its test programme started on 1 December 1954, and continued until 3 October 1957. That second date provides the clue to what it was, as ten days afterwards Jaguar announced that they would no longer field a works competition team. No doubt if the Jaguar works team had continued to exist, sooner or later it would have fielded cars powered by the light-alloy engine – and sooner or later, the light-alloy engine might have become available to the public as well. As it was, the project died when Jaguar pulled out of works competition.

Gearbox

Although engine development was central to the new car, the Jaguar engineers must have been giving some thought to other elements of the powertrain at the same time, and notably to the gearbox. As the new engine was going to deliver lower power and torque than the existing 3.4-litre type, there would be no need for a stronger gearbox than the one that Jaguar was already using. Work was already under way to develop an automatic gearbox option for the 1954-model Mk VII saloons, but there was no indication that the buyers for whom the new smaller saloon was intended would have any interest in such an option. Automatics at this stage were not yet popular anywhere except in the USA, and they did take the edge off performance. The new small Jaguar needed all the performance it could extract from its new and smaller engine.

So Browns Lane took the simplest and cheapest way out: they decided to use the four-speed Moss gearbox that was already standard in the Mk VII and XK120 models. In practice, second and third gear ratios would be altered to suit the torque characteristics of the 2½-litre engine, but the gearbox selected for production was essentially a familiar Jaguar component. The Laycock de Normanville overdrive already optional on existing production Jaguars could also be offered as an optional extra, and would be from the start of compact Jaguar production.

BODY

Styling

William Lyons liked to style his cars by building a full-size, wooden-framed mock-up, on which he would alter details until he was satisfied. It was a method he was certainly using by the time the Mk V Jaguars were being designed in 1947–48, and the Mk VII saloon was done in the same way. So it was only to be expected that Lyons would use this same proven method for the new smaller Jaguar saloon.

Styling was exclusively Lyons' preserve in the early 1950s. Although he worked with a number of assistants who would modify the panelling of the mock-ups according to his instructions, he had direct and personal control over the final shape. Styling was, after all, the skill with which he had made his name in the 1930s. For the new saloon, he started with certain basic dimensions that had been agreed with his chief engineer, Bill Heynes – such as those of the wheelbase, the engine bay and the passenger compartment – and thereafter the decisions were his. No doubt if Lyons felt the car would look better with half an inch added here or there, he would automatically get his way, regardless of the rough dimensions agreed beforehand.

Several photographs survive of the full-size mock-up for the Utah project, but as they are undated it is impossible to establish for certain the stages through which Lyons's ideas evolved, or even the date when he started work. However,

■ DESIGN AND DEVELOPMENT OF THE JAGUAR MK I

The blocks supporting the front bumper and the general air of untidiness suggest that this photograph of the mock-up was set up rather hastily. The old-style wheel trim adds to the same impression: perhaps it was the only one that could be found in a hurry! However, the headlamps of the production design are now in place, the sidelights have moved to their production locations but do not yet have their production shape, and the rather heavy Mk VII-style bumper is clearly on trial. In other photographs taken of this mock-up, it is clear that the bumper really is a Mk VII type, and much too wide for the car. JDHT

The mock-up was looking very assured by this stage, although the rear wheel seems to have acquired an unintended camber.

Did William Lyons really take some inspiration for the 2.4-litre Jaguar from the Aston Martin DB2? It seems quite likely that he did, mixing Aston elements with the Jaguar style established on his own XK120 and Mk VII models.

it would be reasonable to assume that the full-size mock-up was first built towards the end of 1952 or in 1953, and that the design evolved gradually over a period of months.

Lyons himself seems to have referred to the car's shape as a 'rotund style', according to Bob Knight, quoted in Philip Porter's *The Jaguar Scrapbook*. It also seems clear that from the start he did not want the sweeping wing-lines that characterized the Mk VII and XK120. One good reason might have been that there already existed a British-built 2.5-litre saloon with sporting pretensions and that sort of styling, and it was not selling well. That car was the Lea-Francis 18hp, which had been introduced in 1949 and would actually be withdrawn in 1954 after no more than eighty had been built. A more positive inspiration was the modern 'pontoon' styling of cars like the 1949 Jensen Interceptor, the 1950 Aston Martin DB2 and the 1953 Riley Pathfinder. Of these, the DB2, designed in-house by Frank Feeley, seems to have been the greatest influence.

The Aston, of course, was a two-door sports coupé whereas Lyons wanted a four-door saloon with seating for five. However, it is not hard to recognize the basic shapes of the Aston's lower body and passenger cabin in the Jaguar. Lyons added an XK120-like grille, put the headlamps inboard of the wings, added rear spats to give it a family resemblance to the Mk VII and XK120, and hung on some heavy bumpers like those on the Mk VII. On what seem to be the earliest versions of the styling mock-up, there are no panel lines, but one particularly interesting series of later photographs shows panel lines, which make clear that Lyons was considering a forward-hinged front wing and bonnet assembly.

DESIGN AND DEVELOPMENT OF THE JAGUAR MK I

While it is true that the C-type sports-racing Jaguars had such a feature when they first appeared in 1951, it is also true that the Aston DB2 had a forward-hinged bonnet-and-wing assembly a whole year earlier.

However, it would be wrong to overemphasize the influence of Frank Feeley's design for Aston Martin. As Lyons tinkered with the basic shape, so the styling model became more Jaguar and less and less Aston. The bonnet gained and then lost a raised centre section; the heavy Mk VII-style bumpers were changed for a much neater and slimmer pattern painted in the body colour, which was sadly rejected; and the grille and sidelights went through a number of permutations before Lyons was satisfied. Precise dating is problematical, as already explained, but it is clear that the basic styling of the new Jaguar had been settled by the early months of 1954.

Structure

Lyons and Bill Heynes probably decided at an early stage that the new Utah saloon would not have the same body-on-chassis construction as the company's existing products. This traditional method of construction was rapidly losing ground to the newer monocoque structures, and if Jaguar needed to plan for a long production life to make their new saloon viable, they needed to embrace the very latest engineering advances wherever they could so that the car would not become outmoded during its production life. The advantages of a monocoque bodyshell might well have been outlined by Pressed Steel, who were already building the bodies for the Mk VII saloons and were no doubt the automatic choice to build bodies for the new saloons too.

One of the key advantages that a monocoque shell offered was that it allowed a car's overall build to be lower because the lowest point of the body did not have to be placed above a chassis frame that was several inches deep. This was an important consideration for a sporting saloon that needed sleek and low lines. Monocoque shells could also promise greater rigidity than body-on-chassis construction, and this in turn could improve handling by reducing the flexing associated with traditional structures. However, that rigidity could only be achieved by heavy reinforcement of the shell because the understanding of stress engineering was still in its infancy, and that heavy reinforcement brought with it the disadvantage of weight – which of course had a direct impact on performance.

The need for strength in the bodyshell also had some effect on styling, because the universal solution to any doubts about structural strength in the early 1950s was to make the suspect component thicker. Lyons seems to have played for safety by incorporating thick and heavy roof pillars on his styling mock-up, and although these were slightly altered for production, their size certainly robbed the first Jaguar compacts of some of the grace typical of Lyons's designs. When the cars were redesigned at the end of the 1950s to provide the Mk 2 compact Jaguars, one of the most obvious changes was to the window pillars and frames. The need for structural strength may well also have put paid to the idea of an Aston Martin-style forward-hinged bonnet-and-wing assembly. A lack of rigidly-mounted inner wings would have weakened the front of the car, and so Jaguar settled for a more conventional wing structure with a crocodile-type bonnet.

There was a third disadvantage of monocoque structures that Jaguar's engineers had to overcome, too. This was their tendency to act like a large echo-chamber and amplify every noise that was transmitted through the suspension bolted directly to them. Other manufacturers had tackled this problem with varying degrees of success, and Pressed Steel no doubt gave Jaguar the benefit of their experience. However, the Browns Lane team had to get this right, because refine-

It was probably the body engineers who counselled against a flip-front design. Instead, they created a strong structure around the engine bay, shaping the inner wings to cope with the suspension loads. The bonnet was then hinged against those inner wings in conventional fashion, and one of the hinges is seen in this photograph of a car under restoration.

■ DESIGN AND DEVELOPMENT OF THE JAGUAR MK 1

Pressed Steel had the contract to build the production bodyshell for the 2.4-litre Jaguar and in May 1954 they made this three-eighths scale model of it from transparent plastic. Its purpose was to show those elements of the structure that would normally be invisible.

ment was one of the marque's characteristics. So it was that Bob Knight was appointed as development engineer to take charge of what would now be called NVH (noise, vibration and harshness) work on the new car. The end result was a fine testimony to the thoroughness of a man who, a decade and a half later, would be responsible for making the first Jaguar XJ6 such a supremely refined car.

All these problems added to the workload on Jaguar's chief body engineer Bill Thornton and his assistant Cyril Crouch. The design finally came together in the first half of 1954, and production drawings for the bodyshell were certainly ready by May that year, which was when Pressed Steel used them to make a three-eighths scale model of the shell in transparent plastic. According to a report on this model, which followed later in the year, its purpose was 'to reproduce the metal components in sufficient detail (with particular attention to attachment points) to permit of its use in assessing design and production problems as a preliminary to quantity production'. Surviving pictures of the plastic shell suggest that the biggest change before production began was to the shape and position of the front sidelights.

SUSPENSION, STEERING AND BRAKES

The compact saloon's front suspension was drawn up by Bill Heynes. Like the design he had done for the Mk V Jaguars a few years earlier, it depended on equal-length top and bottom wishbones. However, in place of the torsion bars used on other production Jaguars, Heynes chose coil springs this time around. It appears that this was another result of using monocoque construction: finding suitable mounting points

There were no major surprises in the front suspension design, which used upper and lower wishbones with coil springs and concentric dampers. The whole was mounted on a compact subframe that would be bolted to the underside of the bodyshell.

26

DESIGN AND DEVELOPMENT OF THE JAGUAR MK I

for the rear of the torsion bars on the bodyshell proved too complicated.

The real problem was with noise transmission, and ultimately the engineers decided to use a detachable subframe – in effect a miniature chassis – to help insulate the body from the suspension. This subframe was attached to the shell by rubber mountings, soft enough to absorb resonances that reached the subframe from the suspension but hard enough to prevent that subframe from moving and so compromising the car's handling. To make sure that excessive roll did not compromise the car's handling, a front anti-roll bar was fitted ahead of the wheel centreline.

At the rear, first thoughts were to use conventional semi-elliptic leaf springs, but there were doubts about the ability of the monocoque to absorb the stresses from these. So instead, Jaguar developed an intriguing cantilevered arrangement, where only one end of the spring was anchored to the bodyshell, and that in a deep channel under the strong centre section. The axle was attached by brackets to the other end. There were some thoughts about using an A-frame to give additional axle location, but in the end the engineers settled for a pair of trailing arms, each running to a separate mounting point on the body, together with a Panhard rod that controlled the sideways movement of the axle. Hydraulic telescopic dampers were being used on almost all new designs by this stage and were a natural choice for the new saloon.

One curiosity of the rear suspension has never been fully explained, and that is the extraordinarily narrow track that was adopted. That rear track was a full 4.5in (114mm) narrower than the front track – a difference not as extreme as that between front and rear tracks on the Citroën DS introduced in the same year as the 2.4-litre Jaguar, but a big one nonetheless. Citroën adopted these dimensions deliberately, and in the interests of better handling, but of course their car had front-wheel drive and would have handled differently in any case. Perhaps both companies picked up the idea from a common source. In Jaguar's case, it proved not to be a wise choice, as the narrow rear track brought with it some on-the-limit handling problems.

Production Jaguars at the time used a Burman recirculating-ball steering system, and this was an easy choice to make. Rack-and-pinion systems did exist, but they were not common and generally made the steering heavier than Jaguar would have wanted.

Similarly, although disc brakes did exist at the time – and Jaguar was using them on its sports-racing machines – they

The design chosen for the rear suspension was certainly unusual, with inverted semi-elliptic leaf springs in a cantilevered arrangement.

This was the rear axle, complete with drum brakes. The brackets for the two trailing arms are clearly visible on top of the axle casing.

The downward curve of the inverted leaf spring gave the rear suspension a curious appearance when viewed through the wheel arch.

had not yet been developed to the point where they could be used with confidence on a road car. So they settled for drum brakes all round on the new model, allied to a vacuum servo to give greater stopping power. This technology, which was still quite new on production cars, had been seen before on the Mk VII saloons, but it did not make the compact saloon's brakes one of its better features. Jaguar meanwhile continued to work on disc brakes and would have them ready for introduction a couple of years after the compact saloons had gone on sale.

INTERIOR

In developing the passenger cabin of the new compact saloons, Jaguar had to carve out every bit of space that they could find, both to create actual passenger space and to create the illusion of space. The wheelbase of these cars was, after all, more than a foot shorter that that of the Mk VII saloons. By using thinner seat backs and by shortening both front and rear seat cushions by 1in (25mm), the designers managed to make the passenger compartment appear almost extravagantly spacious. The biggest problem they encountered was those thick window pillars, and there was not much they could do to reduce the tendency these had to make the interior feel dark and rather claustrophobic.

The use of wood and leather was of course a foregone conclusion. However, the design of the Jaguar's wooden facia was unadventurous, and very much in contrast to the forward thinking apparent in so many other areas of the car. The main instruments were placed in the centre of the dashboard, which was a deliberate throwback to pre-war fashions at a time when other makers were setting instruments directly ahead of the driver; perhaps production costs were a consideration, as having the instruments in the centre made it unnecessary to use different components for right-hand-drive and left-hand-drive cars. Also antiquated was the huge steering wheel with its cone-shaped horn push in the centre – perhaps Jaguar were hoping to appeal to those who remembered the sports cars of the 1930s and were now looking to purchase a more sensible saloon.

One well-known story about the design of the dashboard explains why the ashtray ended up in a less than ideal location. William Lyons was a non-smoker and simply did not think of incorporating an ashtray when he designed the dashboard for the compact saloons. However, smoking was distinctly fashionable in the 1950s and Lyons was eventually persuaded that the car needed an ashtray. To save redesigning the whole dashboard, an ashtray was therefore added below its centre, concealed behind a wooden fillet. Like so many last-minute solutions to design problems, it was unsatisfactory. As the ashtray was directly below the ignition switch, fobs and other keys on the same ring as the ignition key invariably dangled into the open ashtray and spread cigarette ash all over the floor!

PROTOTYPES

There may have been no more than two full prototypes of the compact Jaguars. Once again, the absence of factory records makes it impossible to be certain. It seems likely that the first prototypes were built over the summer of 1954, as engine test records make clear that at least two prototype cars existed by that September. Both of them had probably been built by hand because Pressed Steel would still have been tooling up for the production bodies at this stage.

Just two cars appear in the known photographs of compact Jaguar prototypes. Some show a dark-coloured car that was almost certainly black, while others show a lighter-coloured car that could well have been grey. Photographs of the grey car show it on test at the MIRA proving ground in Nuneaton, with proprietary round sidelights like those clearly envisaged when Pressed Steel's plastic model had been made. Photographs of the dark car show it in an incomplete state, with hubcaps painted to match the body (as on the Mk VII); the exhaust pipe emerging below the centre of the bumper (it would be offset on production cars); and details of the rear lighting and number-plate lighting still being decided. This car may later have become PVC 302, which Bill Heynes took to France before the public launch (see Chapter 3). At that stage, it had an intermediate style of sidelights, mounted higher up the wings than on production cars, plus Mk VII-style fog lights mounted in the wing fronts where the dummy horn grilles would later go.

Perhaps the most remarkable thing about these two cars is that they appear to differ so little from the eventual production cars, of which the first would be completed on 7 January 1955. Once Lyons had established the styling he wanted on his full-size model, and once the body engineers at Pressed Steel had translated that into a form that could actually be built in quantity, almost nothing changed.

CHAPTER THREE

JAGUAR MK 1 (1955–1959)

The first the public saw of the new Jaguar was at the 1955 Earls Court Motor Show in London, which opened on 19 October. Jaguar had stand number 154 on the ground floor of the exhibition hall where they displayed a single example of the new car alongside a pair of Mk VIIM saloons and an XK140 fixed-head coupé. They had decided to give it a simple name: the Jaguar 2.4-litre. At this stage the 'Mk 1' name did not exist; it was only applied retrospectively after the Mk 2 models had arrived four years later. However, it has become a familiar shorthand for referring to the 1955–59 cars and this chapter uses it in that sense.

The 1955 show car was an example of the most expensive Special Equipment model, complete with whitewall tyres contrasting with its dark paint. From the start, Jaguar offered a standard model at £1,269 0s 10d including purchase tax in Britain, but that was really little more than showroom bait and even though it was listed right through until 1959, very few (if any) were actually built. For £1,298 15s 10d, or £29 15s 0d more, the Special Equipment model came with a collection of extras that most Jaguar buyers would have thought essential. These were a rev counter, a heater, door-operated courtesy lights, vacuum-operated windscreen washers, a rear centre armrest, twin Lucas fog lamps, vitreous enamelled exhaust manifolds and a leaping Jaguar mascot on the bonnet. For an extra £67 10s 0d, which was actually quite a lot of money in 1955, the new Jaguar could also be fitted with overdrive.

The new 2.4-litre was the centrepiece of Jaguar's stand at the 1955 Earls Court Motor Show in London. This was a Special Equipment model, recognizable here by the twin driving lamps and the leaping-Jaguar bonnet mascot. The whitewall tyres were an optional extra.

PVC 302 had been one of the prototype cars, but its engine and registration number were transferred to a production model that became a Jaguar works demonstrator. Here is that second incarnation of PVC 302 in an early publicity photograph.

■ JAGUAR MK I (1955–1959)

Buyers could choose from ten standard paint colours and six interior-trim colours, but they had to wait for delivery. Volume production had barely got under way at Browns Lane and no more than thirty-two cars would be built before the end of 1955. As some of those had left-hand drive (the first of which was completed on 21 November) and others must have been retained as test, development and demonstrator cars, there can have been very few deliveries to customers in the home market before 1956.

THE 2.4-LITRE AND THE PRESS

Even the press had to wait before they were able to borrow examples of the 2.4-litre Jaguar for testing, and the two leading British motoring weeklies – *The Motor* and *The Autocar* (both of which would drop the definite article from their mastheads in the early 1960s) – had to wait until the summer before Browns Lane would part with examples. Both were Special Equipment models, registered SWK 803 and SWK 986, and both had benefited from a small number of improvements that Jaguar had made during the first nine months or so of production. Today, such a long delay between the announcement of a new model and the availability of press demonstrators would probably draw unfavourable comment, but in the gentler 1950s the press were rather more forgiving, even respectful. It was an attitude that allowed manufacturers to sort out teething problems in a new car without incurring bad publicity, and no doubt Jaguar were grateful for the few months' respite.

The Motor tested that Special Equipment 2.4-litre model for its issue of 25 July 1956, and its testers were deeply impressed: 'More than one member of our staff found that a few miles were needed before the car aroused his fullest enthusiasm,' but 'once the mental adjustment is made, the Jaguar becomes more likeable every minute.' The seating position and controls came in for praise, although the nearside wing was invisible past the bonnet, and the performance figures 'related to a full family saloon will stand comparison anywhere'. The actual figures were a mean maximum of 101.5mph (163.3km/h) over the flying half-mile with a best of 102.3mph (164.6km/h), and 0–60mph in 14.4sec.

The engine was 'delightfully smooth – and silent', although it could be reluctant to start when cold. The gear lever was criticized, and the action of the overdrive switch seemed unnatural. If the rear suspension seemed a little old-fashioned in concept, it proved itself with ride comfort 'equivalent to that given by cars tested by *The Motor* with independent rear suspension'. Handling was secure: 'The car has no vices, and feels equally safe and controllable on a slippery road.' The servo-assisted brakes were a little sensitive at town speeds, but gave fade-free stopping from up to 90mph (145km/h).

It mattered in 1956 whether a man could get into a car while wearing a hat and *The Motor* commented that the Jaguar driver could not. Nevertheless, in the passenger cabin, 'the surroundings border on the luxurious' and 'as this is a touring car, it possesses touring accommodation, which implies space for the odds and ends of travelling as well as full-scale luggage.' Overall, there were one or two

SWK 803 was an early production car, again with the Special Equipment specification. Clearly visible in these photographs are the original type of cast front grille and the heavy-looking rear pillars that rather spoiled the graceful lines of the original 2.4-litre car. Whether the heavy bumpers were an improvement over the slim, body-colour items seen on the mock-up is debatable, but they did give a family resemblance to other Jaguars of the time.

If only to prove that the 'standard' 2.4-litre Jaguar did exist, here is its dashboard. Most cars came with the Special Equipment specification, though, with an additional dial (the rev counter) and a sliding control for the heater at the bottom of the dash where this car has only a wood fillet.

'very minor faults' with the new Jaguar but 'no doubt at all attaches to the mechanical design or execution of a car which completely succeeds in the difficult job of furthering a first-class reputation.'

Two months later, in its 21 September issue, *The Autocar* gave its verdict on the car. The test report noted that it 'falls into a category which has a ready-made market, and one for which the Jaguar company is particularly well suited to cater'. It was a 'luxurious five-seater with a high performance and fine handling characteristics' and boasted a 'modern, dignified and efficient' shape. There were no starting problems with this car, although a slight vibration at 80mph (128km/h) was thought to come from the propshaft, and the gear lever was 'not ideally shaped or placed for the average driver'.

The car achieved a higher top speed than the one tested by *The Motor*, with a mean maximum in overdrive of 102.5mph (164.9km/h) and a best of 104mph (167.4km/h). However, in this case the 0–60mph time was not as good, being given as 15.8sec. Like *The Motor*, this magazine praised the comfort of the driving position and commented on the invisibility of the nearside wing. 'The windscreen pillars . . . are unusually thick, but do not seem to interfere with visibility as much as would be expected.' Again, like its rival magazine, *The Autocar* found that:

> the 2.4 is one of those cars whose capabilities are appreciated as the mileage mounts. It is quietly very efficient indeed, providing unstinted luxury, fine performance and roadworthiness, and it is offered at a remarkably low price for the high standards and quality construction for which the make is internationally respected.

In the USA, *Sports Cars Illustrated* was able to test a 2.4-litre for its October 1956 issue. Again the car had the Special Equipment specification. Acknowledging that the new Jaguar had caused a lot of excitement among sports car enthusiasts, the magazine found that it had 'a nice balance between the paired factors of power and roadholding'. *SCI* was unable to better 99mph (159km/h) or 13.4sec for the 0–60mph acceleration test, but had already heard that a 3.4-litre model might be on the way. They were less than enthusiastic about the prospect, arguing that the heavier engine would 'dump 51 more pounds where they aren't needed and apply more power where it can't be fully used'.

Overall, the magazine noted that the car had 'a remarkable feeling of solidity and almost complete freedom from rattles'. The ride was silent and smooth, and the car tracked straight although the steering was heavy at low speeds and the brakes had only 'moderate power':

> The 2.4 controls are sporting but the car's reactions to them are more sedate and sedanlike. It narrowly misses being the perfect machine for the enthusiastic driver who needs family room, but taken strictly as a roomy five-seater, it's exceptionally safe and stable.

PRODUCTION CHANGES (1955–57)

The new Jaguar suffered from surprisingly few teething troubles in view of the amount of new engineering it incorporated. The service bulletins that Jaguar issued to their dealers reveal that many minor changes were made to the car's

JAGUAR MK I (1955–1959)

specification, but that few of these were to counter serious faults. Perhaps the biggest problem was that the Panhard rod mounting on the bodyshell was weak, and a number of breakages were reported. So in May 1956, Jaguar advised dealers to weld a reinforcing plate to customers' cars, and at the same time introduced an adjustable rod on production, which allowed the correct tension to be maintained.

Other problems concerned the rear springs, which could create irritating knocking noises. The first modifications were made in autumn 1956, when a new front mounting plate was added in production and the spring leaves gained rubber ends. Unfortunately, this was not the whole answer, and further reports of problems came in. So early in 1957, Jaguar advised their dealers to check for distortion of the spring mounting clamps. Even that did not cure the problem completely, and the service bulletins would continue to offer suggestions for dealing with the problem right through into 1958.

Performance and handling were generally satisfactory. Longer front springs were fitted at the end of 1955 to reduce front-end cornering roll, and in spring 1956 the carburettors were modified to deal with complaints about flat spots in low-speed acceleration. The twin Solex carburettors gave occasional cause for concern for the rest of the 2.4-litre model's production life, but Jaguar doggedly retained them until 1967. Otherwise, only two engine changes of note were made in this early period. One was in June 1956, when a vibration damper was added to the crankshaft nose to give smoother running, and the other was in November that year when a steel sump replaced the original aluminium type.

Most owners had no cause for complaint about the performance of their 2.4-litre Jaguars. Nevertheless, Jaguar Cars were well aware of their reputation as a maker of performance cars and so, to cater for those who wanted more, they introduced tuning kits during 1956. These never sold very strongly, partly no doubt because few buyers saw the need for any extra performance – particularly on Britain's slow and crowded roads in the pre-motorway era.

The tuning kits came in three stages, each one making a worthwhile difference to top-end performance but – as Jaguar warned – also having an adverse effect on acceleration at low speeds. The Stage I kit boosted power from

TLE 793 was registered in November 1956, but by the time this photograph was taken it had acquired Mk 2-type convex headlamp lenses instead of the original flat-lens type. The yellow headlamp bulbs had been fitted for a continental trip, while the large rear-view mirror is later and more practical than the original.

32

JAGUAR MK I (1955–1959)

This side view shows that TLE 793 carries the optional Ace Turbo wheel trims. The car is finished in Sherwood Green.

the standard 112bhp at 5,750rpm to 119bhp at 5,800rpm and consisted essentially of modifications to the carburettors and the exhaust. Stage II took power up to 131bhp at 5,900rpm and brought high-lift camshafts, stronger valve springs and a new distributor in addition to the Stage I changes. Stage III delivered 150bhp at 6,000rpm by replacing the cylinder head with the new big-valve B-type head that was fitted to the 3.4-litre engine in the XK140 models. With the new head came two SU HD6 carburettors and a twin-pipe exhaust system. Jaguar also recommended fitting (at extra cost) uprated clutch springs to cope with the increased torque of the Stage III conversion.

Gearing came in for early revision, too. The 4.55:1 differential fitted to both overdrive and non-overdrive versions of the 2.4-litre from the start had clearly proved too low for comfortable cruising with the non-overdrive gearbox. So in June 1956, after just 2,188 cars had been built, the non-overdrive models changed to a higher 4.27:1 ratio. At the same time, a conversion kit became available so that owners of earlier non-overdrive cars could add an overdrive. A month after that came a further revision in which a close-ratio gearbox was standardized on cars with overdrive; the non-overdrive models retained the original gearbox.

The cost of these early changes was no doubt absorbed in the price rise of October 1956, with the Special Equipment model soaring from £916 to £976 before purchase tax. After the Chancellor had taken his share, the total cost was now £1,465 7s 0d, and adding overdrive to the specification put that up to £1,532 17s 0d. However, this was a period of general inflation in new-car prices and the increase was not out of line with increases made by other manufacturers. There was another price rise in October 1957 when the Special Equipment overdrive car climbed to £1,061 – £1,597 7s 0d including purchase tax. But by this stage, the 2.4-litre was no longer the only compact Jaguar on the market. It had been joined by an alternative model with the more powerful 3.4-litre engine.

This 1957-model 2.4-litre car has been fitted retrospectively with cut-away rear-wheel spats (first introduced on the 3.4-litre model) – they reveal just how narrow the rear track was on the Mk I.

33

■ JAGUAR MK I (1955–1959)

A COUPÉ PROPOSAL

Jaguar was clearly looking at ways of extending its new saloon range from quite early on and there is evidence that a two-door coupé derivative was under consideration during 1956. However, no running prototype seems to have been built and no pictures of any full-size mock-up have been discovered.

The evidence consists of body drawings from Pressed Steel dated 30 May 1956 and described simply as 'Jaguar Sports'. They show that the saloon's front-end panelling and floorpan would have been retained but the whole of the rear end and the roof panel would have been new. The plan was to give the car a longer tail and larger boot – the design of that boot hints at the design Lyons would later use for the Mk X saloons and subsequently for the S-type and 420 compacts.

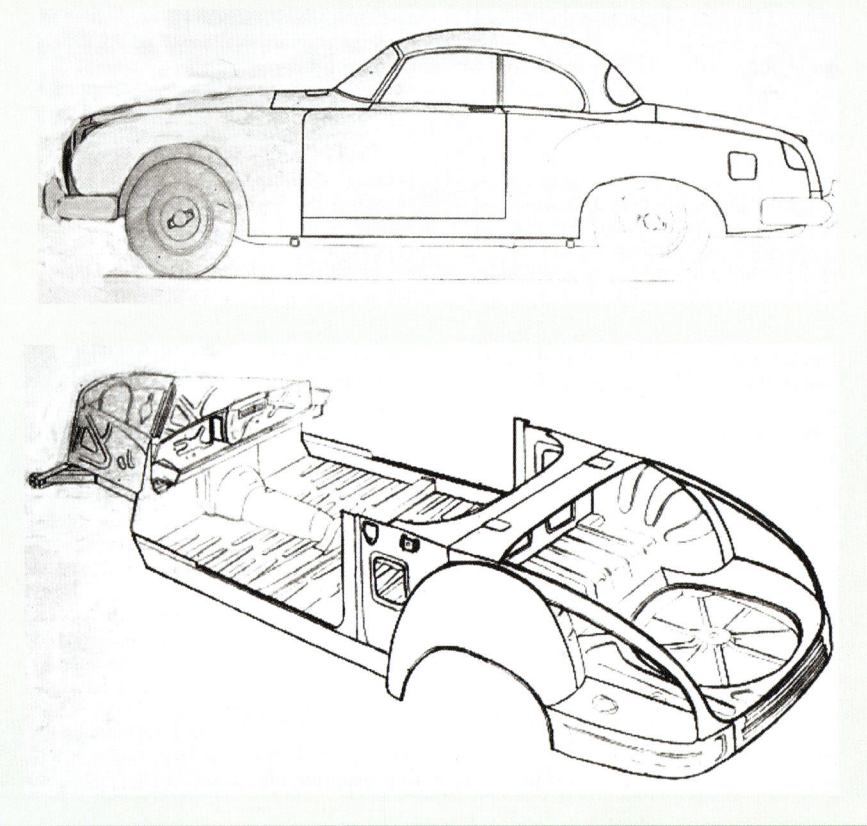

Little information is available about the 'Jaguar Sports' that might have been based on the 2.4-litre car, but these drawings from Pressed Steel give an idea of what might have been.

ENTER THE 3.4

A 3.4-litre edition of the compact Jaguar had been on the cards from a very early stage, and the car's engine bay had been designed to accommodate the 3442cc engine, which was considerably taller than the short-stroke 2.4-litre type. It seems pretty certain that the main reason for the car's development was Jaguar's desire to build on its sales success in the USA.

Well aware that US customers liked both plenty of power and automatic transmissions, William Lyons was certainly planning a 3.4-litre Automatic model for that market by autumn 1955 and he referred to it in a letter dated 4 November that year to John Dugdale of Jaguar's US subsidiary (reproduced in the latter's book, *Jaguar in America*). At that stage, Lyons hoped that the 3.4-litre model might be ready for March 1956. As things were to turn out, however, the car did not enter production until the beginning of 1957.

There was quite a lot more to the development of a 3.4-litre model than dropping the larger engine into a 2.4-litre bodyshell. The bigger engine generated more heat, so a larger coolant radiator had to be fitted. That in turn required a larger grille if it was to get enough cooling air, and to allow for the larger grille the front wings had to be modified. The 3.4-litre engine was also heavier than the 2.4-litre type, so the front suspension needed stronger coil springs. Then a twin-pipe exhaust system proved necessary to allow the engine to give its best.

The 3.4-litre engine delivered much more torque than the 2.4-litre type, and that demanded a stronger rear axle. The Jaguar engineers chose to use one made by Salisbury, in effect using the strong centre section of the Mk VII saloon

JAGUAR MK I (1955–1959)

TOP LEFT: **With the 3.4-litre cars came a wider radiator grille and modified front wings to suit. This early example shows how the grille, which had a greater number of slimmer bars than the original 2.4, helped to make the cars look wider.**

TOP RIGHT: **The 3.4-litre engine was rather taller than the 2.4-litre type. This photograph shows the large black-painted air cleaner box that sat on top of the cam covers.**

MIDDLE: **That narrow rear track is in evidence again here on a late 3.4-litre Mk I attractively painted in Cotswold Blue. Once again, the optional Ace Turbo wheel trims are in evidence.**

All the 3.4-litre cars carried the chrome 'Jaguar 3.4-litre' motif. When an automatic gearbox was fitted, the badge proclaimed the fact.

JAGUAR MK I (1955–1959)

(which already had the 3.4-litre engine) mated to the outer ends of the 2.4-litre's axle casing. Disc brakes were certainly under consideration for the road cars by the time Jaguar were working on the 3.4-litre compact, but they were not yet ready for production. So Browns Lane did what it could with drum brakes. The cut-away rear spats of the production 3.4-litre car were almost certainly not just a ready means of identification, for they also helped to get more cooling air to the rear drums and so minimize brake fade. Not much could be done about the front drums, however, and as a result the early drum-braked 3.4-litre Jaguar was not a car that inspired confidence in high-speed motoring.

By the time the car was ready for production at the beginning of 1957, a number of features distinguished it from the 2.4-litre model. The cut-away wheel spats and twin exhaust pipes were the most obvious of these, but a close look revealed the wider grille with a 3.4-litre emblem at the top, plus a chromed 3.4 badge on the boot lid. Like the almost mythical 'standard' 2.4, the 3.4 had no fog lamps on its front bumper. For the US and some other export markets, this would remain the case, but in Britain fog lamps soon became standard equipment, probably in response to customer demand – a model that was more expensive than even a Special Equipment 2.4 did need to have at least the same levels of equipment! Most 3.4s were also fitted with the extra-cost option of wire wheels, initially with sixty spokes, as on the lighter sports cars, and initially available painted to match the body colour, stove-enamelled in silver, or chromed.

As those badges made clear, the new car was known from its introduction as a Jaguar 3.4-litre. The analogy of the 2.4 and 3.4 names made sense for the two compact models, although it is interesting that the 3442cc engine had earlier been known as a '3½-litre' type. In the 3.4-litre saloons, it came in XK140 tune with the B-type big-valve cylinder head, twin SU carburettors and 210bhp power output. That gave the car astonishing performance, even though it was heavier than the 2.4-litre models. While a 2.4-litre Jaguar could just about exceed 100mph (160km/h) with a following wind, the 3.4-litre model was capable of 120mph (193km/h). In 1957, when small family saloons like the Austin A30 or Standard Eight were flat-out at 65mph (105km/h), that seemed like simply enormous performance. Not surprisingly, it did a power of good for Jaguar's image around the world.

The new 3.4-litre Jaguar could be had with three different gearbox options: four-speed manual, four-speed manual with overdrive (both using the Moss gearbox) or three-speed automatic. The automatics were not quite as fast as cars with manual gearboxes, but the losses were mainly in acceleration. For the 3.4, Jaguar had chosen the same Borg Warner type DG automatic box as they had used in the Mk VII saloons since 1953. Manufactured at Borg Warner's UK plant in Letchworth, Hertfordshire, the type DG incorporated a full-throttle kick-down, a solenoid-operated anti-creep device that held the rear brakes on until the accelerator was depressed, and an intermediate speed hold, or lock-up.

As the automatic cars were expected to appeal mainly in the USA, where full-width front bench seats were still common, the automatic Jaguars came with a split-bench front seat in place of the standard twin bucket seats. To make room for a centre passenger's legs, the automatic selector quadrant was located underneath the centre of the dashboard. Although the arrangement was unusual, the P-N-D-L-R selector positions were conventional; the intermediate-hold switch was separate from the main quadrant and was fitted into the redundant position otherwise occupied by the overdrive switch.

That huge steering wheel dominates the dashboard of this 3.4-litre automatic model. The split-bench type of front seat was standard on automatics, which had a quadrant gear selector at the bottom of the dash centre panel.

Jaguar had planned to put the 3.4-litre saloon on sale in the USA in March 1957 and to follow up with cars for the UK and other markets later in the year. However, rumours about the car's imminent arrival forced them to acknowledge its existence as early as February. It was a most inconvenient time: the company was attempting to build up a launch stock for its US dealers so that customers would not have to wait for their orders to be fulfilled. Only around 200 cars – not enough – had been shipped to the USA when the rumours started. Worse was yet to come. During February, as enthusiastic customers in the UK and elsewhere began to make enquiries about the new 3.4-litre model, a large area of the Browns Lane factory was destroyed by fire.

Several examples of the new car were among those lost in the blaze, but a truly superhuman effort by the Jaguar workforce and by contractors engaged to clear up the mess allowed limited production to restart within nine days and full production to be achieved again after six weeks. Right-hand-drive cars did not become available until May, however, and so *The Motor* had to be content with a left-hand-drive example with automatic gearbox when they asked for a car to test during April. As production was still primarily geared to meet demand from the USA, where the car had been ecstatically received, few British customers took delivery before the autumn, and by that time a number of specification changes had already been made.

The manual models, on the other hand, came with individual front seats, as seen here.

Wood trim and leather upholstery created a luxurious cabin ambience in the back of this 3.4-litre automatic.

THE 3.4-LITRE AND THE PRESS

The earliest published road test of the 3.4-litre model was in *The Motor* of 10 April 1957. The car (registered TRW 316) was a left-hand-drive automatic and the testers found it had a dual personality. While quiet and smooth when driven gently, the car unleashed its 'vast power' when the accelerator was pressed hard:

The initial getaway from rest is impressive, the manner in which the acceleration is then sustained right up to well over 100mph fantastic for such a roomy and refined car, whilst it requires emphasis that obtaining maximum acceleration merely involves pressing the accelerator hard without any need to use a clutch pedal or gear lever skilfully.

JAGUAR MK I (1955–1959)

A valuable advantage was the ability to exceed 80mph (129km/h) in the intermediate gear, 'so that a slower car can safely be passed on surprisingly short stretches of clear road'. The gearbox settings did allow a double-change, 'down and then very quickly up again', but the change down to first at low speeds could be jerky.

The test car's brakes juddered and pulled, and it was considered that 'a braking system able to withstand harder usage without protest would greatly widen the appeal of this car.' It was quite easy to provoke wheelspin, and the heater was poor. However:

> *fundamentally, this is a car which has few superiors in respect of providing smooth, quiet and comfortable travel for five people, yet which has speed and acceleration of the most remarkable order.... No sports car designed as an amusing but impractical plaything for the wealthy, it is a first-class express carriage which will be invaluable to the many men for whom, literally, time is money.*

A couple of weeks later, in its 26 April issue, *Autosport* described the new model as 'sensational' after trying out an overdrive car in the USA. Gregor Grant wrote, 'I cannot remember having driven a car which combines so many admirable features.' He found the roadholding 'beyond criticism', and reported 'no disconcerting pitching, no wavering nor shimmying, and a lightness of steering which makes for completely effortless motoring. This is extremely important in USA and Canada, where the vast distances involved make 600–700 miles a day fairly commonplace.'

At one point in the test, one of the North American Jaguar PR team 'demonstrated the complete silence of the engine and transmission by cutting into neutral at 55mph cruising. There was no discernible difference, and it was extremely difficult to tell when he snicked it into gear again.'

The Americans did love the bigger-engined Jaguar. *Sports Car Illustrated* tested an example in April 1958 and concluded that it was a 'magnificent automobile that no-one in his right mind could seriously fault'. It had performance better than that of American cars with engines twice the size, it had good looks (especially when fitted with wire wheels and whitewall tyres) and it stopped and handled like no other saloon then sold in the USA.

PRODUCTION CHANGES (1957–59)

Between 1957 and 1959, there were dozens of minor production changes to the 2.4-litre and 3.4-litre Jaguars, most of them barely visible. Unquestionably the most important, though, was the introduction of Dunlop disc brakes on all four wheels as an option shortly after production began. In practice, very few 3.4-litre cars would be delivered with drum brakes. Another early change, in September 1957,

Looking distinctly aggressive with its body-colour wire wheels is this 1959 manual-gearbox car in British Racing Green.

The wire wheels could be had with a chrome-plated or stove-enamelled finish, but the serious performance enthusiast preferred the no-nonsense look of the body-coloured option.

saw the 2.4-litre cars take on the larger grille and modified front wings of the 3.4-litre cars and also their cut-away rear wheel spats (although the exact date of this latter change has never been satisfactorily pinned down). November 1957 then brought an automatic gearbox option for the 2.4-litre, with the same Borg Warner gearbox that was used in the 3.4-litre cars.

After that, visible changes were few and far between. From January 1959, the optional wire wheels with their original 60-spoke design were replaced by stronger 72-spoke wheels, and at the same time a new knock-on hubcap without the protruding spinners of the standard type became available with wire wheels for the German market. This was necessary to meet new German safety regulations, but was not made available elsewhere because Jaguar believed the original type with its twin 'ears' had more visual appeal. Then there were a couple of changes to the interior over the summer of 1958: the original cranked gear lever on manual cars gave way to a neater-looking remote shift and the illuminated overdrive switch on the dash was replaced by a metal toggle-type switch. There was little point in changing anything major as late as 1959 because the Mk 2 versions of the compact Jaguars were just around the corner – but there would be changes under the skin of the 2.4-litre and 3.4-litre Jaguars until quite late in production.

Those noisy rear springs remained a problem. Customers continued to complain of knocking noises from the rear of the car, usually most noticeable when the back end was heavily laden. The cures recommended in earlier service literature helped in some cases but not in all of them. In September 1957 Jaguar decided that the handbrake compensator pivot might be the culprit. Dealers were therefore advised to trim the bracket slightly, but this was once again not the whole answer, and the problem was never resolved satisfactorily. No doubt the truth was that there were several different causes of the noise, and several different varieties of it as well. Noise types and their apparent locations on a car have always been a subjective issue.

As far as the 'chassis' hardware was concerned, most items were already well sorted by the time the 3.4-litre models were introduced. There were changes to the dampers in February 1957 and again in November 1958; the front suspension was given progressive bump stops in February 1958 and the free camber of the rear springs was altered that May. In January 1959 came new suspension ball joints with a larger diameter ball and greater angle of movement. The latest Dunlop RS4 tyres with their improved wet-road grip replaced the original RS3s as original equipment on 3.4-litre models built from April 1958, but the change was not reflected on the smaller-engined cars. Lower-geared steering introduced in April 1959 tackled the criticism that the steering was heavy at parking speeds, although the penalty was a certain amount of woolliness at higher speeds – and in truth the steering was still heavy, if less so.

Brakes underwent another important change in April 1959 when all the disc-braked models took on the latest Dunlop bridge-type calipers. Their major advantage was that they allowed the friction pads to be changed very easily, without the dismantling necessary with the older caliper design. However, there had been earlier braking changes too: servos were given an air cleaner in September 1957, and there were modified fixings for the rear caliper adaptor plate from November 1958. Between November 1957 and February 1958, a 5in (125mm) diameter brake servo was fitted in place of the usual 6.875in (175mm) type on cars with drum brakes, although it is not clear whether this was a modification that failed to live up to expectations or simply the result of supply difficulties.

There were drum-braked models right up to the end of production in 1959, although disc brakes were so commonly ordered as to be almost standard. They were so much more effective than the drum type that Jaguar introduced conversion kits in January 1958 so that owners of older drum-braked cars could change to the newer type. At the same time, a kit was introduced to allow owners of disc-braked cars to fit wire wheels.

JAGUAR MK 1 (1955–1959)

Electrical changes in this period began with a new voltage regulator in May 1957 and a new wiper motor in July. There were also some concerns about battery charging, addressed first in September 1957 when a smaller dynamo pulley was fitted to make the dynamo run faster and therefore put out more charge at a given engine speed. This sufficed until May 1959, when a larger 25-amp dynamo became standard on all models. These changes point to concerns about the charging arrangements at this stage; there was certainly no sudden increase in demand from new electrical equipment. There were more powerful 60-watt headlamps from September 1958 (January 1959 on left-hand-drive cars) and an electric

OPTIONAL EXTRAS – JAGUAR MK 1

Brakes
Disc front brakes
Disc brake conversion kit (from early type to later type calipers)

Electrical
Long-life battery
Master battery switch
Uprated headlamps, 40/45-watt Le Mans type
Windtone horns (pair)

Engine performance
High-compression (9:1) pistons for 3.4-litre engines
Lead-bronze engine bearings
Lightened flywheel
Radiator blind (for faster warm-up)
Tuning kits (Stages I to III) for 2.4-litre models
Twin-pipe exhaust system for 2.4-litre models

Exterior
Cut-away wheel spats (replacement for full spats on early 2.4-litre cars)
GB letters in chrome for boot lid
Laminated windscreen
Lockable fuel filler cap
Lock set to enable one key to fit all exterior locks
Rally lamp (by Desmo)
Radio aerial for roof mounting
Radio aerial for wing mounting
Radio aerial for wing mounting (fully retractable by handle inside car)
Rimbellishers (bright metal wheel trim rings)
Tow-bar (by Witter)
Wheel trims, Ace Turbo type (to replace standard trims)
Wire wheels (in body colour, chrome-plated or silver stove-enamelled)

Gearbox
Automatic gearbox
Close-ratio manual gearbox (for 3.4-litre models)
Competition clutch
Overdrive for manual gearboxes

Handling and roadholding
Alternative tyres: Dunlop Town and Country, Dunlop Fort tubeless, Dunlop Road Speed (for 2.4-litre), Dunlop Weathermaster, Duraband, Goodyear Eagle, India Super, Michelin X radial or whitewall
High-ratio steering box
Limited-slip differential (Thornton Powr-Lok) for 3.4-litre models
Uprated anti-roll bar
Uprated dampers

Interior
Automatic choke cut-out switch (for 3.4-litre engines)
Demister for rear window
Fire extinguisher
Gear lever extension
Passenger grab handle on dashboard
Radio (several types)
Radio extension speaker on rear parcel shelf
Rheostat for instrument panel lights
Safety belts (front seats only)
Seat adjustment bracket, to raise height of driver's seat by 1in (25mm)
Speedometer recalibrated for use with Michelin X radial tyres
Split-bench front seat (automatic type) for cars with manual gearbox
Steering wheel in white, for export only
Vanity mirror for passenger's sun visor

rev counter replaced the cable-driven type from June 1959, but neither of these would have been justification for these upgrades to the charging system.

The Moss manual gearboxes remained unchanged between 1957 and 1959, although the selector mechanism was changed for a remote type, as already explained. The automatics, by contrast, were modified twice. In September 1957 they all gained a more effective anti-creep solenoid, and in May 1958 the valve block was changed on those fitted to 3.4-litre models.

There were far more changes under the bonnet. Cooling system changes began in May 1957, when the 2.4-litre cars took on the larger 3.4-litre type of radiator. Then, from November 1958, the original four-blade cooling fan gave way to a twelve-blade type on all engines. January 1959 brought a new fan belt and pulleys for the 3.4-litre engines. There were several modifications to the lubrication system, too. From February 1957, camshaft rattle during a cold start was reduced by drilling a lubrication hole in each cam; July brought a modified oil filter; and November ushered in a new oil pressure relief valve and more durable timing chain dampers. There was a very late switch to more durable lead-indium bearings on all engines in April 1959.

Other changes for the 3.4-litre engines only included longer inlet valve guides in September 1957 and different carburettor needles from May 1958. All engines had a new thermostat from January 1958 and, more visibly, oil-bath air filters became standard on the 3.4-litre cars in November 1957 and on the 2.4-litre models in September 1958.

SALES OF THE FIRST COMPACT JAGUARS

Production figures show just how successful the early compact Jaguars were. Neither the Suez crisis, which blighted the sales of big-engined cars at the tail end of 1956 and during the first months of 1957, nor the factory fire that destroyed so many brand-new cars that February, seemed to have much effect. Production totals for the 1957 calendar year were marginally better than for 1956, the car's first full year on sale, and that was no doubt helped by the introduction of the 3.4-litre car. For 1958, they climbed still higher, and the 1959 totals (which represented a production period of a little under nine months) were high enough to have achieved a record year if the Mk 2s had not taken over in the autumn.

PRODUCTION FIGURES – JAGUAR MK I

Calendar year	2.4-litre	3.4-litre	Total
1955	32		32
1956	8,029		8,029
1957	3,984	4,536	8,520
1958	4,441	7,164	11,605
1959	3,219	5,580	8,799
Total	19,705	17,280	36,985

Although the 2.4-litre Jaguar sold rather more in its four seasons of production than the 3.4-litre in its two-and-a-half seasons, the bigger-engined car was always the stronger seller once the two models were available side by side. Production of the 2.4-litre Jaguar dropped sharply during 1957 and it is clear that the new 3.4-litre model was taking sales away from the older model. In the home market, however, sales of the two cars were probably fairly evenly matched: the real success of the 3.4-litre car was in overseas markets, and especially in the USA.

In fact, the 2.4-litre had had a rather mixed reception when it was launched in the USA in May 1956. While it was undoubtedly a Jaguar to American eyes, it was not the same sort of car as the big Mk VII on which Jaguar's reputation as a maker of luxurious sporting saloons rested. Nor did it have the sort of power that the US market expected. Some of the US dealers actually argued against releasing it in the USA at all, believing that it would be preferable to wait for the 3.4-litre-engined car. And certainly, *Road & Track* magazine's characterization of the 2.4-litre Jaguar as a 'compact, safe-handling family car' suggested that they viewed it as rather less of a sports saloon than Jaguar had intended, even though they were generally enthusiastic about the car and did go on to say that the 'sportscar performance' was a 'bonus feature'.

In his book *Jaguar in America*, John Dugdale revealed that the company's West Coast office wanted to gather some publicity for the 3.4-litre car by tuning it to run at 150mph (240km/h) across a dried-up lake bed in southern California. However, the cost of preparing the car and the need for direct factory involvement put paid to this idea, and instead the 3.4-litre car was introduced rather more quietly as one of Jaguar's 1957 models.

JAGUAR MK I (1955–1959)

Both in the USA and in other markets, the compact Jaguars – the 3.4-litre models in particular – very rapidly acquired the status of coveted possessions. These were cars to respect for their abilities and their good looks, although the rather heavy styling of these early compacts was not universally liked; some people argued that they lacked the feline grace of the Mk VII saloons and their Mk VIII successors.

In Britain, all Jaguars suffered from the rather scornful description of a 'cad's car', applied in more traditional circles. Not only were they trying to outdo the traditional makers of the British sporting motor car (such as Bentley, Alvis and Lagonda), but their much lower prices gave rise to suspicion that their apparent quality was only skin-deep; and besides, their high-performance abilities were really irrelevant and somewhat ostentatious on the crowded roads of Britain before the motorway era. That era began in 1958 with the opening of the M1; in future, high-performance cars would be not only more relevant but also in more demand.

OVERSEAS ASSEMBLY

One little-known aspect of the early compact Jaguars is that just over 200 cars were assembled in Mexico from semi-knocked-down (SKD) kits that had been shipped out from Browns Lane.

The Mexican government levied an import tax on all fully assembled cars entering the country from abroad, making compact Jaguars unattractively expensive. However, Jaguar's importing agent, Mario Padilla, believed he could find a ready market for them if the price could be kept down by having the cars assembled in-territory. So a deal was struck under which partially assembled cars would be brought into the country to be completed at a plant owned by Padilla.

The operation began in August 1957 and ran until July 1960, when the Mexican government decided to limit the number of foreign motor manufacturers operating in their country. In those three years, a total of 214 compact Jaguars were assembled, 152 of them being 2.4-litre models and the remaining 62 being 3.4-litre cars. The final cars were not assembled until nearly a year after the Mk 2 compacts had been introduced, and were therefore probably the last of the Mk I Jaguars to be built.

RIVALS

Outside the UK, Jaguar were not always able to price their compact saloons as aggressively as they might have wished. Import duties, designed to protect domestic products from foreign imports, inevitably pushed up prices. In their own domestic market, however, where Jaguar could do more or less as they wished with prices, their aggressive pricing strategy was much clearer.

Throughout the second half of the 1950s, the compact Jaguars inhabited a sparsely populated sector of the UK car market. They were always very much more expensive than everyday family saloons – often twice the price – and they were also significantly more expensive than even the more upmarket saloons. Nevertheless, they were also very much cheaper than the luxury cars of their day.

The buyer with £1,300 to spend who planned to choose his new car from among the exhibits at the 1956 Earls Court Motor Show was not exactly spoilt for choice. The 4-cylinder 1622cc Lanchester Sprite represented the old guard, at £1,227 19s 0d inclusive of purchase tax. For £1,254 17s 6d there was the Humber Hawk estate, aimed at a developing market sector and as yet of interest to a minority of buyers; it had a 75bhp, 2.3-litre 4-cylinder engine and was stately rather than sporty. At the sportier end of the market was the 110bhp, 2.4-litre Riley Pathfinder at £1,240 14s 2d, but its brakes and steering were already beginning to attract a questionable reputation.

Just two 6-cylinder cars were on show in this price bracket. One was the Rover 75 with its 80bhp 2.2-litre engine, priced at £1,297 7s 6d inclusive of purchase tax. The other was the new 2.4-litre Jaguar, offering 112bhp for £1,298 15s 10d in Special Equipment form. The Rover had a much more traditional appeal than the Jaguar and was deliberately designed for an older and more sedate clientele. For the buyer who wanted performance and refinement, therefore, there was simply no choice: it had to be the Jaguar.

The position changed very little over the next few years. Jaguar did increase the prices of their compact saloons in 1956, but the change did not bring them up against serious new competition. The Rover 90 and 105S straddled the Jaguar's price, but the very different appeal of the two marques remained unchanged. The Riley was still cheaper, but its reputation was getting worse. The 6-cylinder Humber Super Snipe now entered the equation, but it was a large and not very agile car, while the only newcomer that might have made Browns Lane worry was the Armstrong

POLICE JAGUARS

Around twenty British police forces are thought to have bought 2.4-litre Jaguars as patrol cars, and that certainly helped to give the cars a positive image. It suggested both high performance and reliability – both characteristics in demand by police forces. However, none of the 3.4-litre cars seem to have been supplied as patrol cars, although some were supplied for plain-clothes work. Their extra performance was probably not considered necessary for more mainstream police duties in pre-motorway Britain.

Police Jaguars were popularly believed to have benefited from high-performance tuning, but that was not generally the case. Mechanically and bodily they were standard production vehicles. Contemporary photographs suggest that many cars carried no police identification markings (although in the 1950s any sensible motorist would have paid special attention to a black Jaguar that appeared in the rear-view mirror). Some had small blue 'Police' signs at the front, and some had a bell, a loud-hailer or both on the front bumper. Rotating roof beacons were coming into use but large roof signs were still in the future. As always, individual forces modified cars to suit their own requirements.

Among those forces known to have used Mk I cars were the Bedfordshire Constabulary, the Buckinghamshire Constabulary, the Glasgow City Police, the Somerset Constabulary and the West Sussex Constabulary.

The 2.4-litre Jaguar was taken on as a police car from early in its life. This 1956 model belonged to the West Sussex Constabulary. The photograph comes from the Eric McIntosh Collection that is now held by the Police Vehicle Enthusiasts' Club.

Siddeley 236. Sadly for its makers, it proved no match for the Jaguar.

Over the next couple of years, Jaguar retained their strong position in this sector of the market. Rover, Riley and Humber remained the principal domestic competition and the only other cars in the same price bracket were imports. Cars like the second-series Lancia Appia, the Panhard Dyna, the Citroën DS19, the Simca Chambord and the Studebaker Champion stood very little chance at a time when British car buyers had an overwhelmingly patriotic orientation. Likewise, all these cars were designed to sell at lower prices and only came into the Jaguar's price class because of heavy import duties; so they were hardly competitive on specification. In fact, none of them sold very strongly in Britain.

THE MK I IN MOTOR SPORT

The compact Jaguars had a major and lasting impact on motor sport, and the cars are still popular in historic motor sport events today. On the circuits, the Mk I saloons showed up well from the beginning, but their greatest successes were achieved after 1957, when the 3.4-litre models became available. Nonetheless, these early 3.4-litre Jaguars were flawed cars that needed further development. The Mk I saloons were also robust enough to become quite successful as rally cars, although they were always handicapped by their weight and a certain lack of agility.

Works Period (1955–56)

Launched in the autumn of 1955 but not available in quantity until the beginning of 1956, the Mk I saloons made their competition debut as members of the Jaguar works team in the March 1956 RAC Rally. The event demanded both tight time schedules in the navigational exercises on the road as well as speed in the special tests run at a number of racing circuits. The works 2.4 (JWK 753) driven by Bill Bleakley and navigated by Ian Hall put up a good performance to

■ JAGUAR MK I (1955–1959)

The 2.4-litre Jaguar made its first appearance as a works car at Silverstone in the Daily Express Production Car Race in May 1956. Cornering hard – look at the difference in angles between the front and rear wheels! – is Duncan Hamilton, who would finish third. The Mk VII is also a works car, driven by Paul Frère.

take fourth place overall behind the winning Aston Martin, Ian Appleyard's second-placed XK140 and a Morgan. It was the highest-placed saloon and winner of the over-2000cc Production Touring Cars class, which was no small achievement for a completely untried saloon.

The next appearance of the works 2.4 Jaguars was at the Silverstone Production Car Race in May, when one car (RKV 456) was driven by Mike Hawthorn and the second by Duncan Hamilton. Also competing in a 2.4 was Jaguar dealer John Coombs. Hawthorn's car took the lead from the start but dropped out after only two laps with a broken valve spring; Hamilton, however, brought his car home in a creditable third position.

Just a fortnight later, Paul Frère came a convincing first in the Production Car Race at Spa, in Belgium, driving a works-prepared 2.4 with a C-type cylinder head, 2-in SU carburettors and a close-ratio gearbox. Frère's success represented the first outright win for a compact Jaguar. However, that was to be that as far as the works 2.4s were concerned, and the 3.4-litre cars, still unannounced, would never race under the auspices of a Jaguar works team.

On 13 October 1956, Jaguar announced that it would no longer field a works team, at least for the present. The reason given was that the company's engineering division was too heavily committed to forthcoming model developments. That was no doubt at least partly true. Nevertheless, works-prepared cars did race in the hands of privateers and Jaguar continued for many years to provide advice and assistance to drivers who had a good chance of upholding the Jaguar name in motor sport.

Mike Hawthorn's 3.4-litre Mk I Jaguar was a very well-known competition car. A careful look at this photograph reveals that its rear track was wider than standard.

Privateers on the Track (1957–59)

Over the next three years, the 2.4-litre Jaguars remained popular in both circuit and rally events in the hands of privateers, but the better drivers – and the wealthier ones among the others – switched to the new 3.4-litre cars as soon as they became available in the first quarter of 1957.

Saloon car racing the way it used to be: this is Sir Gawaine Baillie in a wire-wheeled 3.4-litre Mk I at Brands Hatch on Boxing Day, 1957.

However, little of significance happened for nearly a year after Jaguar's withdrawal from competition, mainly because the Suez Crisis and the petrol shortages that ensued played havoc with motor sport in Europe. In Britain, five months of petrol rationing was ended in May 1957 and motor sport gradually returned to normal.

Jaguar had prepared three of the new 3.4-litre cars for privateers and these appeared in the Production Car Race at Silverstone that September. The drivers – all names familiar from the Jaguar works teams of old – were Mike Hawthorn, Duncan Hamilton and Ivor Bueb, and they finished first, second and third respectively to win the team prize for Jaguar and start the 3.4's competition career with a flourish. Perhaps almost equally impressive was that fifth place in the race went to Ron Flockhart, who was driving John Coombs's 2.4-litre car.

It took a skilful and courageous driver to pilot one of these early 3.4s to victory. Hawthorn's RVC 592, Hamilton's VDU 384 and Bueb's VDU 385 all suffered from brake fade, a problem that had become apparent during the very first outings of the 2.4-litre cars in 1956. Fortunately, the new disc brakes, already a production option by the time of the Silverstone event, would make the cars quite a different proposition.

The 3.4s starred in just one more important event before the 1957 season ended. Tommy Sopwith and Sir Gawaine Baillie had both bought themselves 3.4-litre Jaguars, and at the Brands Hatch touring car race held on Boxing Day, they finished first and second. Sopwith's first-placed car, registered EN 400, was one that racegoers would see very much more of.

During 1958, he and Baillie delighted the crowds with their Jaguars, as did Hawthorn, Bueb and Hamilton. It was a 1-2-3 victory for the Jaguars of Hamilton, Sopwith and Flockhart at the Silverstone touring car race in May 1958, and by now the news about the 3.4 was spreading. So it was that US sports car champion Walter Hansgen, a member of the Briggs Cunningham team, entered a Coombs-prepared 3.4 in the saloon car race held on Grand Prix day at Silverstone in July. Sopwith's Jaguar led until it lost a wheel at about half-distance, when Hansgen in TWK 287 inherited the lead and retained it with ease to the end. He was followed past the finishing line by a procession of three more 3.4-litre Jaguars, driven by Baillie, Jack Crawley and Jeff Uren.

That year was a great one for Tommy Sopwith, who raced as team leader for Equipe Endeavour, and allowed him to end his distinguished racing career on a high note. At Crystal Palace, where a saloon car event was held for the first time during a BRSCC event, he took first place and fastest lap honours in his 3.4 and was followed over the line by Baillie and Uren, both also in 3.4 Jaguars. At Brands Hatch in October he won again, and at Snetterton later that month he took his 3.4 to the chequered flag for the last time.

With Sopwith no longer in the running, and Hawthorn tragically killed at the wheel of his 3.4-litre Jaguar on the road early in the new year, 1959 was bound to be different. Moreover, it was to be the final year of production for the Mk Is, which paved the way splendidly for their Mk 2 successors by continuing their dominance of saloon car events.

The Coombs racing team was now boosted by other 'name' drivers, including Formula 1 driver Roy Salvadori, who was most often seen behind the wheel of a 3.4-litre

JAGUAR MK I (1955–1959)

BUY I was one of the Coombs racing Jaguars, and was often driven for the team by Roy Salvadori. The car has survived and races in historic events today.

registered as BUY 1. Meanwhile, at Equipe Endeavour, Ivor Bueb took over from Tommy Sopwith as team leader and repeated his success on the tracks. Bueb's 3.4, bearing the fictional registration plate IVA 400, took first place in the production car races at Silverstone, Aintree and Goodwood, in each case leaving second place to Roy Salvadori in the Coombs-prepared 3.4 (287 JPK) and third place to Sir Gawaine Baillie in another 3.4 (UXD 400). (At Silverstone, the next three places also fell to compact Jaguars, fourth and fifth going to Dick Protheroe and Dixon in 3.4s and sixth to Peter Bland in a 2.4-litre car.) Finally, on the other side of the Atlantic, where the 3.4-litre Jaguar was enjoying huge popularity, Walter Hansgen managed to persuade Jaguar to prepare him an example, which he then drove to victory in the support race for the US Grand Prix, the compact sedan race.

Privateers in Rallying (1957–59)

The stars of Jaguar rallying in the late 1950s were the brothers Don and Erle Morley, although they were certainly not the only team to take honours with the Mk I saloons. In 1957, 1958 and 1959 they made the Tulip Rally their own, driving first a 2.4- then a 3.4-litre Jaguar and working their way up from third in class, through a class win and eighth overall, to outright victory. Both the 2.4, which they drove in the 1957 and 1958 events, and the 3.4 they had for 1959, wore the same registration number, DJM 400.

Brothers Don and Erle Morley on their way to victory in the 1957 Tulip Rally. DJM 400 was a 3.4-litre model.

JAGUAR MK I (1955–1959)

IDENTIFICATION – JAGUAR MK I

Identification numbers are stamped on a plate in the engine compartment, attached to the right-hand inner wing. The engine number, body number and gearbox number are repeated elsewhere, as shown below.

Car Number
The car number, also known as the chassis number or VIN (Vehicle Identification Number), is found only on the plate on the right-hand inner wing. A typical car number would be 905302 DN. The numerals are the car's serial number and the letters show the transmission type.

The serial number sequences are:

	RHD	LHD
2.4	900001–916250	940001–943742
3.4	970001–978945	985001–993461

The suffixes decode as follows:

BW   Borg Warner automatic gearbox
DN   Laycock de Normanville overdrive

Engine Number
The engine number is stamped on the right-hand side of the cylinder block above the oil filter and again at the front of the cylinder head casting, beside the front spark plug hole.

A typical engine number would be BC 3501/8. This breaks down into three elements:

BC   Engine type identifier (see below)
3501   Serial number
/8   Compression ratio (/8 for 8:1 compression, /9 for 9:1)

The type identifiers are:

BB, BC, BD and BE   2.4-litre engines
KE and KF   3.4-litre engines

Body Number
The body number is stamped on a small plate attached to the right-hand side of the bulkhead, under the bonnet. It generally has four digits.

Gearbox Number
On all manual gearboxes, the gearbox number is stamped on a small shoulder at the left-hand rear corner of the gearbox casing, and on the top cover around the rim of the core plug aperture. On automatic gearboxes, the number is stamped on a plate attached to the left-hand side of the gearbox casing.

That 3.4-litre car remained in everyday use for a further six years, but it was never rallied again. Impressed by the brothers' winning performance in the 1959 Tulip Rally, Marcus Chambers of the BMC competitions department made them an offer they were more than happy to accept, and thereafter their rallying career was pursued at the wheel of an Austin-Healey 3000.

The 1957 rallying season was truncated by the Suez Crisis – the Monte Carlo rally was cancelled – and the compact Jaguars scored no more rally successes that year. However, 1958 showed more promise. The large number of hopefuls who entered that year's Monte in Jaguars was a clear demonstration of the respect in which the car was then held, but the results were unspectacular. The highest-placed Jaguar was the 3.4 of Carris and Beeziers, which came second in its class but was a lowly twenty-fourth in the overall classification. The RAC, Acropolis, Scottish and Liège–Rome–Liège rallies all produced class wins but no more for the compact Jaguars, and by the end of the season it was beginning to look as if the cars would not be able to duplicate their circuit successes in international rally events.

Yet 1959 produced its share of victories. Not only did the Morley brothers take first overall in the Tulip Rally, but Nano da Silva Ramos also drove his 3.4 to first place in the Tour de France. In the Monte and the Scottish Rally that year, compact Jaguars again recorded class wins, and in the minor Sestrières Rally, the German team of Plat and Heinemann took a second in class with their 3.4.

SPECIFICATIONS – JAGUAR MK 1

Engines
2.4-litre
Type XK 6-cylinder, with cast-iron block and aluminium-alloy head
2483cc (83 x 76.5mm)
Twin overhead camshafts, chain-driven
Seven-bearing crankshaft
Compression ratio 8:1 (7:1 available)
Two Solex B32 PBI-5 carburettors
112bhp at 5,750rpm
140lb ft at 2,000rpm

3.4-litre
Type XK 6-cylinder, with cast-iron block and aluminium-alloy head
3442cc (83 x 106mm)
Twin overhead camshafts, chain-driven
Seven-bearing crankshaft
Compression ratio 8:1 (7:1 and 9:1 available)
Two SU HD6 carburettors
210bhp at 5,500rpm (with standard compression)
216lb ft at 3,000rpm

Transmission
Hydraulically operated clutch with 9in diameter (manual) or torque converter (automatic)
Four-speed Moss manual gearbox
  Ratios 3.37:1, 1.98:1, 1.36:1, 1.00:1 (for 2.4-litre)
  Ratios 3.37:1, 1.86:1, 1.28:1, 1.00:1 (for 3.4-litre)
Optional overdrive with 0.77:1 ratio
Three-speed Borg Warner type DG automatic
  Ratios 4.97:1, 3.09:1, 1.00:1
Four-speed close-ratio manual gearbox (optional on 3.4-litre only)
  Ratios 2.98:1, 1.36:1, 1.21:1, 1.00:1

Axle ratio
2.4-litre
4.55:1 with four-speed manual gearbox
4.27:1 with overdrive
3.54:1 with automatic gearbox
3.4-litre
3.54:1 with four-speed manual, close-ratio and automatic gearboxes
3.77:1 with overdrive

Suspension, steering and brakes
Independent front suspension with wishbones, coil springs and anti-roll bar
Live rear axle with radius arms, Panhard rod and cantilevered semi-elliptic leaf springs
Burman recirculating-ball, worm-and-nut steering
Drum brakes with 11.125in diameter front and rear as standard; front discs with 12in diameter optional from late 1957

Dimensions
Overall length	180.75in (4,591mm)
Overall width	66.75in (1,695mm)
Overall height	57.5in (1,460mm)
Wheelbase	107.375in (2,727mm)
Front track	54.625in (1,387mm)
Rear track	50.125in (1,273mm)

Wheels and tyres
15in steel disc wheels standard, with 4.5in rims
15in wire-spoke wheels optional
6.40 x 15 cross-ply tyres

Kerb weights
2.4-litre	2,960lb (1,343kg)
3.4-litre	3,192lb (1,448kg)

PERFORMANCE FIGURES – JAGUAR MK 1

2.4-litre overdrive
0–60mph	13.5sec
Maximum speed	104mph (167km/h)
Fuel consumption	20–23mpg (12–14ltr/100km)

3.4-litre automatic
0–60mph	11.2sec
Maximum speed	120mph (193km/h)
Fuel consumption	19–21mpg (13–15ltr/100km)

Note that these figures are representative only.

PAINT AND TRIM COLOURS – JAGUAR MK I

The same options were available on both models. Some cars were painted and trimmed to special order.

September 1955 to March 1956
There were ten standard body paint colours and six interior-trim options:

Body	Interior
Battleship Grey	Grey or Red
Birch Grey	Grey, Blue or Red
Black	Biscuit, Grey, Red or Tan
British Racing Green	Green or Tan
Dove Grey	Biscuit or Tan
Lavender Grey	Green or Red
Old English White	Red
Pastel Blue	Blue or Grey
Pastel Green	Green
Suede Green	Green

April 1956 to December 1956
Three new paint colours were added, bringing the total to thirteen. The same six interior-trim options were available. The new combinations were:

Body	Interior
Carmine Red	Red
Maroon	Biscuit or Red
Pearl Grey	Blue, Grey or Red

January 1957 to October 1957
Four more paint colours were added to make a total of seventeen options. During this period, Maroon was generally known as Imperial Maroon. The same six interior-trim options were available. The new combinations were:

Body	Interior
Claret	Red or Tan
Cotswold Blue	Blue or Grey
Indigo Blue	Blue or Grey
Sherwood Green	Green

November 1957 to December 1957
Three of the original paint colours were now dropped, leaving fourteen options available. The six interior-trim options remained unchanged, as did the combinations of paint and trim. The three colours no longer available were Battleship Grey, Birch Grey and Pastel Blue.

January 1958 to (approximately) March 1959
There were again fourteen standard paint colours, although Forest Green replaced Sherwood Green. The same six interior-trim options remained available. The full list was:

Body	Interior
Black	Biscuit, Grey, Red or Tan
British Racing Green	Green or Tan
Carmine Red	Red
Claret	Red or Tan
Cotswold Blue	Blue or Grey
Dove Grey	Biscuit or Tan
Forest Green	Green or Grey
Imperial Maroon	Biscuit or Red
Indigo Blue	Blue or Grey
Lavender Grey	Green or Red
Old English White	Red
Pastel Green	Green
Pearl Grey	Blue, Grey or Red
Suede Green	Green

March 1959 (approximately) to September 1959
The number of paint options was reduced to eight, and the same six interior-trim options remained available. The six colours no longer available were Claret, Dove Grey, Forest Green, Lavender Grey, Pastel Green and Suede Green.

Note that Pearl Grey existed in at least three slightly different shades between 1956 and 1959.

JAGUAR MK I (1955–1959)

SO YOU WANT TO BUY A MK I COMPACT JAGUAR?

You'll love the car's combination of fifties ambience with smooth power delivery that allows you to potter in traffic and gives you a real shove in the back when you floor the accelerator on the open road. Yes, the 2.4 delivers less accelerative thrust, but it's still a blast to drive.

However, this is an early monocoque design and rusts just about everywhere. Repairs can be both tricky and very expensive. At the front, check the 'crow's feet' wing supports behind the wheels. The whole area behind the wheels can rust, exposing the A-pillar, inner sill and lower front wing to further corrosion. Sills are structural and must be sound; check particularly around the jacking points. The whole floorpan can rust, too. Look for problems in the door skins and lower door frames, and check for doors that have dropped.

Most expensive to put right will be rust around the rear spring hangers, Panhard rod assembly and rear seat pan. Check the inner wings, and the outers, too, behind the removable spats. Some cars even rust around front and rear screens, and the bonnet and boot lid can go, as well.

Oil pressure is a guide to the engine's health and should read between 35 and 45psi when the oil is hot. Watch for leaks from the crankshaft rear seal (major work needed), the back of the sump and the back of the cam covers. Regular oil changes are critical. Even the best ones use some oil: a light-blue tinge to the exhaust is quite normal.

All engines should start instantly. Uneven running will probably be a carburettor problem; 2.4s had Solexes and 3.4s SUs, but many 2.4s now have SUs. Listen for noise from the timing chains. If it's at the top, the cure is relatively easy and inexpensive, but noise from the bottom chain can prove costly to rectify.

The four-speed Moss gearbox has long throws, no synchromesh on first, and a vintage whine in first and reverse. It may also whine less noticeably in second and third. Wear can make second impossible to select, but these gearboxes are generally long-lived and reliable. Many manual cars came with overdrive, a Laycock de Normanville type that is engaged electrically. Make sure it works properly – delayed engagement spells bad news. Clutches wear quite quickly, especially on a 3.4, and changing the plate is a major job.

The three-speed automatic option was a Borg Warner DG, which is robust but slow and clunky by modern standards. Worn brake bands can slip. Check the colour of the transmission fluid: red or light brown is acceptable, but black means the gearbox is worn. Parts are harder to find than for later Borg Warner gearboxes, but persistence pays.

Early cars had all-round drum brakes, with a servo. Discs arrived soon after the 3.4 was introduced – and make a huge difference. Some early cars will have been converted. The handbrake on disc-braked cars has its own pads and was never much good.

Problems inside the passenger cabin will be obvious – lifting and cracking wood veneer, rotten carpets, worn and cracked leather. Everything can be repaired or replaced at a price, but those prices can make your eyes water. A poor interior may be a bargaining point when you're buying, but it will probably be a long time before you can afford to put it right.

CHAPTER FOUR

DEVELOPING THE JAGUAR MK 2

Even though the early compact Jaguars had been extremely well received, they had certainly not been above criticism. Some of that criticism had focused on outmoded and bloated styling, tricky high-speed handling, old-fashioned interior design, inadequate heating and ventilation, and poor visibility for the driver. These, then, were the areas that Jaguar needed to address if initial strong sales were to be maintained.

Exactly what Sir William Lyons (who had been knighted in 1956) instructed his engineers and designers to do is not clear, but he probably told them to make the car look as fresh as possible and address all its mechanical shortcomings while making the minimum possible number of alterations. He may also have asked them to give the car more luxury features, but in the background there must have been budget considerations. Major changes to the bodyshell would be very expensive and were probably ruled out from the start.

Exactly when work began on these improvements is hard to pin down, but Jaguar historian Andrew Whyte was probably right in believing that the Utah facelift, or Utah Mk 2, took shape over the summer of 1958. The revised car would go on sale in autumn 1959.

MECHANICAL CHANGES

One of Jaguar's great strengths had always been strong performance supported by first-rate handling and braking, so criticism of the latter two levelled at the early compact saloons must have hurt. As Chapter 3 shows, several running changes were made to the original cars to improve things – such as the introduction of disc brakes and the modification of the front suspension – but the biggest obstacle to better handling lay in the narrow track of the rear axle. At moderate speeds, it could make the car feel disconcertingly unresponsive through a series of S-bends, while at higher speeds it was responsible for a degree of instability.

The Browns Lane engineers were already working on a new independent rear suspension but this would not be ready in time for the revised compact saloons so the existing system had to be modified. The car's handling was greatly improved simply by fitting a wider rear axle and retaining the existing suspension – a change that had been made

Mk 2 assembly lines at Browns Lane. Nearest the camera on the left, the car wears whitewall tyres, suggesting that it may have been destined for the USA. JDHT

DEVELOPING THE JAGUAR MK 2

to Mike Hawthorn's racing Jaguar and probably to others as well. At the front, the suspension was modified to reduce roll in corners, and the car's roll centre was raised by placing the pivots of the upper and lower wishbones slightly further apart and by angling both wishbones downwards.

Jaguar had already been offering disc brakes on the front wheels of their compact saloons. The wider rear axle now enabled Jaguar to fit disc brakes to the rear wheels and to make the all-disc set-up with its vacuum servo standard on all models.

As for the criticisms of heavy steering, power assistance was the obvious solution. Jaguar had already introduced it on the Mk VIII models in April 1958; for the Mk 2 compacts they would turn once again to Burman for the steering box (which was smaller than on the Mk VIIIs to suit the space available) and to Hobourn-Eaton for the engine-driven hydraulic pump. However, in practice the system was not made available until a year after production began.

There had to be performance improvements, of course, and these were not difficult to achieve with existing hardware, although Jaguar did miscalculate rather badly with the 2.4-litre engine. They assumed that fitting the big-valve B-type cylinder head to give 120bhp would make a difference, and were somewhat shamefaced when they discovered that the extra weight of the revised cars (a Mk 2 2.4 weighed as much as a Mk 1 3.4) more than countered the extra power. The 2.4-litre Mk 2 was markedly slower than the original car, and would not even reach 100mph. As a result, there were no 2.4-litre Mk 2 road test cars for the press to try!

The 3.4-litre engine had more than enough power to maintain the performance of the original cars with that engine, but Jaguar knew that there was a demand for even greater performance. This was especially so in the USA, which was one of the company's most important markets. So the decision was taken to create a third and even more powerful variant of the Mk 2 saloon, this time using the 3.8-litre version of the XK engine that was the largest Jaguar then had available.

First announced in 1958 for the XK150 sports cars and the Mk VIII saloons, the 3.8-litre engine was really a big-bore 3.4-litre. It offered substantial increases in both power and torque, but for the Mk 2 Jaguar it was used in the same 220bhp twin-carburettor tune as the Mk IX models. The external dimensions of the 3.4-litre and 3.8-litre engines were identical, so there were no installation problems. However, it soon became clear that the massive torque of the 3.8-litre engine would very easily provoke wheelspin, so the Powr-Lok limited-slip differential was plucked from the options list and made standard on cars with the new engine.

STYLING CHANGES

Although the inner structure of the existing bodyshell was essentially unchanged, there were some minor modifications to the structure. The most radical styling changes affected the passenger cabin, where the original car's heavy window pillars were replaced by slimmer pillars with a much larger glass area. A new rounded rear quarter-light picked up an earlier Jaguar styling trademark and reached back into the stodgy rear pillar that had so spoiled the original car's looks, and the side windows were made to look even bigger by adding chrome-plated frames.

Heavy window pillars had rather spoiled the appearance of the Mk 1 Jaguars. For the Mk 2 body, the rear door windows were extended into the rear pillars and all the windows gained bright metal frames. It made all the difference that was needed.

The roof panel was altered, too. It was made slightly flatter than before and its apparent height above the door opening was reduced by chromed rain gutters that ran right around the new line of the windows. At the front, a taller windscreen took 1in (25mm) from the metal of the roof, and at the rear a much larger window added 7in (175mm) of width and 3in (75mm) of depth to the original.

These changes required only minimal alterations to the Pressed Steel body tooling but their overall effect was simply astonishing. From all angles, the car looked lighter and slimmer than before, and yet the basic lines remained familiar. The slightly awkward lines of the original had given way to a style that was actually pretty as well as more modern in appearance.

Below the waistline, less was changed. The exterior door handles were now more curvaceous and less 'antique' in style – and, importantly, they were less prone to freezing up in cold weather, a design aim as important as any cosmetic considerations. The rear wing panels and rear valance changed slightly to accommodate the wider rear axle, but they looked much the same as before. The rear wheel spats, too, retained their basic shape, although a subtle alteration at their trailing edges gave them a rather happier appearance.

Also subtly different was a wider rear bumper, necessitated by the wider rear axle but generally similar to the earlier type. It did have one important addition, though: a circular emblem warning following drivers that this car had disc brakes – and was therefore likely to stop more quickly than they could! Neater exhaust tailpipes tidied up another area of the rear, and there were new and larger rear lamp clusters of a style similar to those on other models, although not interchangeable with those on either the XK or Mk VIII saloons.

At the front, the wing panels were modified to accommodate new lighting arrangements. Sidelights were fitted in pods on the wing crowns to enhance the family resemblance to other Jaguars, and new circular indicator lamps were added to the wing fronts. The horn grilles gave way to fog lamps that fitted neatly into the recesses, as seems to have been the original intention for the Mk 1 cars. Last but not least, the overriders were moved outwards to make the car look wider, and a new grille with prominent central bar was added.

INTERIOR CHANGES

There had been little to criticize about the interior of the original compact Jaguars beyond the anachronistic dashboard layout and the huge four-spoke steering wheel. Vintage touches such as these still had a certain appeal in 1955, but by 1959 they had become a liability, and they had to go. However, the interior redesign for the Mk 2 models did not

For the Mk 2 design, the sidelights moved to streamlined fairings on top of the wings. A major advantage was the red 'pip', which picked up light from the bulb and reassured the driver that the light was working.

New and larger tail lights gave additional distinction to the rear of the car. They incorporated an amber section for the turn signal, as required by the latest UK legislation.

DEVELOPING THE JAGUAR MK 2

The dashboard was completely redesigned and the result was a triumph – at least visually. Finding the right switch in the dark required practice.

stop there. Customers wanted more of the luxury associated with the bigger Jaguar saloons, and so Browns Lane restyled not only the dashboard but also the seats and the door trims. In the end, the restyle was so extensive that very little of the original interior was left unchanged.

The dashboard was completely reworked, with the instruments positioned directly ahead of the driver. Although this made the provision of LHD and RHD versions slightly more complicated, it made the instruments easier to use and removed the old-fashioned feel of the Mk 1 dash altogether. The wooden panel containing speedometer and now-standard rev counter was matched in size by a passenger-side panel incorporating a lockable glovebox with drop-down lid. By careful arrangement of the surrounding panels Jaguar were able to minimize the number of different dashboard panels they had to manufacture.

The master strokes in the redesign were a more modern-looking steering wheel and a neat, black centre panel that contained the auxiliary instruments and switchgear. The new two-spoke wheel was set off by a chromed half-ring that operated the horn, and the arrangement of the four auxiliary instruments with toggle switches below created a classic layout that would be carried over in its essentials to the XJ6 of 1968. Even though the toggle switches were labelled, it was easy to confuse one with another, but that barely mattered: in this case, it was their suggestion of an aircraft's controls that carried the day.

Radios in cars had been the exception rather than the norm when the Mk 1 dashboard had been designed, but they had become increasingly popular. So provision for a radio was made in a neat downward extension of the dashboard that met up with a centre console between the front seats and incorporated space for both a radio and its speaker. Heating and ventilation controls were tidily arranged on either side and a large ashtray was fitted into the horizontal surface ahead of the gear lever. The idiosyncratic selector quadrant of automatic cars gave way to a steering-column selector, with a window in the shroud to show which mode had been selected. This same window, moulded as part of the shroud, was also used on cars with manual transmission: on four-speed cars, the lettering behind it simply read 'Jaguar', while on overdrive models it read 'Overdrive' and was illuminated when the overdrive was engaged.

DEVELOPING THE JAGUAR MK 2

The new dashboard had a dark walnut veneer, which was also used for the wooden door cappings. Below these, the door trims were also completely redesigned, with new armrests and new fluting to give a less spartan look than the originals. The rear seat remained substantially unchanged (although its top panel was now a single piece of leather rather than in two sections), but the front seats were quite radically altered. With wider cushions and deeper squabs, they looked more luxurious than the earlier type, although in practice they gave less lateral support. In keeping with the greater emphasis on luxury fittings, they also had fold-down picnic tables in the backs, made of veneered wood to match the rest of the trim in the passenger cabin.

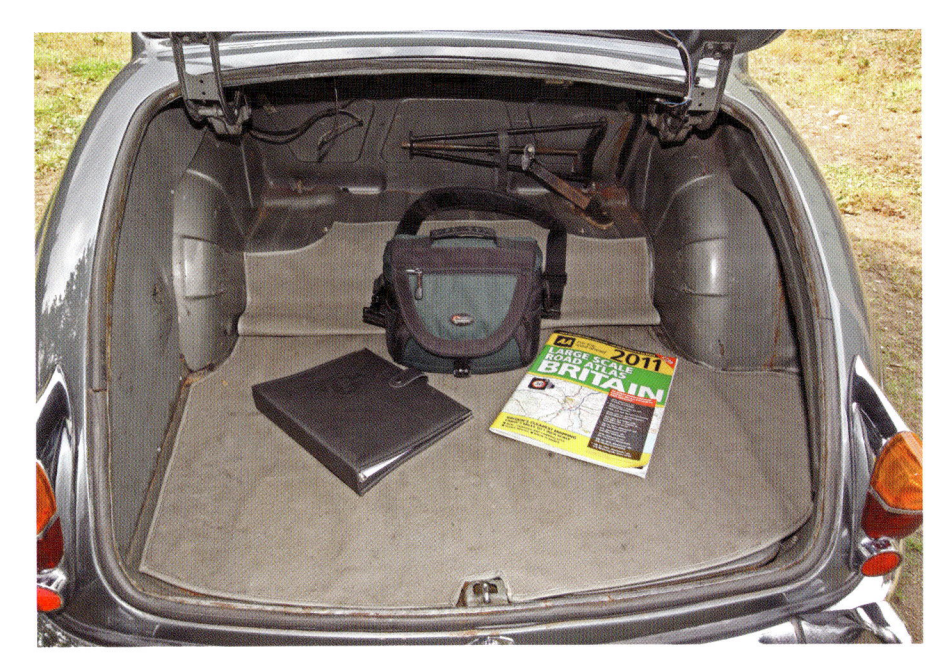

The boot of the Mk 2 provided plenty of room, as before.

PROTOTYPES

Rather less information has survived about the Mk 2 prototypes than about the earlier Mk 1 prototypes. The dates of their construction can be no more than guesswork, but no doubt 1958 would have been the key year in Mk 2 development.

The initial Mk 2 prototypes were simply modified Mk 1 cars, and among them was a black 3.4-litre known at Browns Lane as the 'wide-track car'. As the name suggests, this was used for development of the Mk 2's wider rear axle. The same car was fitted experimentally in July 1959 with Lucas petrol injection in place of its twin carburettors, but nothing came of these experiments as far as the Mk 2 was concerned.

The 3.8-litre Mk 2 was also developed on a Mk 1 'mule', this one a Sherwood Green 3.4-litre that carried registration number TVC 420. Its new engine (number NC4243/8) was a modified production 3.8-litre type, which was fitted as late as 4 June 1959. This was just a few months before the 3.8-litre Mk 2 was announced, so Jaguar clearly did not anticipate any major problems in fitting the larger engine.

Among the development cars listed in a July 1959 memo (reproduced in Philip Porter's *The Jaguar Scrapbook*) was a car identified as 'no 3' (presumably prototype number 3), a 3.4-litre with independent rear suspension. At this stage, IRS had not been revealed on any production Jaguar – it would make its appearance two years later on the E-type in 1961. So this 3.4-litre seems to have been an early indication that Jaguar was thinking about using IRS on their compact saloons, although no such car entered production until the S-type in 1963, some four years later (*see* Chapter 9).

That same July 1959 memo also lists a black 3.4-litre convertible, which did not carry a chassis number. Absolutely nothing more is known about this car, although in later years some quite attractive convertibles have been made from 'beheaded' Mk 2 cars. The design would certainly have worked visually, but perhaps there were issues with body rigidity and cost. (Lyons was certainly not averse to big convertibles – he had arranged for a pair of Mk VII Jaguar convertibles to be built in the early 1950s, although these also did not progress past the experimental stage.)

Production records suggest that a small run of off-tools prototypes of the Mk 2 were built in August, September and October 1959. These were then followed by volume production to get cars into the showrooms in anticipation of demand after the public announcement of the new models at the start of October.

CHAPTER FIVE

JAGUAR MK 2 (1959–1967)

In 1986, when Jaguar's chief engineer Jim Randle was introducing the then-new XJ40 saloon, he described the Mk 2 as 'an outstandingly beautiful car [which] clearly established the company's position as a class leader in terms of value for money, performance, state-of-the-art handling, high-quality interior appointments and distinctive exterior styling.' Nearly thirty years later, in 2014, the company's design director Ian Callum chose a Mk 2 as the car on which to execute a subtle redesign for his own personal use. Even though the compact saloon was the least expensive Jaguar available when it was new, it went on to have a major impact on the company and its future.

The very first Mk 2 to be built appears to have been a right-hand-drive 3.4-litre model, completed on 15 July 1959.

The identity of the new model was conveyed by this badge on the boot lid.

Equipped with the options of wire wheels and whitewall tyres, a Mk 2 finds the limelight at the centre of the Jaguar stand at the 1959 Earls Court Motor Show. In the foreground is one of the old-model 2.4-litre cars that would remain available through the showrooms until Mk 2 production had got into its stride.

56

JAGUAR MK 2 (1959–1967)

The first 2.4-litre car followed in August. However, these two were isolated examples and were probably used to test build methods. Volume production of Mk 2s did not begin until September, and the first cars then were left-hand-drive 3.8-litre models for the US market that was so important to Jaguar. Right-hand-drive 2.4s and 3.4s followed in October, while right-hand-drive 3.8s were the last to arrive, in November.

The launch announcement of the Mk 2 models was made on 2 October 1959, just under three weeks before the Earls Court Motor Show, where the new model would be given its first public airing. The timing allowed the press to publish their initial reports and so whet the appetites of potential Mk 2 customers. In most countries, however, cars were simply not available in the showrooms before the end of November or the beginning of December. Even in the USA, where initial production of the 3.8-litre models was used to build up dealer stocks before the launch announcement, no cars were sold before the end of October.

So the customers just had to wait. The original 2.4-litre and 3.4-litre saloons remained on sale and what Jaguar now called a 'standard' 2.4-litre car (in other words a Mk 1) was on the Earls Court stand alongside examples of the 2.4-litre and 3.4-litre Mk 2s. The run-out examples of these earlier cars were available only with what had earlier been the Special Equipment specification, and tided Jaguar's dealers over until the Mk 2 models became available in quantity. Any Mk 1s that remained in the showrooms after the end of the year must have been difficult to sell, because the Mk 2s offered huge advances for a price increase of only around 6 per cent.

THE MK 2 AND THE PRESS

The first full road test of a Mk 2 Jaguar was published in *The Autocar* at the end of February 1960. Not surprisingly, Jaguar had offered them the most expensive variant, a 3.8-litre

The favourite Mk 2 Jaguar has always been a 3.8-litre overdrive model with wire wheels. This 1961 example also sports narrow-band whitewall tyres and a racing mirror on the driver's side wing.

JAGUAR MK 2 (1959–1967)

model with overdrive; equally unsurprisingly, the magazine's testers were enthusiastic about the car. Nevertheless, their enthusiasm was carefully reined back in the manner so characteristic of the British motoring press at the time, and it was certainly not untempered by criticisms.

The magazine praised the car's performance, braking, handling, refinement, and its new interior and exterior appearance. But they also found the seats insufficiently supportive during hard cornering, commented on the car's marked understeer at speed, disliked the long travel of the clutch pedal and were dismayed by the low-geared steering.

In many ways, that first road test was definitive. Subsequent English-language tests added little to it, and even tests of the 3.4-litre and 3.8-litre automatic models simply seemed to be variations on a theme. The 2.4-litre cars were never given the full road-test treatment by a major magazine for reasons explained in Chapter 4, and after 1963 there was the new S-type to interest readers of the motoring press. Yet it was the Mk 2s that retained the sports-saloon image, and the public in general continued to see them as offering excellent value for money, while the 3.8-litre overdrive car remained every young man's dream of a fast and stylish saloon.

MK 2 SALES

Sales of the new Jaguars certainly got off to a good start. Production figures for 1959 show that just over 2,500 Mk 2s were built before the end of the year, which, when added to the 8,799 Mk 1s, kept the 'compact Jaguar' totals similar to the 1958 figures (11,605). In 1960 the real impact of the new models became apparent, for in that year production jumped by nearly 55 per cent to meet demand. Very noticeable was that the new 3.8-litre models accounted for some 85 per cent of the increased sales. The figures for 1961 were even more impressive, and overall production of the compact saloons was 21 per cent up on 1960 at a total of 21,236.

This dramatic peak was one that Jaguar would never even approach again. In 1962 sales of the compact models collapsed and only 12,743 cars were built. Jaguar responded very quickly with strong new products to keep its overall place in the market, introducing a Daimler derivative of the Mk 2 at the end of 1962 (see Chapter 7) and the new S-type models a year later (see Chapter 9). But the real success of the compact Jaguars had been short-lived, and from 1962 their sales continued to decline.

One reason must have been that other manufacturers had determined to secure a slice of the Jaguars' market. In Britain, the newly revitalized Rover 3-litre range began to take sales away from the Jaguars, although the Rover competed mainly on price and never pretended to be a sports saloon like the Mk 2. On the European continent, the Mk 2's main rivals were probably the Alfa Romeo 2600 saloons and coupés, the Fiat 2300S coupés and the new Mercedes-Benz 300SE saloons. In the USA, meanwhile, the first cheap 'muscle cars' had put in an appearance, offering enormous straight-line performance even if they handled badly and were crude by Jaguar's standards.

During 1963, Mk 2 production slipped again, although sales lost to Jaguar were largely recouped by the new Daimler 2.5-litre V8 models, which used the same bodyshell. That year, Daimlers accounted for 19 per cent of all 'compact' production. There were further losses for 1964, balanced by further defections to Daimler and to the new S-class Jaguars, themselves also derivatives of the Mk 2 compacts. Then 1965 saw another major collapse, orders justifying the production of fewer than 5,000 Mk 2 Jaguars, only just over 20 per cent of the total built in the record year of 1961. Daimler production was down that year too, although S-type Jaguar sales hit their peak year and these cars had probably taken many sales away from the Mk 2s.

The following year, 1966, was a bad year all round. Mk 2 Jaguar produc-

PRODUCTION FIGURES – JAGUAR MK 2

	RHD	LHD	TOTAL
2.4-litre	21,768	3,405	25,173
3.4-litre	22,092	6,571	28,663
3.8-litre	15,383	14,757	30,140
Overall total	**59,243**	**24,733**	**83,976**

Note that the RHD models include a proportion of export models. Not every RHD as built was destined for the UK!

JAGUAR MK 2 (1959–1967)

dominated. The figures in the table on page 58 show that the 3.8's biggest success was outside the UK, and notably in the LHD markets (which of course included the USA). The 3.8-litre nevertheless probably lost many sales to the new S-types after 1963. Least successful were the 2.4s, although only 3,490 cars separated them from the stronger-selling 3.4s.

MK 2 PRODUCTION CHANGES (1959–67)

Jaguar made scores of minor changes to the Mk 2 saloons during the eight years of their production, but there were major changes at only three points: in September 1960, when power-assisted steering became optional; in the summer of 1965, when new manual and automatic gearboxes were introduced; and in September 1966, when economy changes were made, including a switch from leather to vinyl upholstery (though leather was retained as an optional extra).

Parts commonization with other Jaguars became more frequent from 1963 when the S-type models entered production. From 1966, there would also be elements in common with the 420 and Daimler Sovereign.

From the passenger's side of the car, the new dashboard design gave a very strong impression that the driver was in control – which was probably exactly what many drivers wanted!

tion was lower again, Daimler sales slipped and the S-types were now on the downhill slope as well. It was not surprising that Browns Lane took a number of economy measures that autumn to reduce the production cost of the Mk 2s, as low production meant that each car cost correspondingly more to manufacture. By the time Mk 2 production stopped in 1967, in favour of the further cheapened 240 and 340 models, the public was more than ready for the all-new Jaguar that would appear as the XJ6 in 1968. The basic design of the Mk 2 had, after all, been on sale for twelve years by this stage.

In terms of overall sales, the 3.8-litre cars proved the most popular in the long term, but they were not the most popular in the home market, where the 3.4-litre

Not many cars could pull up as fast as a disc-braked Jaguar, so the rear bumper carried this neat badge – which was as much a boast as it was a warning to following drivers. The studs on either side of this badge were not a standard feature, but were a common way of plugging holes in the bumper after a towbar had been removed.

59

■ JAGUAR MK 2 (1959–1967)

As before, the grille carried a badge showing the size of the car's engine. There was of course a 3.8-litre badge as well as the 2.4-litre and 3.4-litre types shown here.

1960 Season

January 1960 brought improved sump sealing to reduce oil loss, and in March the 100psi dashboard oil pressure gauge was changed to a 60psi type; the smaller scale allowed the needle to register in the middle of the gauge when all was well, and stopped owners worrying unnecessarily.

In April, the fixed interior mirror stem was replaced by a telescopic type that gave a wider range of adjustment. In May, the steering column stalks swapped sides to suit export market expectations, so that the indicator stalk was now on the left and the overdrive switch on the right. May also brought stiffer front springs.

The Mk 2's heating arrangements were never good, and as a first step Jaguar advised dealers to make sure that all the heater flaps closed properly to exclude cold air. Then in July 1960 they added a water valve to the system (which was originally permanently in circuit) to counter the opposite problem of unwanted heat seeping through from the heater when the air flaps were in the 'off' position. In July, two changes were also made to counter complaints about petrol smells in the car: a breather pipe was fitted to the filler neck, together with a non-vented filler cap.

The style of the identification badges on the boot lid changed, too. Compare this with the Mk I style illustrated in Chapter 3.

The original black paint on the dash centre panel was very prone to scratch damage from the ignition key, so in July 1960 the panel took on a black Rexine finish instead. Also in July, the oil-bath air filter on 3.4 and 3.8 engines gave way to a paper filter housed in a large pancake casing with twin intake trumpets – although Jaguar kept the oil-bath type available to order as a precaution.

1961 Season

At the start of the 1961 season, in September 1960, power-assisted steering became an option. It brought stronger steering arms to resist damage if the wheels were turned against an obstruction, such as a kerb. The system was only ever offered for the 3.4-litre and 3.8-litre models, because the lighter engine in the 2.4-litre models made it unnecessary. The original 4.5in wheel rims gave way to 5in rims, and a polythene reservoir for brake fluid replaced the corrodible steel type.

In November 1960, the front door window frames gained a reinforcing fillet at the bottom that prevented the frames being sucked outwards at speed and creating wind noise. New sun visors appeared, reshaped and now on a pivot mounting at their outer edges so that they could be swivelled to shield the side windows. As the original ashtray had tended to deposit its contents all over the floor, the spring loading of its lid was changed to keep it shut rather than open. The steering column was lowered slightly to give a more comfortable driving position, and an organ-type accelerator pedal replaced the original pendant type. (The organ-type pedal had also been fitted on a few earlier cars – it was intended to appeal to more sporting drivers who were unable to heel-and-toe with the pendant type.) Also in November, a different type of fuel pump was fitted and the optional engine block heater moved to the right-hand side of the block because it was inaccessible below the exhaust manifold in its original position.

The crankshaft rear cover was modified in January 1961 to reduce oil leaks. February brought more rigid forged wishbones to replace the pressed type, while the optional uprated anti-roll bar now became standard. A dipstick guide tube was added this month, which also saw a range of new paint colours that included Jaguar's first-ever metallics.

In June 1961, cast-iron brake calipers replaced the malleable-iron type and came with improved adjusters. The dipstick for the automatic gearbox was relocated from its position under the transmission tunnel carpet to a more accessible position under the bonnet. Rubber buffers fitted to the door sills and bonnet edges that month were probably a response to complaints of rattles or chafing, and June also saw a zone-toughened windscreen become standard across the Mk 2 range.

The 1961 season's final changes were in August that year, when a new PAS pump became standard and a larger-capacity oil pump was fitted. Water deflectors were added to protect the front hubs and drilled camshafts minimized rattle during cold starts by improving lubrication.

1962 Season

For the 1962 season, seat belt mounting points became standard, although they would not become a mandatory fitting in Britain for another three years. In October 1961, automatic fan-belt tensioners removed one routine maintenance chore, and a cast-iron crankshaft pulley replaced the original alloy type. Also in October, a rope-type oil seal replaced the scroll type at the back of the engine. December brought a larger universal joint on the propshaft and a new cover over the exhaust camshaft to improve oil sealing.

The February 1962 changes were improved exhaust manifold gaskets and the introduction of an optional high-output dynamo for 3.4-litre and 3.8-litre models (presumably there was no demand from 2.4-litre buyers). From April 1962, the brake servo gained a two-stage air valve to eliminate the sighing noises characteristic of the earlier type.

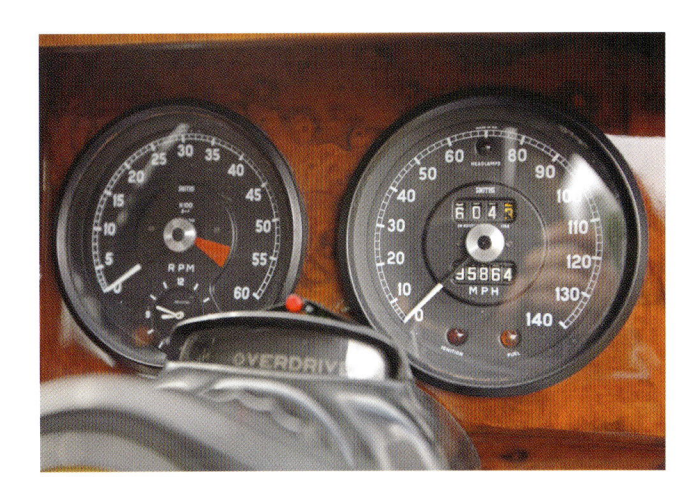

This indicator on the steering column lit up when the overdrive was engaged on cars so equipped.

JAGUAR MK 2 (1959–1967)

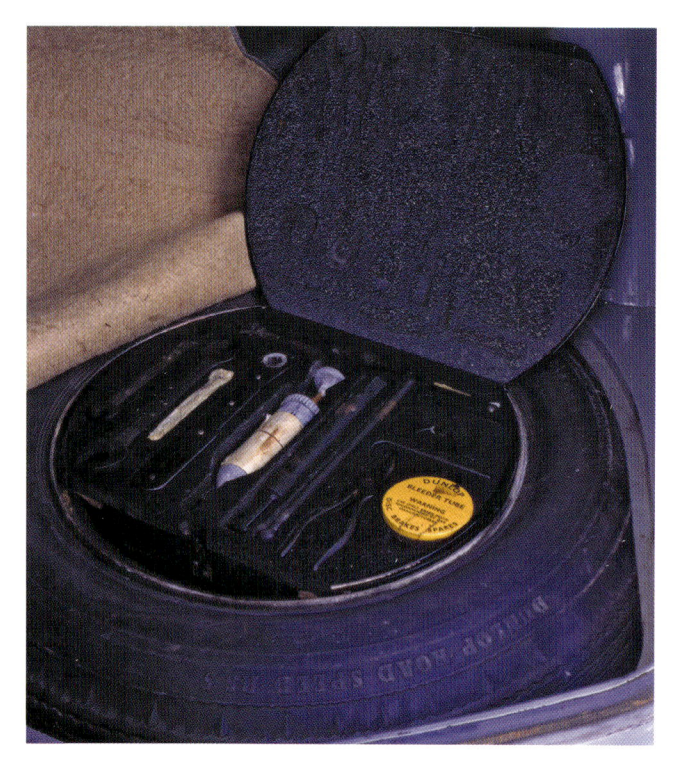

As always, the neat toolkit stowed in the centre of the spare wheel was a source of delight.

1963 Season

The September 1962 changes ushered in the new season, bringing sealed-beam headlamps, which were becoming increasingly common on cars of all types because they offered greater power and longer life than earlier types with separate bulbs. The new lamps had convex lenses, whereas the older types had flat lenses. That same month, the 3.8-litre engine's reputation for burning oil was tackled with new piston scraper rings. October then saw longer main bearing cap dowels on the left-hand side and the arrival of the season's new paint colour range.

In November, the dipstick gained a longer handle to reduce the risk of burning hands on the hot exhaust manifold, and a five-bolt oil filter casing replaced the four-bolt type, probably to reduce oil leaks.

In January 1963, the Panhard rod mounting bracket was reinforced, and then in February stiffer Girling dampers were fitted, to reduce fade in hard use. From March, the Mk X-type steering column became standard on all Mk 2s, and in April a high-output dynamo was standardized.

May 1963 brought dust excluders around the headlamps, and some changes to the cooling system. A new top hose and clip, together with a change to a 9lb radiator pressure cap, were intended to tackle overheating problems, while the 3.4-litre and 3.8-litre engines took on the Mk X-type water pump.

A final change during the 1963 season was to the backs of the front seats, which had a greater cut-away at the bottom to give rear passengers more foot room.

1964 Season

Customers who examined the 1964 model Mk 2 at the Earls Court Motor Show in October 1963 would have seen that the new season's cars had a new steering wheel, the same as that fitted to the Mk X and the brand-new S-type saloons that were announced at that show. Its spokes were slightly different in shape from the earlier type, and the horn was operated by the centre boss as well as the horn ring. The

This March 1964 small advertisement from the motoring press traded on the immediate availability of new Jaguars – and the dealership had clearly managed to obtain delivery of some in the popular Opalescent Silver Grey colour.

spark plug leads had also been rerouted (since September), and there were tougher mounting rubbers for the front cross member in October. November then brought a rectifier for the clock and stronger bracketry for the brake vacuum tank.

The 3.8-litre engines still burned oil, and Jaguar tackled that by modifying the pistons in January 1964. Supply difficulties around this time explained why a number of early 1964 cars had carpets with PVC heel pads instead of the usual Hardura type.

The Mk 2s gained S-type fuel pumps in March 1964, and new interior lamps on the B-pillars. From April there were S-type oil cleaners and flywheels, and waterproofed distributors. In May came the S-type's 4lb radiator pressure cap, fused overdrive circuit (or intermediate-hold circuit in automatics) and single-piece carpets in the footwells, with press-stud fittings instead of the earlier 'bow' type.

1965 Season

The 1965 season opened in October 1964 with no visible changes except the removal of the 'Automatic' badge from cars with the Borg Warner gearbox. Under the bonnet, engines now took on the S-type sump pan. Changes to the paint options were held over until December 1964, and the gearbox changes already outlined kept Jaguar busy over the summer of 1965.

Shields were added to the brake discs in October 1964, apparently because the inner pads tended to wear faster than the outers. Overheating problems were addressed yet again in December 1964, when all Mk 2s took on larger radiators and larger fan cowls.

There were two changes in April 1965. Polythene reservoirs for windscreen washer fluid arrived that month because component manufacturers were moving away from breakable glass types. The second change was caused by an interesting problem: the battery tray drain tube was lengthened to prevent water dripping onto a brake pipe and promoting corrosion.

Right at the end of the 1965 season, in June, the latest Borg Warner type 35 three-speed automatic gearbox replaced the same company's DG type. The newer gearbox gave smoother changes, both up and down.

The neat centre console and impressive-looking switch panel on the dashboard gave the Mk 2 interior a distinction that the Mk 1 had lacked. The smaller-diameter steering wheel helped, too. This is the earlier type.

■ JAGUAR MK 2 (1959–1967)

1966 Season

That change to the automatic gearbox was followed just a few months later by a change to the manual gearboxes. These were changed in September, when the old Moss box with its unsynchronized first gear gave way to Jaguar's own all-synchromesh four-speeder, as already seen in the Mk X and S-type saloons. Once again, the improvement was very welcome, even if the long travel of the gear change was not universally viewed as an improvement.

Disposable oil filters from November 1965 reflected another industry trend, and that same month problems with rear quarter-vent catches working loose and even falling off were solved by adding Loctite glue to the screws during production. At the same time, Jaguar provided an additional notch in the opening mechanism of the front quarter-vents, allowing them to be fixed open in two different positions.

All the other major changes during the 1966 season occurred in April. They brought an improved handbrake mechanism, a dashboard switch for the heated rear window, which had been operated directly by the ignition switch on earlier cars, and different horns and indicator switches.

1967 Season

The third and last set of major changes came in September 1966, when Jaguar introduced a number of economy measures to keep manufacturing costs down. These were announced at the Earls Court Motor Show in October 1966.

On the outside, the 1967-model cars could be recognized most easily by their dummy horn grilles in place of the twin recessed fog lamps, although the lamps could still be bought at extra cost. They also had a simplified, single-piece chrome moulding on the B-pillar, and rubber door seals instead of the weather strip on the chrome beading around the door tops.

Leather upholstery disappeared in favour of Ambla vinyl, which no doubt saved quite a lot in manufacturing costs but certainly took away some of the traditional British character of the cars. Anticipating that this might be a problem, Jaguar kept leather available, although as an extra-cost option. The picnic tables were removed from the front seat backs, too. The material used for the headlining and sun visors was also changed for the cheaper type already seen in the S-type saloons and, shortly afterwards, Velcro strip carpet fasteners replaced the stud type used since 1964.

The 2.4-litre models had a distinctive air cleaner, which is seen here on a 1967 car.

December 1966 saw a simplification in 2.4-litre engine assembly when the separate crankshaft vibration damper and fan-belt pulley were replaced by a pulley with integral damper.

More changes arrived in March 1967, headlined by a change to the paint options. At the same time, the optional power-assisted steering changed to the Variomatic type that had been pioneered on the Mk X. Then in July, right at the end of production, there were yet more changes. However, very few cars were built with these final modifications.

The standard steel wheels were replaced by the type used on the 420 models, and the optional wire-spoked type now had forged hubs and straight spokes. There was a switch to Girling brakes, because Girling had bought out Dunlop's braking interests. The last cars also picked up the red over-drive telltale light from the 420.

Curiously, one quite major annoyance went unchanged until nearly the end. This was the tendency of the boot lid to spring open on rough roads taken at speed. It certainly could be cured with a great deal of patience by adjusting the catch, and so it was not until July 1967 that Jaguar fitted a different catch that finally eliminated the problem.

RIVALS

Just as the original compact Jaguars had largely been without rivals, so the Mk 2s had almost no serious competition – at least, in the beginning and in their own domestic market. Although the market sector in which these cars and their Daimler equivalents competed between 1959 and 1967 was rather more densely populated than it had been in the 1950s, the Browns Lane machines continued to stand out because of their unique blend of qualities.

In Britain, the Mk 2 Jaguars and compact Daimlers remained very much more expensive than ordinary family saloons but still considerably cheaper than the large luxury cars of the day. Their main competition on price came from the big Humber Super Snipe and Rover 3-litre models, although both of these were sedate luxury saloons without the high-performance characteristic of the Jaguars, and the Rover moved up a rung on the price ladder when the new Mk II models arrived in 1962. There was no domestic competition from a sports saloon on performance.

Italian imports presented a more sporting challenge but lacked the luxury features of the Jaguars. The third-series Lancia Appia and Fiat 2300 never really gained a foothold among British buyers. Alfa Romeo could offer only the 1600cc Giulia models at this price level, and although these cars had excellent performance they could not offer the refinement and luxury of the Jaguars.

From Germany came the stolid Mercedes-Benz 190, which was only a competitor because import taxes boosted

---

OPTIONAL EXTRAS – JAGUAR MK 2

Electrical
Fog lamps (standard on some models)
High-output dynamo (3.4 and 3.8 engines only, 1962–63)

Exterior
Ace Turbo wheel trims
Competition wire wheels (in body colour or silver stove-enamelled)
Laminated windscreen
Lockable fuel filler cap
Radio aerial for roof mounting
Radio aerial for wing mounting
Radio aerial for wing mounting (fully retractable by handle inside car)
Rimbellishers (bright metal wheel trim rings)
Steel sunroof
Sundym tinted glass
Tow-bar
Wing mirrors (standard or Paddy Hopkirk sports style)
Wire wheels (in body colour, chrome-plated or silver stove-enamelled)

Handling and roadholding
Power-assisted steering

Interior
Childproof locks for rear doors
Column-mounted combination ignition and starter switch
Heated rear window
Radio
Radio speaker for rear shelf, with balance control
Reclining front seats
Reclining front seat kit (to convert fixed type to recliners)
Safety belts (front seats only)

■ JAGUAR MK 2 (1959–1967)

The two bigger-engined Mk 2s had this type of pancake air cleaner, shown in this case under the bonnet of a 3.8-litre automatic.

OVERSEAS ASSEMBLY OF MK 2 JAGUARS

There was only one CKD operation involving the Mk 2 Jaguars, and that was in South Africa. Early Mk 2 models were exported to South Africa as fully built cars, but the country's new Local Contents Programme encouraged overseas car makers to look at in-territory assembly after 1960.

Jaguar reached an agreement with Car Distributors Assembly (Pty) Ltd, which had been established in East London as long ago as 1948 and assembled cars for a wide variety of companies. CDA took on assembly of the 2.4-litre, 3.4-litre and 3.8-litre models. Although assembly of the 2.4-litre had ended by 1964, the other two cars remained available until 1969 and a grand total of 2,050 Mk 2 Jaguars were built in South Africa.

Mk 2 Jaguar assembly in South Africa was carried out alongside that of Renaults and Fiats.

its price to Jaguar levels, and later the small BMW 1500 and its 1800 and 1800TI derivatives. However, such cars were always critical rather than sales successes in a Britain still convinced it made the best cars in the world. Sports coupés from Volkswagen and Volvo, in the shape of the Karmann Ghia 1500 and the 1800S respectively, also fell into the same price bracket as the Jaguars but were generally viewed as seriously overpriced and were certainly unable to compete on performance.

Outside the UK, the story was quite different. Import duties, which worked in Jaguar's favour in the home market, worked against them abroad. On price, Jaguar were unable to compete with Mercedes-Benz or BMW in Germany, with Alfa Romeo in Italy and with any number of domestic makers in the USA, where high performance took on a new importance in the 1960s. However, only Jaguar offered the luxury of a wood and leather interior combined with high performance and with seats for five people – the 'Grace, Pace, Space' equation of their advertising – and this uniqueness undoubtedly kept them afloat in highly competitive overseas markets.

THE MK 2 IN THE USA

The most important of those overseas markets for Jaguar was the USA, and in that country the Mk 2 was reduced to a single model – the 3.8-litre, available with either the automatic or the overdrive gearbox. This gave US customers a very different perspective on the Mk 2 from the one that existed among British buyers. It positioned the Jaguar at the top end of the imported cars market, giving it an exclusivity that was never complicated by the availability of cheaper 3.4-litre and 2.4-litre models. (In practice, a few 3.4-litre cars were imported to special order, but the 2.4-litre Mk 2 never crossed the Atlantic as a new car.)

That market positioning is best illustrated by comparing the showroom price of the 3.8-litre Mk 2 with that of its contemporaries in the USA. The car cost around $5,000 dollars in 1960 when equipped with the desirable extras of power steering, wire wheels and the automatic gearbox, at a time when few standard-sized American family cars of the time cost more than half that figure. Even the desirable Chevrolet Corvette roadster cost well under $4,000, and around $5,100 bought into the lower reaches of the Cadillac range. So US buyers perceived the car even more as a sign of wealth and status than their equivalents in Britain.

This was the gold-plated Jaguar that introduced the 3.8-litre Mk 2 to US buyers at the 1960 New York Auto Show. Note that the US cars came with dummy horn grilles instead of the fog lamps that were standard for other markets.

The 3.8-litre Mk 2 was announced on 29 October 1959 at the New York showrooms of Jaguar Cars Inc on East 57th Street and Madison Avenue. This was just a week after the Mk 2 had been introduced at the Earls Court Motor Show in London and it was in fact the first public showing anywhere for the 3.8-litre model, which had not been on the Earls Court stand. But the Jaguar laid claim to its special position in the US market at the 1960 New York Auto Show that spring with a specially made show car.

This was the brainchild of US advertising manager Everett Martin, who took a white 3.8-litre Mk 2 and had every piece of external chrome plate on it replaced by gold plate. At the show's opening, the car was accompanied by an elegant

■ JAGUAR MK 2 (1959–1967)

model wearing a complementary formal gown of 24-carat gold thread and a Napoleonic tiara containing over 1,000 diamonds. The image, captured by press photographers from all over the American continent, was unforgettable: this car was clearly intended for the wealthy few. (Sadly the car was later stripped of its gold fittings and sold, but in 1998 it was located and restored, complete with gold trim.)

When the Mk 2 became available in the USA at the end of 1959, US sales of imported cars were still on the increase and Britain still provided most of them. However, things were about to change: the US domestic manufacturers had begun to fight back strongly during 1959 with their new compact sedans – Chevrolet had the Corvair, Ford the Falcon, and Chrylser the Plymouth Valiant. Moreover, the success of Volkswagen and Mercedes-Benz meant that the West Germans would become the number one exporters of cars to the USA during 1960, a position they would retain for the rest of the decade.

The 3.8-litre Mk 2 won 'best imported car' awards for several years running, but it did not sell in huge numbers in the USA. Precise figures are not available, but if as many as 50 per cent of the 14,757 left-hand-drive cars built between 1959 and 1967 had gone to the USA, sales would still have averaged fewer than 1,000 cars a year. In such a vast country, these were tiny numbers.

Two features distinguished the US versions of the 3.8-litre Jaguar from those sold elsewhere: the amber lenses in the front indicator lamps were replaced with plain glass and the fog lamps in the front wing recesses were replaced with dummy air-intake grilles. After September 1965, all Mk 2s destined for the USA also had a hazard-warning-light system to meet local requirements, a feature not fitted for other models. Otherwise, US-market cars simply drew on the range of options available elsewhere. Most had automatic gearboxes, power-assisted steering and wire wheels, and probably the majority of cars were also delivered with the whitewall tyres so popular in the USA at the time. Many cars were also fitted with aftermarket air-conditioning systems, some of which had the disadvantage of taking up an unacceptable amount of space in the boot.

By the time the 3.8-litre Mk 2 ceased production in 1967, the US government had already announced the first of its new measures obliging motor manufacturers to improve safety features and reduce noxious exhaust emissions. The Mk 2 disappeared before these new regulations came into force and so it was never developed to meet them.

Rather less flamboyant than the gold-plated Jaguar, but somewhat more typical of the US cars, this well-preserved example was photographed at a Jaguar dealership in the 1970s.

THE MK 2 IN MOTOR SPORT

From the moment the 3.8-litre Mk 2 was announced in 1959, those who used saloons in motor sport events knew it was the car they wanted. The older 3.4-litre cars already enjoyed a formidable reputation, and here was a car with even more power and torque, plus vital improvements in handling and roadholding. The drivers could hardly wait to get their hands on it.

Mk 2 on the Tracks (1960–64)

The 3.8-litre Jaguar first appeared on the circuits during the 1960 racing season. In that and the following year it proved all but unbeatable. Its domination of saloon-car racing in Europe continued throughout 1962 and 1963, but the competition by this time was becoming tougher. The first big American racing saloons had reached British circuits during 1961, when the Chevrolet Impalas had given the 3.8s a run for their money. In May 1962 a 3.8 was beaten on the tracks for the first time by a Chevrolet (a Chevy II model), and during 1963 the Jaguars often had to give best to the thundering 7-litre Ford Galaxies driven by former 3.8 Jaguar drivers Jack Sears, Peter Jopp and Sir Gawaine Baillie, among others. By 1964 it was all over. The new Ford Lotus Cortinas swept the field, leaving the Jaguars trailing in their wake.

Yet in those four years, the 3.8-litre Jaguars had created a legend. They were highly respected by competition drivers, and it was not uncommon to see starting grids very nearly

THE INSPECTOR MORSE JAGUAR

The television series *Inspector Morse*, based on the novels of Colin Dexter about the fictional Oxford-based Detective Inspector Morse, starred a Mk 2 Jaguar. This car has gone on to become one of the best-known examples of the type, and at the time of writing was being used for promotional work.

The car is an early 2.4-litre overdrive model, registered in July 1960 as 248 RPA. It was bought by Carlton TV in the mid-1980s and featured in all thirty-three episodes of the series, which was aired between 1987 and 2000. In the novels, Morse drove a Lancia, but actor John Thaw, who played Inspector Morse in the television series, insisted on having a British car.

Throughout its television life, the car sported a non-standard black vinyl roof covering. This was probably fitted by an owner in the 1970s when vinyl roofs became popular on cars in Britain. The Coombs Jaguars could be ordered in the 1960s with a leather roof covering that looked very similar.

The Inspector Morse Mk 2 was pictured in a posed scene for this photograph. The black vinyl roof was a fashionable 1970s addition.

■ JAGUAR MK 2 (1959–1967)

MK 2 POLICE CARS

As Britain's motorway network began to expand in the early 1960s, the need arose for patrol cars that were capable of high speeds. These cars also needed to carry special equipment, both to maintain radio communication with a control centre and to deal with incidents and accidents on the motorway. The traditional black of the police patrol car was considered too inconspicuous, so these cars were painted in high-visibility white.

The Jaguar Mk 2, particularly in 3.8-litre form, proved ideal as a motorway patrol car. It was fast enough for high-speed chase duties, and its good roadholding and braking offered a valuable safety margin in extreme situations. However, many police forces switched to cheaper cars with similar performance as soon as they could because the Mk 2 was an expensive machine. By the end of the 1960s, the Triumph 2.5 PI and Rover 3500 were taking over the motorway patrol role. Some police forces nevertheless took on Mk 2s for lower-profile duties. During their heyday in the first half of the 1960s, there were Mk 2s on the strength of no fewer than thirty-seven British police forces.

The typical motorway patrol 3.8 Mk 2 was an overdrive model and carried a large light box on its roof, bearing police signs and a flashing light. It would have police signage on its sides and rear, and might have twin chromed air horns and a loud hailer mounted

The Mk 2 furthered the popularity of the compact Jaguars with police forces in the UK. This 1963 car belonged to the Somerset Constabulary and appears black in the photograph, but was probably dark blue. Note the anti-mist panel on the rear window.

The Leicester and Rutland Constabulary owned this 1965 car, DJU 950C. It figured in a Jaguar advertisement, which is inset in this composite picture. Note the air horns attached to the front bumper.

JAGUAR MK 2 (1959–1967)

on the front bumper. The rear seat was often removed to make room for the cones and other paraphernalia needed to cope with motorway problems, while there would be a calibrated speedometer (against which an offending driver's speed could be checked), and radio-telephone equipment on the dashboard.

Although police Jaguars were commonly believed to be specially tuned for speed, in practice they were not. At most, some had stiffer springs to offset the weight of equipment carried in the back and an uprated dynamo to power the additional electrical equipment.

Below is a list of those police forces for which there is photographic evidence of their use of the Mk 2 Jaguar – it is reproduced by courtesy of the Police Vehicle Enthusiasts' Club:

Angus Constabulary
Ayrshire Constabulary
Buckinghamshire Constabulary
Dumfries and Galloway Constabulary
Durham Constabulary
Flintshire Constabulary
Glasgow City Police
Gloucestershire Constabulary
Lanarkshire Constabulary
Leicestershire and Rutland Constabulary (which became the
   Leicester and Rutland Constabulary in 1967)

Manchester City Police
Metropolitan Police
Scottish North-Eastern Counties Constabulary
Somerset Constabulary
Staffordshire Constabulary
States of Jersey Police
Warwickshire Constabulary
West Sussex Constabulary

ABOVE: **This photograph of a Mk 2 that was new to the Manchester City Police in 1966 flags up the vivid contrast between the low, sleek Jaguar and the elderly 1948 Austin alongside.**

BELOW: **This Lanarkshire Constabulary Mk 2 reflects the move towards high-visibility white for police cars. 436 GVD was new in 1963. This photograph is from the Alan Matthews Collection now held by the Police Vehicle Enthusiasts' Club.**

JAGUAR MK 2 (1959–1967)

full of 3.8s, or to see two, three, or even four of these cars among the first five places at the finish. They succeeded mainly because they were both fast and durable, and even when the big American cars started to leave them behind on the straights they were usually able to catch up on the corners because of their excellent handling and roadholding. In the end, it was weight that was their undoing. During their heyday, they were notoriously heavy on tyres (one set might last no longer than a single race), and once the much lighter and more nimble Lotus Cortinas arrived, the 3.8s were simply outclassed.

Although dozens of individuals raced Mk 2 Jaguars in the 1960s, the major successes went to the racing teams, which could employ top-class drivers. The two leading teams were Equipe Endeavour and Coombs; but some individuals also did remarkably well and the names which stand out are those of Sir Gawaine Baillie and Peter Lindner, the German Jaguar dealer who managed to secure factory support and put together a team to contest the new European Touring Car Challenge in 1963.

Equipe Endeavour

Tommy Sopwith's Equipe Endeavour had already established a name for itself with the 3.4-litre Mk 1 cars (see Chapter 3) and it proceeded to maintain its reputation with the 3.8-litre Mk 2s. Its best-known car carried the registration number JAG 400, and its regular driver for the 1960 season was Jack Sears; Stirling Moss also put in a single appearance with JAG 400 that season. For 1961 Mike Parkes was the team driver and Graham Hill guested, while 1962 saw Parkes again driving for Equipe Endeavour and Sears returning to the fold. The team did not show for 1963.

The very first appearance of the Mk 2 in competition was at the Goodwood meeting on Easter Monday, 1960. Sears put up a fierce fight in the Equipe Endeavour car but was eventually placed third behind Roy Salvadori in the Coombs team car, and both conceded victory to Stirling Moss in an Aston Martin DB4. However, Moss himself took over JAG 400 for the Silverstone production touring car race in May and carried off second place, again behind Salvadori in the Coombs car. JAG 400 raced again at Silverstone in July,

This scene was fairly typical of saloon car races at Goodwood in the early 1960s. There are seven Mk 2 Jaguars among the ten cars visible, including some well-known examples – JAG 400 belonged to Equipe Endeavour.

taking second place in the touring car race when driven by Sears and then a further second place with Parkes at the wheel in the production cars event.

Equipe Endeavour showed well at the May 1961 Silverstone meeting, too. Parkes managed second place while the race was won by Hill, driving a second Equipe Endeavour car. Parkes was Sears's co-driver when the Jaguar raced at the Lombard Trophy meeting at Snetterton and the pair would have won if they had not run out of petrol on the very last lap while leading the race. Then it was Parkes once again who represented Equipe Endeavour in the Circuit of Ireland road race, where he carried off a class win.

Both Parkes and Sears entered Jaguars in the races supporting the British Grand Prix at Aintree in 1962 and Sears took first place. He also raced in the Oulton Park Trophy, but without result. However, Parkes won at Snetterton and Brands Hatch, and Sears pulled off a second place at Crystal Palace in June. But the best result by Equipe Endeavour that season was in the six-hour endurance race sponsored by *The Motor* magazine and held at Brands Hatch in October. This was the first long-distance saloon car event to be held in Britain and ended with a first place for Mike Parkes and his co-driver Jimmy Blumer in JAG 400.

John Coombs

Like Equipe Endeavour, the Coombs team had also made its name racing Mk 1 Jaguars in the late 1950s. The best-known Coombs 3.8-litre Mk 2s were registered as 6 PPF and

Two well-known Mk 2 competition cars storm uphill at Brands Hatch. BUY12 is a Coombs car, and VCD400 is driven by Jack Sears.

This time the scene is Silverstone, where driver P.J. Woodruffe is driving a Coombs-modified 3.4-litre Mk 2. The car was later modified further, to run a 3.8-litre engine.

JAGUAR MK 2 (1959–1967)

BUY 12, which raced in the Coombs team colour of Pearl Grey. Roy Salvadori was the team's main driver for 1960 and 1961, although Colin Chapman (of Lotus fame) also put in one appearance at the wheel of a Coombs car during 1960. For 1962 Salvadori was joined by Graham Hill, who had previously driven 3.8s for Team Speedwell. For 1963 the Coombs team turned its attention elsewhere.

The 1960 season began with promise as Salvadori came second in 6 PPF to Moss's Aston Martin at the Goodwood meeting on Easter Monday. At Silverstone in May, he won the International Trophy race; but it was Colin Chapman who piloted 6 PPF to victory at the races supporting the British Grand Prix at Silverstone in July. The Coombs cars put up several good fights during 1961, but this was a less successful season for them. In 1962 they bounced back, however, now with Graham Hill in the team. Hill secured first places at Oulton Park, Aintree, Goodwood, Silverstone, Mallory Park and Snetterton to become that season's outstanding Jaguar saloon driver. Salvadori also pulled in some good results, taking BUY 12 to first place at Crystal Palace in June, losing nobly to the big American cars at the Oulton Park Trophy Race, but coming in second behind Charles Kelsey's Chevy II at the Brands Hatch meeting in May.

Sir Gawaine Baillie

In the early 1960s Sir Gawaine Baillie, another driver who had tasted success with the Mk 1 3.4-litre cars, campaigned his new 3.8 (GB 448) to good effect. To him went the honour of the first outright win by a Mk 2 Jaguar anywhere, at Snetterton during 1960. That year he also took a first in class at Oulton Park, came third in the May meeting at Aintree and was placed fourth in the International Trophy Race at Silverstone that month – behind the 3.8s of Salvadori, Moss and Hill.

During 1961 Baillie continued to turn in some entertaining performances with the 3.8 and was usually well up with the race leaders, though outright victory came his way only once. That was at the Lombard Trophy support race at Snetterton, when a last-lap failure by the leading Equipe Endeavour Jaguar allowed him to cross the finish line first. For 1962 his performance was much the same, embracing a fourth place at Crystal Palace in June, another fourth place in the Oulton Park Trophy Race and a third behind Salvadori and the winning Chevy II at Brands Hatch in May.

Endurance Racing

Peter Lindner's main contribution to the racing history of the 3.8 Jaguars was in long-distance endurance rac-

In Germany, Peter Lindner and Peter Nöcker campaigned the Mk 2. Here they are with the car at the 1962 Nürburgring 12-Hours race.

ing. He had raced in Jaguars during the late 1950s in his native Germany, but after teaming up with Peter Nöcker he decided to enter a 3.4-litre Mk 2 for the first-ever endurance race to be held at the Nürburgring in 1961. Despite suffering serious clutch trouble and a broken steering column mounting, the Lindner/Nöcker Jaguar crossed the line first – a very clear indication of what was to come. Indeed, Lindner went on to win every race he entered in 1961, and that year became combined German National GT and Touring Car Champion.

Lindner went on to repeat his success with Jaguars in 1962. With Hans-Joachim Walter in the co-driver's seat, he won that year's Nürburgring 12-Hours, and then came second with Nöcker in the Brands Hatch 6-Hours. For 1963, however, things became much more serious. The endurance races had been grouped together to form the new European Touring Car Challenge, later to become the European Touring Car Championship (ETTC), and Lindner was determined to do well. To help him in his aim, he sought assistance from Browns Lane.

THE MONZA RECORD CAR

The initiative for an attack on the international long-distance driving records during 1963 seems to have come from the oil company Castrol, who secured Jaguar's agreement to use a modified 3.8-litre Mk 2 for the job. For Jaguar, success would bring valuable publicity, which was always welcome.

The original plan was to take as many records as possible over a period of seven days, and to that end the Monza racetrack in Italy, with its banked circuit, was booked for the beginning of March. However, things did not run smoothly. The 3.8 twice suffered damage around the area of the Panhard rod mounting on the rear axle tube and eventually the run had to be aborted while the axle was replaced.

With time running out because the circuit was booked by another team from the middle of the following week, the Castrol-Jaguar team were forced to limit the number of records they were attempting to break. Nevertheless, the final runs were successful. By the time they were over, the car had taken four International Class C records, with the following average speeds:

10,000 miles (16,100km)	at 106.58mph (171.58km/h)
15,000km (9,320 miles)	at 106.61mph (171.64km/h)
Three days	at 107.02mph (172.3km/h)
Four days	at 106.62mph (171.66km/h)

The car used for the record runs was a silver-grey 3.8 Mk 2 with wire wheels, registered 3116 VC and prepared for the event by Jaguar. The interior was stripped out to competitions standard and a third windscreen wiper (mounted centrally above the screen) and large spotlamps were added. Mechanical changes included a high 2.93:1 final drive and an XK-type exhaust, while the overdrive was locked out to prevent failure at high speed.

After the Monza event, the car was driven to Geneva, where it was displayed on the Jaguar stand at the 1963 Motor Show.

An extra-large fuel tank was one of the modifications to the Monza record car.

JAGUAR MK 2 (1959–1967)

That year, the Lindner/Nöcker 3.8 stormed to victory at the Nürburgring 12-Hours after being held up for thirty-seven minutes by repairs to its Panhard rod mounting. It was second again in the Brands Hatch 6-Hours, and then at Zolder, in Belgium, Lindner crashed early on. Nöcker, driving another car, went on to win; and for the remaining races of the 1963 ETCC, the two Jaguar drivers cooperated so that (under the points system then in operation) Nöcker had the distinction of becoming the first-ever European Touring Car Champion. This result was a major coup for Jaguar, particularly as some of the most telling victories had been scored against their arch-rivals from Germany, Mercedes-Benz.

Mk 2 in Rallies

Although 3.8-litre Jaguars were entered for almost every major rally in the early 1960s, the optimism of their crews was rarely rewarded with good results. The Mk 2 was nowhere near as good a rally car as it was a track racer, although over the years it was well-placed in a number of events.

The best result during 1960 was a fourth overall and class win in the RAC Rally, achieved by Jack Sears and Willy Cave in a 3.8. José Behra and René Richard won the Touring Car class and a Coupe des Alpes in that year's Alpine Rally, which also saw Mike Parkes and Geoff Howarth placed fifth overall and third in class in their 3.8. Bernard Consten and Jacques Renal won their class in the Tour de France by a small margin from Peter Jopp and Sir Gawaine Baillie in another 3.8, while Boardman and Whitworth won their class and came eleventh overall in the Tulip Rally. Altogether less successful were the Jaguar entries for the Monte Carlo Rally, an event that never did prove kind to the Mk 2s.

During 1961 the Jaguars were once again limted to class wins. Baillie and Jopp shared a car again on the Alpine Rally

The scene looks tranquil enough, but this is a French village during the 1960 Tulip Rally and that is the 3.8-litre Mk 2 of Parkes and Howarth.

to claim one of them, and Consten won his class for the second year running on the Tour de France. Other Jaguars took second, third and fourth places behind him. In the RAC Rally and the Monte, however, there were no Jaguar results of any sort, even though 3.8s were among the cars that completed both events.

The picture was similar in 1962. Consten won his class for the third year running in the Tour de France and Jaguars took the next four places in the class as well. Otherwise, it was already clear that the Mk 2s were not proving to be good rally cars. For 1963, results were steady: the Tour de France was again the Jaguar's best showing, Consten again winning the Touring Car category while Annie Soisbault and Louisette Texier claimed second in class with their Mk 2. In the Tulip Rally, Jaguars came second and third in their class, driven by Lundberg with Lindström and John Sprinzel with Barry Hughes respectively.

By 1964, however, things had begun to slide. Bernard Consten managed only third place on the Tour de France while Louisette Texier and Marie-Louise Mermod won the Ladies' Award in the Touring Car class. After that, very little was heard of the rallying Mk 2s.

IDENTIFICATION – JAGUAR MK 2

Identification numbers are stamped on a plate in the engine compartment, attached to the right-hand inner wing. These numbers are repeated elsewhere, as shown below.

Car Number
The car number, also known as the chassis number or VIN, is stamped into the bonnet catch channel, just ahead of the radiator header tank. A typical car number might be 202389 BW. The numerals are the car's serial number and the letters show the transmission type.

The serial number sequences are:

	RHD	LHD
2.4	100001–121768	125001–128405
3.4	150001–172095	175001–181571
3.8	200001–210000	210001–224758
	230001–235383	

The suffixes decode as follows:

BW   Borg Warner automatic gearbox
DN   Laycock de Normanville overdrive

Cars fitted with power-assisted steering have a P prefix; for example, P 202389 BW.

Engine Number
The engine number is stamped on the right-hand side of the cylinder block above the oil filter and again at the front of the cylinder head casting, beside the front spark plug hole. A typical engine number would be KG 5320/8. This breaks down into three elements:

KG	Engine type identifier (see below)
5320	Serial number
/8	Compression ratio (/8 for 8:1 compression, /7 for 7:1, /9 for 9:1)

The type identifiers are:

BG, BH and BJ	2.4-litre engines
KG, KH and KJ	3.4-litre engines
LA, LB, LC and LE	3.8-litre engines

Body Number
The body number is stamped on a small plate attached to the right-hand side of the bulkhead, under the bonnet. It has four or five digits. On cars built after 1963, the body number is stamped on a small plate attached to the right-hand side of the body behind the rear bumper. (It should not be confused with a similar plate on the left-hand side that shows the Pressed Steel reference number.)

Gearbox Number
On all manual gearboxes, the gearbox number is stamped on a small shoulder at the left-hand rear corner of the gearbox casing, and on the top cover around the rim of the core plug aperture. On automatic gearboxes, the number is stamped on a plate attached to the left-hand side of the gearbox casing.

JAGUAR MK 2 (1959–1967)

SPECIFICATIONS – JAGUAR MK 2

Engines

2.4-litre
Type XK 6-cylinder, with cast-iron block and aluminium-alloy head
2483cc (83 x 76.5mm)
Twin overhead camshafts, chain-driven
Seven-bearing crankshaft
Compression ratio 8:1 (7:1 and 9:1 available)
Two Solex B32 PBI-5 carburettors
120bhp at 5,750rpm
144lb ft at 3,000rpm

3.4-litre
Type XK 6-cylinder, with cast-iron block and aluminium-alloy head
3442cc (83 x 106mm)
Twin overhead camshafts, chain-driven
Seven-bearing crankshaft
Compression ratio 8:1 (7:1 and 9:1 available)
Two SU HD6 carburettors
210bhp at 5,500rpm (with standard compression)
216lb ft at 3,000rpm

3.8-litre
Type XK 6-cylinder, with cast-iron block and aluminium-alloy head
3781cc (87 x 106mm)
Twin overhead camshafts, chain-driven
Seven-bearing crankshaft
Compression ratio 8:1 (7:1 and 9:1 available)
Two SU HD6 carburettors
220bhp at 5,500rpm (with standard compression)
240lb ft at 3,000rpm

Transmission
Hydraulically operated clutch with 9in diameter (manual) or torque converter (automatic)
Four-speed manual gearbox (Moss type with no first-gear synchromesh to August 1965; Jaguar all-synchromesh type with same ratios thereafter)
Ratios 3.37:1, 1.86:1, 1.28:1, 1.00:1
Optional overdrive with 0.77:1 ratio.
Three-speed Borg Warner type DG automatic (type 35 from September 1965)
Ratios 4.97:1, 3.09:1, 1.00:1
Four-speed close-ratio manual gearbox (optional on 3.4-litre and 3.8-litre only)
Ratios 2.98:1, 1.36:1, 1.21:1, 1.00:1

Axle ratio

2.4-litre
4.27:1 with four-speed manual gearbox
4.55:1 with overdrive
4.27:1 with automatic gearbox

3.4-litre
3.54:1 with four-speed manual, close-ratio and automatic gearboxes
3.77:1 with overdrive

3.8-litre
3.54:1 with four-speed manual, close-ratio and automatic gearboxes
3.77:1 with overdrive

Suspension, steering and brakes
Independent front suspension with wishbones, coil springs and anti-roll bar
Live rear axle with radius arms, Panhard rod and cantilevered semi-elliptic leaf springs
Burman recirculating-ball, worm-and-nut steering
Disc brakes with 11.125in diameter front and 11.375in rear, with servo assistance as standard

Dimensions

Overall length	180.75in (4,591mm)
Overall width	66.75in (1,695mm)
Overall height	57.5in (1,460mm)
Wheelbase	107.375in (2,727mm)
Front track	55in (1,397mm); 55.5in (1,410mm) with 5in rims
Rear track	53.375in (1,355mm); 53.875in (1,368mm) with 5in rims

Wheels and tyres
15in steel disc wheels standard, with 4.5in rims to September 1960 and 5in rims thereafter
15in wire-spoke wheels with 5in rims optional
6.40 x 15 cross-ply tyres

Kerb weights

2.4-litre	3,192lb (1,448kg)
3.4-litre	3,304lb (1,499kg)
3.8-litre	3,360lb (1,524kg)

PERFORMANCE FIGURES – JAGUAR MK 2

2.4-litre overdrive
0–60mph 17.5sec
Maximum speed 96mph (154km/h)
Fuel consumption 18–21mpg (13–16ltr/100km)

3.4-litre overdrive
0–60mph 10.0sec
Maximum speed 118mph (190km/h)
Fuel consumption 17–21mpg (13–17ltr/100km)

3.4-litre automatic
0–60mph 12.0sec
Maximum speed 113mph (182km/h)
Fuel consumption 16–20mpg (14–18ltr/100km)

3.8-litre overdrive
0–60mph 8.5sec
Maximum speed 125mph (201km/h)
Fuel consumption 16–19mpg (15–18ltr/100km)

3.8-litre automatic
0–60mph 10sec
Maximum speed 120mph (193km/h)
Fuel consumption 15–18mpg (16–19ltr/100km)

SO YOU WANT TO BUY A MK 2 COMPACT JAGUAR?

Though it doesn't go, handle or stop like a modern car, a Mk 2 Jaguar always feels fast. It has a much more modern feel than the Mk 1, from which it is derived, and it is widely acknowledged as one of the great classic cars of the 1960s. As a result, the best ones are now very expensive indeed. However, this popularity has aided the growth of an aftermarket parts and servicing industry.

Like the Mk 1 models, the Mk 2s rust badly. A car that looks good on the outside may conceal expensive problems, so check carefully. Replacement panels can be bought, but good ones are expensive; many people use part-panels to replace rust damage, but these demand skilled fitting. Check the alignment of the doors – misalignment may be caused by a weakened body that is sagging. Look at the floorpan, the sills, the wheel arches and the wings. Underneath, examine the chassis legs, cross members and box sections, the Panhard rod and suspension mountings, the spare-wheel well and the fuel tank.

Engine and gearbox choice are down to personal preference. The acknowledged favourite is a 3.8-litre model with overdrive, and these tend to command the highest prices. However, in a car bought as a classic, the additional performance is not really very important – and in any case, many cheap modern cars will easily out-accelerate and out-handle even a 3.8-litre Mk 2. The 2.4-litre models are slowest, and usually least expensive to buy, but their more modest performance is not to be sniffed at.

A well-maintained engine will last well and regular oil changes are the key to longevity. Decent oil pressure is important: the gauge should settle at around 40psi when the engine is at working temperature; it may go as high as 50psi when the engine is cold. If the oil level is low, check for leaks – especially from the rear crankshaft oil seal, when there will be oil all over the underside of the car. A major engine rebuild will be needed if this has gone. Excessive blue smoke from the exhaust might be caused by blockages in the filter or the breather pipes.

As on the Mk 1 models, the four-speed Moss gearbox is distinctly old-fashioned in feel, but makes nice vintage noises. Brakes are better on the Mk 2s, with discs all round. However, discs and calipers can rust, and pistons and cylinders corrode. Make sure there is a shield protecting the brake servo, as it can rust away.

If a car has wire wheels, check for wear of the splined hubs and that the spokes are not damaged or loose. Many cars will have modern tyres fitted, and if these have a different rolling radius from the originals the speedo will read incorrectly. Check that they do not foul the wheel arches.

As on the Mk 1, interior problems will be obvious. The burr walnut is a veneer on a softwood base – it cracks and peels with age and exposure to sunlight or to water leaking into the car. Seats crack, sag and split, and a full professional retrim will be very expensive. Door trims discolour and warp if they get wet, while headlinings discolour and become tatty with age.

■ JAGUAR MK 2 (1959–1967)

PAINT AND TRIM COLOURS – JAGUAR MK 2

The same options were available on all three models. Some cars were painted and trimmed to special order. Note that there is still some controversy over the colours and trims available, and that sales catalogues and service bulletins often seem to be contradictory.

October 1959 to January 1961

There were eight standard paint colours and two extra-cost options, indicated below by an asterisk (*). White was probably mainly specified for police cars. Six interior-trim options were listed.

Body	Interior	Body	Interior
British Racing Green	Champagne, Suede Green or Tan	Imperial Maroon	Red
Carmen Red	Black or Red	Old English White	Red or Tan
Cotswold Blue	Dark Blue or Grey	Pearl Grey	Dark Blue, Grey, Light Blue or Red
Dove Grey	Grey, Red or Tan	Sherwood Green	Suede Green or Tan
Embassy Black*	Red or Tan	White*	Black

February 1961 to November 1964

There were fourteeen standard paint colours and two extra-cost options, indicated below by an asterisk (*). Six of the standard colours were new 'opalescent' (metallic) types. White was probably mainly specified for police cars. The six interior-trim options were unchanged.

Body	Interior	Body	Interior
British Racing Green	Champagne, Suede Green or Tan	Opalescent Bronze	Red or Tan
Carmen Red	Black or Red	Opalescent Dark Green	Champagne, Suede Green or Tan
Cotswold Blue	Dark Blue or Grey	Opalescent Gunmetal	Red or Tan
Dove Grey	Grey, Red or Tan	Opalescent Silver Blue	Dark Blue, Grey, Light Blue or Red
Embassy Black*	Red or Tan	Opalescent Silver Grey	Grey, Red or Tan
Imperial Maroon	Red	Pearl Grey	Dark Blue, Grey, Light Blue or Red
Old English White	Red or Tan	Sherwood Green	Suede Green or Tan
Opalescent Blue	Dark Blue, Grey, Light Blue or Red	White*	Black

December 1964 to March 1966

There were ten standard paint colours and two extra-cost options, indicated below by an asterisk (*). Five of the standard colours were opalescent (metallic) types. White was probably mainly specified for police cars. There were nine interior-trim colours.

Body	Interior	Body	Interior
Carmen Red	Black or Red	Opalescent Maroon	Beige or Maroon
Cream	Dark Blue, Light Blue or Red	Opalescent Silver Blue	Dark Blue or Grey
Dark Blue	Grey, Light Blue or Red	Opalescent Silver Grey	Grey, Red or Tan
Embassy Black*	Red or Tan	Sherwood Green	Light Tan, Suede Green or Tan
Opalescent Dark Green	Beige, Light Tan, Suede Green or Tan	Warwick Grey	Red or Tan
Opalescent Golden Sand	Light Tan or Red	White*	Black

80

JAGUAR MK 2 (1959–1967)

April 1966 to August 1966
Colours and trims remained unchanged except that Black was now listed among the standard paint colours and could now be had with Grey, Light Tan, Red or Tan interior trim. There were therefore eleven standard colours, one special-order option (White, probably mainly used on police cars) and nine interior-trim options.

September 1966 to February 1967
Colours and trim colours were unchanged, but Ambla upholstery now became standard and leather became an extra-cost option.

March 1967 to August 1967
The paint options were reduced to just eight standard colours, and all the opalescent options were dropped. No special-order options were listed. Interior-trim materials and colours remained as before.

Body	Interior	Body	Interior
Beige	Light Tan, Red, Suede Green or Tan	Cream	Dark Blue, Light Blue or Red
Black	Grey, Light Tan, Red or Tan	Dark Blue	Grey, Light Blue or Red
British Racing Green	Beige, Light Tan, Suede Green or Tan	Warwick Grey	Dark Blue, Light Blue or Tan
Carmen Red	Beige or Red		

Mk 2 Jaguars are still raced with enthusiasm in classic events today.

CHAPTER SIX

JAGUAR 240 AND 340 (1967–1969)

By 1967 the Jaguar saloon range was becoming overcomplicated. As that year began, the compact saloon range consisted of six models: 2.4-litre, 3.4-litre and 3.8-litre Mk 2s; 3.4-litre and 3.8-litre S-types; and 4.2-litre 420s. Then there were the Daimler V8s and the Daimler Sovereign version of the 420, plus the big Mk X-derived 420G. So for the 1968 season that began in autumn 1967, Jaguar rationalized their saloon ranges.

With the elimination of the 3.8-litre Mk 2 and some price adjustments, the company removed the overlap between the top end of the Mk 2 range and the bottom end of the S-type range. And, pursuing the process that had already begun with the 1967-season Mk 2s, Browns Lane further trimmed the specification of the remaining 2.4-litre and 3.4-litre Mk 2s, both to keep manufacturing costs down and to permit the keen pricing on which the company had always depended.

Beginning a year earlier, Jaguar had embarked on a policy of giving numbers to its saloon models, the first examples being the 420 and 420G. John Dugdale's book *Jaguar in America* explains that this policy was adopted to help Jaguar's US sales and was an attempt to emulate the success of the Mercedes-Benz model-naming system. So with effect from the end of September 1967, the Mk 2 saloons were renamed 240 and 340 respectively – although at Browns Lane they seem to have been more generally known as 'Mk 2 240' and 'Mk 2 340' models.

CHANGES FROM THE MK 2

Exterior Changes

The 240 and 340 models were easily distinguished from their predecessors by their slimmer bumpers. Those at the

ABOVE: **This close-up of the nose of a 340 shows the new bumpers and the dummy horn grilles, which had been available earlier on some models, such as the 3.8-litre Mk 2s sold in the USA.**

LEFT: **Were it not for the '240' number plate, this publicity picture would be almost believable! The smaller-engined version of the facelifted Mk 2s is seen here, looking fresh with its new slimline bumpers.**

JAGUAR 240 AND 340 (1967–1969)

front came from the S-types, and although the matching rear bumper was actually unique to the 240 and 340 (and their Daimler equivalents), it did wear S-type overriders. Both front and rear valance panels were modified to suit. Metallic paints disappeared from the options list, so helping to distance the 240 and 340 from the more expensive S-types. In addition, 240 and 340 had new hubcaps with black plastic badges in the centre, exactly like those introduced in 1966 on the 420 and 420G. Boot-lid badges that read '240' or '340' completed the exterior changes, other details like the dummy horn grilles being carried over from the 1967-model Mk 2s.

Interior Changes

Basic interior details were the same as on the 1967 Mk 2s, with Ambla upholstery as standard. However, there was a smaller colour palette and the picnic tables had gone, and were not even available as an option. Carpets, too, were now made of cheaper tufted nylon instead of wool, while the wood trim now came in a lighter shade with less prominent figuring – this latter a sign of changing public tastes rather than a cost-saving measure. Even the toolbox in the boot had been cheapened and was now a moulded plastic type instead of the earlier wood-and-metal variety.

Mechanical Updates

Some people who had not noticed the start of the cheapening process in mid-1966 now realized what was happening and a few complained bitterly and publicly through the press. But the process was not entirely downhill, because both 240 and 340 also took on some very worthwhile mechanical updates.

The more significant changes affected the 240, whose engine now boasted a power increase from the earlier 120bhp to 133bhp and a small torque increase from 144lb ft to 146lb ft at 3,700rpm. The main benefits of this were that the car could now exceed 100mph with ease for the first time and that its high-speed acceleration was improved. The heart of these improvements lay in the straight-port cylinder head of the 4.2-litre E-type engine that had replaced the old B-type cylinder head. However, the 240 engine also had a new water-heated inlet manifold, which carried two SU HS6 carburettors in place of the Solexes on earlier 2.4-litre engines. A paper-element air cleaner with twin intake trumpets replaced the old oil-bath type, and a new dual-pipe exhaust system made the most of all these changes.

The 340 engine also took on the straight-port cylinder head and a paper-element air cleaner, although the latter came from the S-type and differed slightly from the one in the 240. Although Jaguar did not claim any power or torque increases over the Mk 2, this may have been to reinforce the distinction between 340 and 3.4-litre S-type; comparisons suggested that the new 340 was noticeably quicker than the old car.

Wood trim and a wool headlining were traditional Jaguar fare – it took a close look to reveal that the upholstery was no longer in leather but rather in Ambla vinyl.

JAGUAR 240 AND 340 (1967–1969)

Engines in the 240 and 340 models took on smart ribbed cam covers with the Jaguar name cast into them. This is a 2.4-litre engine, now with SU carburettors instead of the Solexes used on earlier versions.

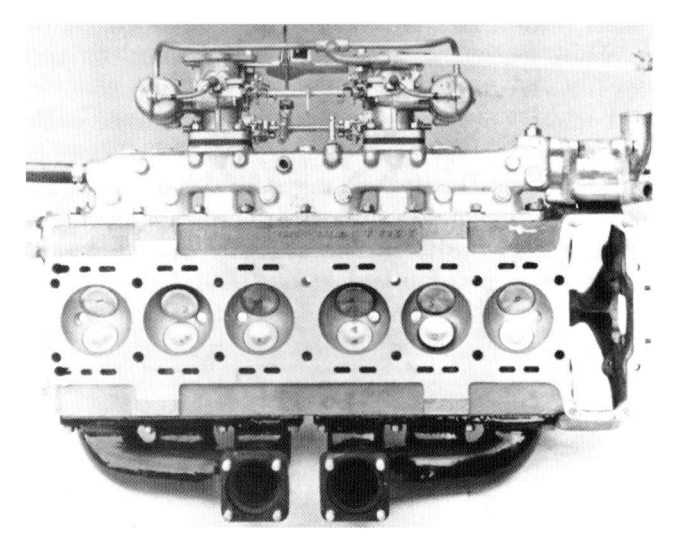

The 2.4-litre engine was also improved by the addition of the straight-port cylinder head, as shown here. The improved gas flow made some differences to performance, but the 240 was nobody's favourite getaway car.

Both 240 and 340 engines sported the latest style of ribbed camshaft covers, both had distributors with side-entry rather than top-entry leads, and both had a new thermostat arrangement in their cooling systems. This closed off the radiator bypass when it opened, so allowing the full flow of coolant from the water pump to pass through the radiator for more effective cooling without an increase in radiator size. Servicing intervals for both engines had been extended from 2,500 to 3,000 miles (4,000 to 5,000km) – an improvement, but still not up with the industry leaders in 1967.

The 240 came with manual, manual-plus-overdrive, or automatic gearbox, and Jaguar announced that supplies of the latter would be more plentiful. This was probably their way of saying that they hoped the extra power and torque would help it to sell better than it had done before. The 340 came with the same three gearbox options. In addition, as Chapter 7 explains, there were three versions of the Daimler V8-engined car. So even though the old Mk 2 range had been trimmed for 1968, there were still no fewer than nine different versions on offer!

Pricing

Perhaps most striking of all was the pricing of the new models. The much-improved 240 cost £23 more than the superseded 2.4-litre Mk 2, but in automatic form it now cost £16 less than an automatic 2.4. The manual-gearbox 340, meanwhile, cost the same as the last of the 3.4-litre Mk 2s, and as an automatic was now £40 cheaper than before. As ever, the whole range represented remarkable value for money – although there was no denying that the cars were beginning to show their age. Their basic design, after all, dated back to 1955.

THE 240 AND 340 ON SALE

Although Jaguar listed only the 240 and 340 models from the end of September 1967, the newcomers did not finally supplant the Mk 2s for several months because examples of the older cars lingered on in the showrooms until early 1968. On the production lines, the changeover was nevertheless very rapid indeed: after a single pilot-build example of each model had been assembled in June 1967, volume production of 240s and 340s began in mid-August.

At one stage it was intended that the 240 should not be built at all. Philip Porter's *The Jaguar Scrapbook* refers to a document written by competitions manager 'Lofty' England outlining the 1966 Jaguar product programme, which shows that Jaguar had intended to replace the 2.4-litre car with a model with a 2.6-litre engine that would have been called the 260. It did not happen – and no trace of that anticipated 2.6-litre engine has been found, either.

The 240 and 340 models sold steadily. Both were available for the whole of the 1968 season, but production of the 340 stopped in September that year as the new XJ6 was launched, and sales naturally tailed off. The 240 remained available until the following summer and the last example was built on 9 April 1969, but the total of 692 cars built in that first quarter of 1969 suggests that demand was no lower than in the previous year. Nevertheless, the compacts had to go: they were expensive to produce and Jaguar was keen to move over to the more cost-effective XJ6 range as soon as possible.

PRODUCTION CHANGES (1967–69)

With only two years of production ahead of them, Browns Lane hoped to make as few production changes as possible to the 240 and 340 models. However, their hopes were thwarted by new legislation affecting motor vehicles that was now proliferating in markets all around the world. As no two countries' regulations ever seemed to be the same, this was a difficult period for motor manufacturers because they were obliged to build multiple different varieties of the same model.

Some of the production changes made to the 240 and 340 were in response to this new legislation. West Germany demanded that sidelamps be integral with headlamps, so from July 1968 the 240s and 340s destined for customers there had new headlamps incorporating sidelight bulbs. The original sidelamp pods remained on top of the wings, but the lamp units were not wired up. A further change in December 1968 illustrated the sort of problems new legislation was beginning to cause: although Jaguar were able to simplify production a little by fitting a common type of 'European' headlamp to left-hand-drive cars, Austrian cars now became the exception because they retained the older type of headlamp.

PRODUCTION FIGURES – JAGUAR 240 AND 340

	RHD	LHD	Total
240	3,716	730	4,446
340	2,265	535	2,800
Overall total	**5,981**	**1,265**	**7,246**

Note that a small number of 340 models were built with 3.8-litre engines; see panel on page 89.

OPTIONAL EXTRAS – JAGUAR 240 AND 340

A much-reduced range of optional extras was listed for the 240 and 340 models, although no doubt old-stock options from the 2.4-litre and 3.4-litre days were still available for persistent enquirers. The options listed were:

Dunlop SP41 radial tyres
Heated rear window
Leather upholstery
Overdrive
Power-assisted steering (340 only)
Radio
Reclining front seats
Seat belts
Special paint finishes
Spotlamps
Wire wheels (chrome-plated or silver stove-enamelled only)

JAGUAR 240 AND 340 (1967–1969)

Jaguar's careful cost-paring exercise moved some items to the options list. The purchaser of this 340 was happy to pay extra to have the fog lamps reinstated and to upgrade to stove-enamelled wire wheels.

No expense spared here: there is a badge bar as well as the optional fog lights on this 340.

West Germany had insisted some years earlier that the knock-on hubcaps that came with wire wheels should not have protruding spinners; now a new design of knock-on hubcap was standardized to meet new requirements in Denmark, Japan, Sweden and Switzerland. This was another July 1968 arrival and was also added to cars for West Germany, but all other countries retained the home-market type with its twin 'ears' until production ended. Relatively few cars were affected, in any case, and relatively few cars were affected by the standardization of a cylinder block heater on all cars for Canada in July 1968: the 340s, in particular, had only another two months of production life left.

More minor changes were made in six stages between January 1968 and May 1969. First came a renewable petrol filter element in place of the gauze type. Then from July 1968 all cars had a new water temperature gauge with simplified 'normal' and 'danger' zone markings instead of the earlier calibrations. At the same time, push-fit terminals replaced the screw-in type on coils, and on the 340 engine there were different struts for the oil suction and delivery pipes. These changes were the last ones to affect the 340s.

By the time the next changes were made in December 1968, only the 240s remained in production. Engines gained sintered valve seats with a reduced depth; a new type of Lucas starter solenoid was fitted; and there was also a new non-hydrostatic clutch slave cylinder. This was something of a mixed blessing because it did not compensate automatically for clutch wear. Then, from January 1969, new connecting rod bolts and nuts with a higher tensile strength were introduced.

In March 1969, a modified gearbox plug on overdrive cars reduced the risk of the overdrive being starved of oil in certain conditions. Then the sixth and final set of changes came in May, when the water pump spindle was changed and the petrol pipe between filter and float chamber was modified;

on left-hand-drive cars, a different choke cable was fitted as well, because the old type had tended to stick.

Lastly, it looks as if a few 240s and 340s were fitted with a black PVC padded roll on the tops of their dashboards, exactly like that in the contemporary Daimler V8-250. There is no record of this in Jaguar literature, but it was probably a response to shortages of the standard type right at the end of production.

THE 240 AND 340 AND THE PRESS

It was the 240 that attracted press attention when the cars were new, perhaps partly because of its revised engine, but it was clear that Jaguar wanted maximum publicity for its least expensive model. *Autocar* magazine tested one in its issue of 4 January 1968 and assessed the car as 'remarkable value'. They pointed out that the basic list price was now 'only £133 more than it was twelve years ago, which is a remarkable achievement considering how costs in every other field have escalated so much more'. Age was beginning to count against the 240, though:

> What were once very brisk acceleration and a high top speed can now be matched by several cars with engines of under 2 litres. Nevertheless, from behind the wheel there is never a moment's doubt that this is a full-blooded Jaguar with all the virtues of a thoroughbred.

This was an overdrive car, and it distinguished itself by losing all the oil from that overdrive when an oil seal failed during the test. There was no comment on that fault, but the magazine did point out that 'the latest all-synchromesh [gearbox] is hard to fault on any score'. It even made nice noises: 'each of the indirect gears has its own characteristic whine ... but these are all subdued and introduce a pleasant note to the mechanical ear.'

The 240 was 'rather ponderous around town perhaps but superb on the open road and ideal for journeys'. The lack of power-assisted steering – not available even as an option – was criticized: 'The marked nose heaviness ... makes it hard to turn the wheels, but it gives excellent stability.' No doubt the SP41 radials on the test car played their part in making the steering heavy. As for the latest version of the 2.4-litre engine, *Autocar* felt that flexibility had not suffered at the expense of top-end power. The cooling fan was noisy, 'otherwise the 240 is a very quiet car'.

Motor also remarked on the 240's quietness in its test dated 27 January 1968. 'The power unit was outstandingly smooth and quiet,' they said, 'better in this respect than most other Jaguars we have tested over the past few years.' However, the age of the design again occasioned comment. 'The 240 is about half a ton heavier than many more recent designs offering the same passenger space and comfort ... [so that] the engine must do the work that is now quite satisfactorily done by engines of 2-litres capacity or less.'

Steering was again criticized as too heavy at parking speeds, even though it gave 'nimble, responsive handling' at

The badges on the boot lid changed once again. The badge fitted on the 340 had the same style as this one.

■ JAGUAR 240 AND 340 (1967–1969)

Although the basic design of the compact saloons dated back to the mid-1950s, it was still attractive and distinctive by the time this 340 was built in 1968.

THE 3.8-LITRE 340

As far as the general public was concerned, the old 3.8-litre model was no longer available after the end of the 1967 season. However, Browns Lane was always receptive to special requests and it appears that a small number of 340 models were built with the 3.8-litre engine. Nigel Thorley (in *Jaguar Mk I & Mk II – the Complete Companion*) believed that nine such cars were built between December 1967 and May 1968, although the factory records are silent on the matter. At least two of these cars have survived. One has wire wheels, inset fog lamps and an overdrive gearbox and carries '340 3.8' badges on its boot lid. The other is a former Somerset and Bath Constabulary traffic car, with standard steel wheels.

speed. The ride quality was acceptable but 'not outstanding' when compared to that of the S-type Jaguars, and not all the testers liked the front seats, which some felt were too upright and gave inadequate lumbar support. Controls were sometimes difficult to find in the dark.

Autocar went on to use a 240 as a long-term test car, and liked it enough to sign off in its issue of 12 February 1970 with the comment that 'one fears that there will never again be a compact Jaguar to replace the 240. In its absence, it is not surprising that there is a healthy demand for well-preserved used examples.'

In Britain, the only test of a 340 was conducted by *Autosport* for its issue dated 16 February 1968. 'Now that the S and 420 models satisfy the luxury market, the simpler 340 brings 120mph motoring within the reach of the man of medium income,' wrote John Bolster. He found that the acceleration figures were 'better than ever', with 8.8sec for the 0–60mph standing start, and that fuel consumption normally worked out around 20mpg (14ltr/100km) – although performance testing reduced that to 17mpg (16.6ltr/100km). 'The 340 is therefore not only cheap to buy but cheap to run as well.'

Overall, this was a car in the true Jaguar tradition. 'It feels, sounds, and looks like a very costly car, and everything about it is rich except its price. Once again, I am astonished at the Jaguar miracle of value for money.'

RIVALS

Jaguar's policy of keeping showroom prices for the 240 and 340 models as low as possible certainly helped to keep these by now elderly models attractive to buyers, but it also pitched them into a different and much more competitive sector of the market. Throughout the 1950s and early 1960s, the Mk 1 and Mk 2 saloons had occupied an almost unique position, but during the early 1960s the growth of the so-called executive saloon market had put a variety of new models just below the prices of the Jaguars. Pioneers in Britain had been the Rover 2000 and Triumph 2000, both introduced in 1963, and by the middle of the decade they had been joined by several others. While the prices of the Jaguars remained static, prices of the new executive cars began to rise. As a result, the Jaguars found themselves competing against much newer designs that were similarly or more cheaply priced.

A look through new-car prices at the 1967 Earls Court Motor Show makes the change quite clear. Inclusive of purchase tax and without extras, the Jaguars ranged from £1,365 for a manual 240 to £1,537 for an automatic 340. In that price range there were also attractive models by BMW, Citroën, Fiat, Ford, Opel, Reliant, Rover, Vauxhall and Volvo. None of them offered quite the same blend of qualities as the Jaguars, but all of them were newer designs, and that counted for a lot.

For the buyer who wanted a four-seater sports saloon, the Fiat 2300 at £1,354 might have looked tempting, but in practice it sold poorly in Britain. The BMW 1800 would certainly have looked attractive at £1,498, for although its interior was somewhat spartan, it boasted excellent handling, roadholding and acceleration. Other possibilities would have included the rapid Opel Commodore at £1,380 and the Vauxhall Viscount automatic at £1,483, a large car with acres of interior space and better performance than its barge-like appearance suggested, but without the roadability or refinement of the Jaguars.

New on the scene was the twin-carburettor Volvo 122S at £1,415, no great beauty and in fact the latest iteration of an old design, but a very solidly built car with good performance and road manners. The Rover 2000TC at £1,451 was neatly priced between the 240 and 340 Jaguars and allied new levels of performance to the 2000's established qualities of good handling and restrained luxury, although it fell down on refinement. Nevertheless, the single-carburettor 2000 was a very attractive alternative to a 240 at just £1,357.

JAGUAR 240 AND 340 (1967–1969)

THE 240 AND 340 IN POLICE SERVICE

By the time the 240 and 340 Jaguars were introduced, the new XJ6 was only just over a year away and prototypes would have been shown to many potential police buyers in the UK. As the 3.8-litre Mk 2, which had been a police favourite, was no longer available, several forces probably decided to wait for the XJ6 before placing further orders. However, as noted elsewhere, at least one police force placed a special order for a 340 with a 3.8-litre engine. The Somerset and Bath Constabulary was probably in a unique position as it had been formed in 1967 from the merger of the Somerset Constabulary and the Bath City Police and may have needed new vehicles urgently.

Both the 240 and 340 found homes with other UK police forces. Some of course served as unmarked police vehicles, but most served in the all-white livery of motorway patrol cars. Like their Mk 2 predecessors, they were typically equipped with a calibrated speedometer, two-way radio equipment and an illuminated police sign with blue flashing lights on the roof. However, the precise specification differed from force to force, to meet local preferences.

ABOVE RIGHT: **Smiling policemen – and why not? These members of the Dunbartonshire Constabulary pose for an official photograph with their 340, which was a 1969 model.**

ABOVE LEFT: **One of several Kent Police 340s doing duty on the A20(M). Note the white-painted wing mirrors, as on the other Kent car (below). This car has a single fog light with the standard dummy horn grille on the other side.**

LEFT: **The change of model designation made no difference to police users. This 340 was another purchased by the Kent Police, whose museum kindly provided this photograph. Tyre pressures were marked at the top centre of each wheel arch.**

JAGUAR 240 AND 340 (1967–1969)

The Police Vehicle Enthusiasts' Club has photographic records of 240 and 340 Jaguars being used by the following thirteen police forces:

Angus Constabulary
Ayrshire Constabulary
Dumfries and Galloway Constabulary
Dunbartonshire Constabulary
Durham Constabulary
Hertfordshire Constabulary
Kent County Constabulary

Somerset and Bath Constabulary
Staffordshire and Stoke-on-Trent Constabulary
Staffordshire Constabulary
Scottish North-Eastern Counties Constabulary
Warwickshire and Coventry Constabulary
Warwickshire Constabulary

The crew of a Kent Police traffic division Jaguar pose with the equipment carried in their car.

■ JAGUAR 240 AND 340 (1967–1969)

> ### THE 340 IN THE USA
>
> Only the 340 model was available in the USA, where the car was perceived as a slightly modified 3.4-litre Mk 2 rather than a new model. Sales declined in favour of the S-types and 420s, and relatively few of the 535 left-hand-drive 340s built were sold in the USA.

THE END OF PRODUCTION

The 340 models went out of production after just twelve months, to avoid competition with the new 2.8-litre version of the XJ6 saloon that went on sale towards the end of 1968. The 240s lasted a little longer, but the last car was built in April 1969 and by the end of the year there were probably no more in the showrooms.

Sadly, there was no official end-of-line ceremony for these cars, which had done so much for Jaguar's fortunes in fourteen years of production. One reason must have been that the Daimler V8-250 derivative remained in production (and would do so until August). So the last car came off the lines unnoticed by all except the Jaguar employees directly associated with it. The car itself was sold on through a dealer in the normal way and has now, in all probability, been scrapped.

If a two-door coupé would fit the bill, then the Reliant Scimitar with its Ford 3-litre V6 engine looked attractive. By the time of the 1968 Earls Court Show, there was another serious rival for the Jaguars, this time the Triumph 2.5 PI with its fuel-injected 6-cylinder engine, priced at a few shillings less than £1,450.

Overseas, where Jaguar prices tended to be higher and those of their locally built rivals lower, the 240 and 340 fought a losing battle. Sales of the 340 held up quite well, but the 240 was outclassed in many markets and was simply not offered in others.

RIGHT: **The police were not the only ones who used 340s with 3.8-litre engines. This 1967 340 was given a 3.8-litre engine in later years to make it competitive in club racing events. The car had a number of other modifications as well, such as ventilated front brake discs and lowered suspension, together with engine performance improvements.**

LEFT: **The 3.8-litre engine in the racing 340 was balanced, had a lightened flywheel and a gas-flowed cylinder head, and is seen here with a pair of 2in SU carburettors. With a big-bore exhaust, it developed 203bhp at the wheels and was estimated to have a top speed of 140mph (225km/h).**

IDENTIFICATION – JAGUAR 240 AND 340

Identification numbers are stamped on a plate in the engine compartment, attached to the right-hand inner wing. These numbers are repeated elsewhere, as shown below.

Car Number
The car number, also known as the chassis number or VIN, is stamped into the bonnet catch channel, just ahead of the radiator header tank. A typical car number might be 1J 30048 BW. This breaks down into three elements:

1J	240 or 340 model
30048	serial number (see below)
BW	transmission type (see below)

The serial number sequences are:

	RHD	LHD
240	1J001–1J4716	1J30001–1J30730
340	1J50001–1J52265	1J80001–1J80535

(The special-order 3.8-litre cars appear to have been numbered within the 340 sequences.)

The suffixes decode as follows:

BW	Borg Warner automatic gearbox
DN	Laycock de Normanville overdrive

Cars fitted with power-assisted steering have a P prefix; for example, P1J 30048 BW.

Engine Number
The engine number is stamped on the right-hand side of the cylinder block above the oil filter and again at the front of the cylinder head casting, beside the front spark-plug hole. A typical engine number would be 7J 2700/9. This breaks down into three elements:

7J	Engine type identifier (used for both 240 and 340 engines)
2700	Serial number (see below)
/9	Compression ratio (/9 for 9:1 compression, /7 for 7:1, /8 for 8:1).

The serial number sequences are:

7J 1001 upwards	240 engines
7J 50001 upwards	340 engines

(The special-order 3.8-litre cars appear to have had engines drawn from the 3.8-litre S-type sequences.)

Body Number
The body number is stamped on a small plate attached to the right-hand side of the body behind the rear bumper. (It should not be confused with a similar plate on the left-hand side that shows the Pressed Steel reference number.)

Gearbox Number
On all manual gearboxes, the gearbox number is stamped on a small shoulder at the left-hand rear corner of the gearbox casing, and on the top cover around the rim of the core-plug aperture. On automatic gearboxes, the number is stamped on a plate attached to the left-hand side of the gearbox casing.

PERFORMANCE FIGURES – JAGUAR 240 AND 340

240
0–60mph	12.5sec
Maximum speed	106mph (170km/h)
Fuel consumption	18–21mpg (13–16ltr/100km)

340
0–60mph	8.8sec
Maximum speed	120mph (193km/h)
Fuel consumption	17–22mpg (13–17ltr/100km)

JAGUAR 240 AND 340 (1967–1969)

SPECIFICATIONS – JAGUAR 240 AND 340

All specifications were as for the final Mk 2 models, with the following exceptions.

Engines
240
Compression ratio 8:1 (7:1 available)
Two SU HS6 carburettors
133bhp at 5,500rpm
146lb ft at 3,700rpm

340 3.8
The engines in these special-order models appear to have been 3.8-litre S-type engines (*see Chapter 9*)

Transmission
Close-ratio manual gearboxes not listed

Axle ratio
3.4-litre
3.54:1 with four-speed manual and automatic gearboxes
3.54:1 with overdrive

PAINT AND TRIM COLOURS – JAGUAR 240 AND 340

The same options were available on both models. Some cars were painted and trimmed to special order.

September 1967 to April 1969
There were six standard paint colours, none of which was metallic. White was not listed but was certainly used on police cars. Four interior-trim colours were listed; upholstery was in Ambla, and leather an extra-cost option.

Body	Interior	Body	Interior
Beige	Beige, Black, Blue or Red	Cream	Beige, Black, Blue or Red
Black	Beige, Black, Blue or Red	Dark Blue	Beige, Black, Blue or Red
British Racing Green	Beige or Black	Warwick Grey	Beige, Black, Blue or Red

SO YOU WANT TO BUY A JAGUAR 240 OR 340?

The 240 and 340 models are essentially the same as the earlier Mk 2 types, and the buying advice given in Chapter 5 for Mk 2s applies to them as well. Note, as an additional complication, that damaged Ambla upholstery may be harder to repair and more expensive than the optional extra leather. Not surprisingly, some restored cars now have leather upholstery that they did not have when new!

CHAPTER SEVEN

DAIMLER V8 (1962–1969)

Daimler did not do well during the 1950s. Founded in 1896 and owned since 1910 by the Birmingham Small Arms Company (BSA), in 1950 Daimler lost the Royal Warrant that it had held for nearly fifty years. Recognizing that the market had changed and that it would no longer be able to survive on sales of the low-volume, high-quality luxury cars that had made its reputation, the company attempted to break into a new market by offering smaller luxury saloons. But cars like the 1953 Conquest did not sell in large enough numbers to sustain the company; by 1955, it had to drop its 'middle-class' Lanchester models, and by the middle of 1956 it was clear that the time had come for drastic action. The decision was taken to develop a new saloon with a V8 engine – a configuration almost certainly chosen with thoughts of expansion into the American market in mind.

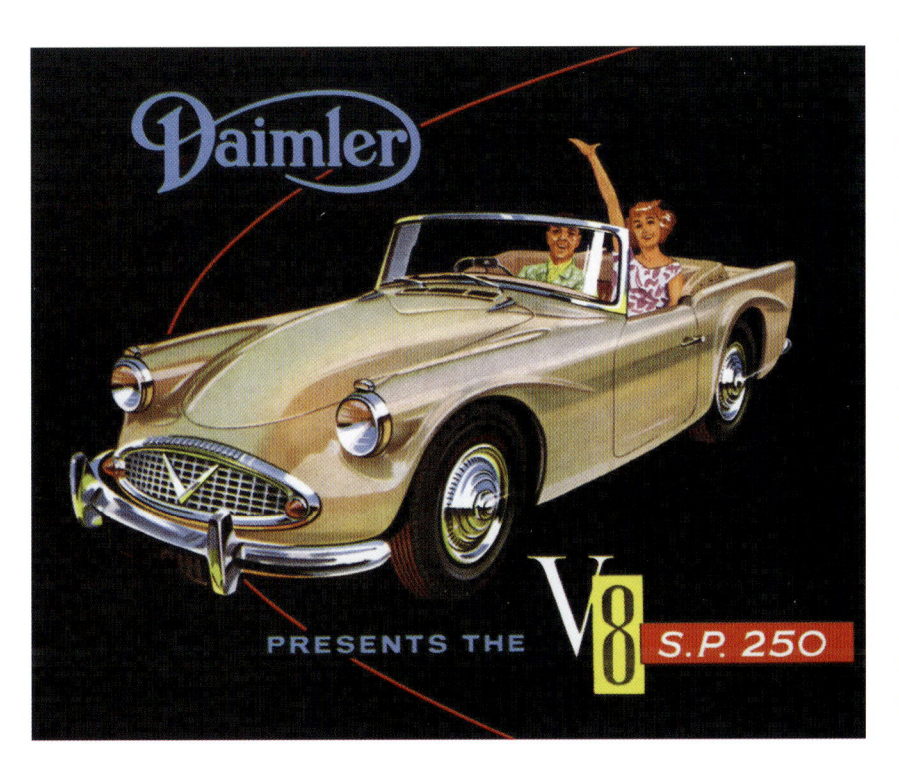

DAIMLER V8 ENGINE

The managing director of BSA's automotive division was Edward Turner, who had been a noted designer of motorcycle engines earlier in his career. He took on the job of designing the new V8 engine, and took as his inspiration the well-proven Cadillac V8 engine; as Brian Long notes in *Daimler V8 SP250*, Turner himself owned a Cadillac at the time. So he decided to set the cylinder banks at 90 degrees to one another, and to use a simple overhead-valve layout with a single central camshaft operating the valves by pushrods.

Turner also drew on his own earlier work with motorcycle engines. His most highly acclaimed design had been a V-twin engine for the 1937 Triumph Speed Twin, and from this he took the combustion chamber design and certain dimensions that married up happily with the 2.5-litre capacity he wanted for the Daimler engine. There was considerable urgency behind the whole project, and the new engine came together remarkably quickly. First drawings were done in October 1956, and the first prototype engine ran just eight months later. So accomplished was the design that it seems to have needed very little further development.

The first Daimler V8 engine went on mileage test in a Conquest Century saloon during 1957, but there were no plans to use this combination in production. Daim-

Although the V8 engine had originally been intended for a saloon model, in practice its first appearance was in the 1959 SP250 sports car.

DAIMLER V8 (1962–1969)

Edward Turner's 2.5-litre V8 engine drew on its designer's extensive experience in motorcycle engine design, but also shared some design solutions with American Chrysler V8 engines of the time.

The rocker covers have been removed from this sectioned display example of the V8 engine in order to reveal the valve gear.

ler wanted a completely new saloon, and by the end of 1958 were planning to base it on the bought-in bodyshell of the Vauxhall Cresta PA. However, this project, codenamed DN250, was dead by the middle of 1959.

Meanwhile, Daimler had decided during 1957 that the new V8 engine should also appear in a sports car aimed primarily at the American market. What Daimler called the SP250 model was running in prototype form by the beginning of 1958 and, when the DN250 saloon project was abandoned, Daimler decided to use the sports car's chassis and running gear as the basis of a small sports saloon as well. This took on the code name DP250, and the prototype appeared as a Daimler V8 2.5-litre Close Coupled Saloon on the stand of Hooper, the coachbuilders who had made its body, at the 1959 Earls Court Motor Show. Also new at that show was Jaguar's Mk 2 compact saloon, which would later play an important role in the Daimler story.

ENTER JAGUAR

The DP250 saloon did not progress beyond the prototype stage. Sales of the SP250 sports car, which had been announced at the New York Auto Show in April 1959, failed to live up to expectations and BSA, already disillusioned with Daimler's progress, decided to dispose of its lame duck. Jaguar was then in need of more factory space and bought Daimler primarily for that reason in mid-June 1960.

There were obligations to Daimler dealerships to consider and, for the time being, Jaguar allowed the existing models to remain in production. Sir William Lyons hated the productionized DP250 saloon prototype he was

DAIMLER V8 (1962–1969)

This was the first publicity picture of the new Daimler model, issued in 1963. Note how the 'D' badges on the hubcaps have been neatly arranged in a vertical position. In this view, the car was clearly a Mk 2 Jaguar with Daimler badges – but there was far more to it than that.

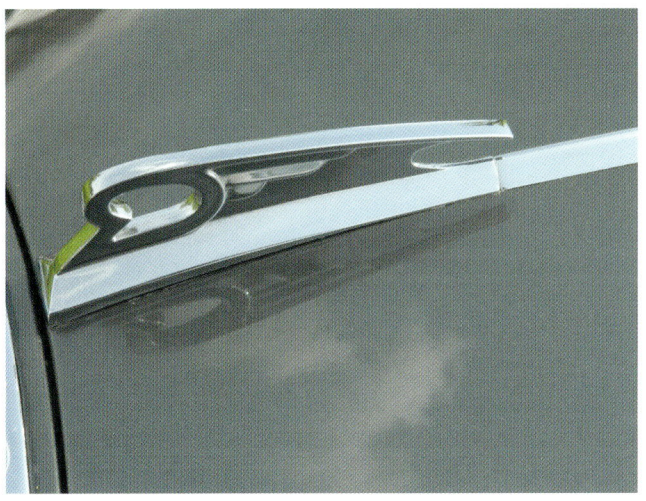

ABOVE LEFT: **A winged 'D' badge served both as identifying mascot and as a handle for raising the bonnet.**

ABOVE RIGHT: **The Daimler models were distinguished by this rather elegant grille, similar in shape to the Jaguar type but featuring the fluting that had become a Daimler hallmark. Lights, bumpers and other details were the same as on the Jaguars.**

The Daimlers had an exhaust pipe like this on each side, with a special rear valance panel to suit.

DAIMLER V8 (1962–1969)

shown and ordered the whole project to be scrapped, but he did listen when his engineers told him that their tests of the small-block Daimler V8 engine had shown it to be thoroughly sound and well-engineered. The fact that the engine was already in production and was relatively new probably then gave rise to the idea of fitting it into the bodyshell of a Mk 2 Jaguar to provide Daimler with the new saloon it had been struggling to create since 1956.

Browns Lane did not take long to get to grips with the idea. The project was allocated code number ZX530/112 – it never did get a Daimler model code – and by November 1960 Phil Weaver's team in the experimental department had transplanted a Daimler V8 into one of their existing Mk 1 Jaguar hacks. This car was put through the usual rigorous test procedures over the next sixteen months and turned in a performance that was very much better than anyone expected.

It would appear that Jaguar briefly considered trying out a Mk 2 saloon with the larger Daimler V8 engine, also designed by Edward Turner and already in production for the Majestic Major. However, that idea seems not to have gone beyond the drawing board. The 4.5-litre Daimler V8 was a wide engine and fitting it into a Mk 2 bodyshell would have demanded changes to the engine bay. Although the big V8 might have had some appeal in the USA, it delivered only 220bhp when Jaguar's 3.8-litre XK already had 265bhp, and an enlarged XK engine (which became the 4.2) was probably already under consideration.

The 2½-litre project did become serious, however, and the experimental department built a second prototype, this time using a Mk 2 bodyshell. By now, the project had attracted the code XDM2. The second car had the latest Borg Warner type 35 automatic gearbox, and proved very successful. Its major problem was a throbbing and intermittent drumming, which Jaguar discovered was caused by flexing of the gearbox transmission unit. The problem was quickly solved by fitting a stiffener plate between the bottom of the bellhousing and the sump.

The Browns Lane engineers made a few more alterations. They replaced the cylinder-head studs of the Daimler design with set bolts so that the heads could be removed with the engine still in the car. They relocated the water pump centrally on the front face of the cylinder block, with split outlets to each bank of cylinders, and inserted an extra pulley between crankshaft nose and fan to drive the auxiliaries. They reduced the size of the main bearings to make room for balancing weights on the crankshaft. New exhaust manifolds were also drawn up, although their design suggests that maximum power was not a consideration; perhaps there were fears that a more efficient design would give the V8-engined car too much of a performance advantage over the 2.4-litre Jaguar.

Meanwhile, a Daimler version of the Mk 2 bodyshell was prepared. This gained a radiator grille with a fluted top; a number-plate lamp on the boot lid with similar fluting; a 'flying D' mascot on the bonnet; and 'D' emblems on the wheel-trim centres. There was another 'flying D' in the centre of the rear bumper, where the early Mk 2s had their disc brake warning sign. Wheels gained rimbellishers as standard (they were optional on the Jaguars), and the boot lid was given a chromed 'Daimler' script and a stylized 'V8' badge. There was also a minor change to the rear valance panel to accommodate a twin-outlet exhaust.

The basic design of the Daimler dashboard was that of the Jaguar, but note here the radio installation. The Daimler front seats were arranged as a split bench rather than as separate seats, theoretically giving room for a third passenger in the centre.

DAIMLER V8 (1962–1969)

Closer examination would be rewarded with details such as this: a fluted boot-lid handle that also carried a reversing light with the Daimler name in its glass lens.

Although the interior remained fundamentally unchanged, the Jaguar team did give it some special features. Most obvious were a split-bench front seat and the absence of a centre console, which between them gave a more limousine-like, less sporting appearance. Without the console, there was nowhere to conceal the rear heating ducts, so these were simply omitted, to the benefit of foot room for the rear passengers. There were no picnic tables on the front-seat backs, either, probably mainly for economy reasons.

The dashboard was altered only in detail. It had the 120mph speedometer of the 2.4-litre Jaguars, but its rev counter was red-zoned between 6,000 and 6,500rpm to suit the higher-revving V8 engine. In the centre, a veneered extension below the main dashboard housed the radio, heater controls and ashtray. The steering wheel was Mk 2, but with a gold-on-black 'D' symbol in its centre boss, and the automatic gearbox selector lever was on the steering column rather than on the floor as in Jaguar models. Otherwise, the only changes were to the headlining, which was mounted on a sprung frame, and to the courtesy lights, of which the Daimler had three rather than the Jaguar's four. The heated rear window that was optional on Jaguars was also made a standard feature for the Daimler.

THE 2.5-LITRE V8 ON SALE

Jaguar's directors were formally told of the planned new model during February 1962 and it entered production as a Daimler 2.5-litre V8 just in time to be on the Daimler stand at the Earls Court Motor Show that October. Production was very slow to get under way and only eight cars were built before the end of the year. Most of these actually had modified SP250 engines that were numbered in the five-digit sequence reserved for the sports car; the proper saloon version of the engine did not become available until December. As far as buyers were concerned, the cars were therefore not available until the beginning of 1963. Examples for road testing were not available until even later and it was not until May 1963 that *Autocar* published the first test of the new Daimler.

The compact Daimler was priced between the 2.4-litre and 3.4-litre Mk 2 Jaguars, but its market position would not always stay the same. In later years, its price relative to the Jaguars increased – without any visible benefits – and by 1964 it had become more expensive than a 3.8-litre Mk 2. All the Daimlers built before 1967 had the Borg Warner automatic gearbox and a manual alternative was simply not offered. Nor did traditional Daimler customers expect one:

'Here is the kind of Daimler which provides prestige motoring in the modern manner' – or so said this March 1964 advertisement for the 2.5-litre V8.

99

DAIMLER V8 (1962–1969)

PRODUCTION FIGURES – DAIMLER V8

Calendar year	2.5-litre V8	V8-250	Total
1962	8		8
1963	2,444		2,444
1964	3,969		3,969
1965	3,430		3,430
1966	2,200		2,200
1967	967	803	1,770
1968		2,871	2,871
1969		1,223	1,223
Total	13,018	4,897	17,915

Figures provided by the Jaguar Daimler Heritage Trust.

Daimler had been wedded to the idea of automatic (and, before that, semi-automatic) transmissions for many years.

Throughout its production life, the compact Daimler provided an upmarket small saloon for retired couples who appreciated its qualities of style, comfort and quiet refinement. However, the Daimler also offered a fair turn of speed and was faster than the contemporary 2.4-litre Jaguar. Browns Lane had performed its usual trick of finding a market niche for the car where there was almost no competition. However, it was a niche of limited size. The Daimler's appeal outside Great Britain was small, and one consequence of this was that relatively few left-hand-drive examples were built. The car was never sold in the USA, where the Daimler name had no standing.

Like sales of the Mk 2 Jaguars, sales of the compact Daimlers peaked in the early 1960s and declined quite rapidly after that. Their best year was 1964, when 3,969 were built, but in 1967 fewer than half that many left the lines at Browns Lane. By then, the cars had been supplemented in the Daimler range by the new and more powerful Sovereign model (see Chapter 11).

PRODUCTION CHANGES (1962–67)

Like their Jaguar counterparts, the compact Daimlers underwent very few major changes before 1967, although scores of minor changes were made. The first of the big changes came in December 1963, when the latest version of the Borg Warner gearbox with its D1-D2 control system was fitted. The next one was not until February 1967, when a manual gearbox option was made available for export only. This became available on UK-market cars in February 1968, by which time the 2.5-litre V8 had become a V8-250 (see below). The manual gearbox came from the Mk 2 Jaguar and was offered with overdrive at extra cost, although it seems that very few cars had overdrive from new. When overdrive was ordered, a 4.55:1 final drive replaced the standard 4.27:1 type.

Minor changes generally paralleled those made to the Mk 2 Jaguars, as was only to be expected. Unique to the Daimlers, however, was a change very early in production from the original air filter with side-intake trumpets to a more attractive type with twin forward-facing intakes; quite possibly the change was made for aesthetic reasons.

A strike at the Salisbury company that made Jaguar's axles disrupted supplies after the middle of November 1964, with

OPTIONAL EXTRAS – DAIMLER 2.5-LITRE V8

Ace Turbo wheel trims
Childproof locks for rear doors
Column-mounted combined ignition and starter switch
Laminated windscreen
Limited-slip differential (from 1965)
Lockable fuel filler cap
Power-assisted steering
Radio
Radio aerial (for roof or wing; also wing-mounted manually retractable type with winding handle under the dash)
Radio speaker for rear shelf, with balance control
Rimbellishers for wheels
Safety belts (front seats only)
Steel sunroof
Sundym tinted glass
Tow-bar
Wing mirrors (standard or Paddy Hopkirk sports style)
Wire wheels (with chrome finish)

the result that a number of cars had to be completed with 4.27:1 axles instead of the 4.55:1 type. Although this change was made purely to keep the assembly lines moving, the customers liked the result, and so Jaguar standardized the 4.27:1 axle from mid-May 1965. Its taller gearing gave the Daimler slightly better fuel economy at a barely noticeable cost to acceleration, which suited traditional Daimler customers very well. Interestingly, demand persuaded Jaguar to offer the Powr-Lok limited-slip differential for the Daimler after 1965, although this was probably more because it reduced wheelspin in the wet than because it enabled faster getaways.

The Daimlers did not suffer the economy measures that affected the Jaguars in autumn 1966 and therefore retained their leather upholstery and fog lamps for the time being. As explained later, the original 2.5-litre V8 model was replaced during 1967 with a revised version called the V8-250, although in practice the two models overlapped on the assembly lines by some five months. The last of the original left-hand-drive cars was built in June 1967; assembly of the new V8-250 began in July; and the very last of the original Daimlers left the lines in November.

These twin air cleaners are part of the second type of air-filtration system used on the V8 engine – in this case in a V8-250 model.

V8-250

As Chapter 6 explains, the Mk 2 Jaguars became 240 and 340 models in September 1967. Some of the changes made for those models also rubbed off on the compact Daimler. The announcement of the V8-250 name was made a week after the 240/340 announcement, that delay being intended to allow Browns Lane two bites of the publicity cherry.

Since August 1966, what Jaguar called the XDM2/2 (second version of the XDM2) had existed in prototype form; the first production cars were assembled in July 1967. Left-hand-drive types followed in August. All of the new Daimlers carried their new name on the boot lid, with the earlier 'V8' badge now sitting alongside a separate '250' badge.

The Daimlers were rather less obviously cheapened than the contemporary Jaguars, although Ambla upholstery did become standard while leather was relegated to an extra-cost option. The Daimlers took on the same slimmer bumpers and overriders as the Jaguars, plus the new style of hubcaps (in this case with a 'D' central motif). The rim-bellishers remained standard and the Daimlers did not lose their fog lamps. Although metallic paints disappeared from the options list, new solid colours were added.

This was the later design of wheel trim, with the Daimler 'D' symbol replacing the Jaguar's head logo that appeared on Jaguar versions.

■ DAIMLER V8 (1962–1969)

The Daimler fulfilled the role of the compact luxury saloon very well, offering good performance, a smooth power delivery and a well-appointed interior. The mirror mounted on the quarter-light frame here is a modern addition.

ABOVE LEFT: **Just visible behind the grille of this V8-250 is an auxiliary fan – the car had presumably suffered from cooling problems.**

ABOVE RIGHT: **From the rear there was little to mark out the Daimler model from its Jaguar equivalent without a closer examination. The twin exhausts are hard to spot in this photograph.**

LEFT: **A further special feature of the later Daimlers was this badge, which read 'V8 250'. The V8 badge had also been on the earlier cars, along with a Daimler script logo; the 250 had not.**

DAIMLER V8 (1962–1969)

This later V8-250 wears the wheel trims introduced in 1968, with raised centres. The slim bumpers of these later cars looked particularly good with the Daimler grille, but they were of course the same as those on contemporary Jaguar models.

Inside the cabin, meanwhile, reclining front seats became standard and the upholstery now had perforated 'breathing' panels like those on the Daimler Sovereign introduced a year earlier. The heated rear window was still standard, and the dashboard top was now padded and upholstered in black Rexine, while padding that matched the interior-trim colour was continued around the wooden door cappings in the style pioneered by the Sovereign and its Jaguar 420 equivalent.

There were mechanical changes, too. Marles Variomatic power-assisted steering (see Chapter 10) replaced the original Burman type. An alternator and negative-earth electrical system replaced the dynamo and positive-earth system. And the engine gained twin air filters instead of the single pancake type to simplify maintenance.

V8-250 PRODUCTION CHANGES

The Daimler V8-250 was in production for a fraction over two years and was never built in large quantities. Overseas sales were minimal, with only 105 left-hand-drive cars being

■ DAIMLER V8 (1962–1969)

This early publicity photo for the revised Daimler V8-250 shows the car with the original type of wheel trims, which remained in use for a year.

built, while fewer than 5,000 right-hand-drive examples left the lines. Production was brought to an end in summer 1969, the last left-hand-drive car being built on 9 July and the last V8-250 of all a month later on 5 August.

There were no major changes during V8-250 production. However, stronger new pistons were added during 1968 because there had been service failures from overheating – something to which the engine was never prone in the SP250 sports car. Possibly, the issue had been provoked by enthusiastic use of the saloon with the newly available manual gearbox. Further changes included a different camshaft, a modified cylinder block and a modified sump.

The 2.5-litre Daimler V8 engine died with the V8-250 saloon. The SP250 sports model had gone out of production some five years earlier, so the

The V8 engine was a very neat fit under the bonnet of Utah Mk 2. This rather cumbersome-looking air intake filter was fitted from 1966.

OPTIONAL EXTRAS – DAIMLER V8-250

Overdrive
Power-assisted steering
Radio
Radio aerial
Seat belts
Special paint finishes
Wire wheels (chrome-plated)

saloon was the only car for which Edward Turner's V8 was being built. Although it was a fine engine that could have been further developed, there was no need for it in the latest Daimlers based on the Jaguar XJ6.

THE COMPACT DAIMLERS AND THE PRESS

'I doubt whether I have ever sat behind a better power unit than the 2½-litre Daimler V8.' So wrote John Bolster in the 9 August 1963 issue of *Autosport*. 'With plenty of torque all through the range and the smoothness of a dynamo at 7,000rpm, it is also about as quiet as a reciprocating engine can be.'

The test car, registered 4545 VC, also delighted Bolster with its performance, which he described as 'remarkable'. Although 'the getaway from standstill is not rapid, due to the characteristics of the torque converter … once on the move the car just tucks down its tail and goes.' Handling was excellent, too: 'Owing to its revised weight distribution, the Daimler handles particularly well and can out-corner a Jaguar.' It was 'just as delightful to drive when one is not in a hurry'.

Even so, Bolster felt that the engine would be better suited to a really good all-synchromesh gearbox. 'It would be fun … to play tunes with the gear lever as that exciting little V8 pushed the hand round the rev counter dial.' Meanwhile, 'the marriage of a Daimler engine and a Jaguar chassis has produced not a hybrid but a superb quality car.'

Nearly three years later, *Autocar* tried an example for its issue dated 20 May 1966. The magazine had tried one earlier, in May 1963, and had thought that a higher final drive ratio would be beneficial. The 1966 test car had the new 4.27:1 final drive, as well as the later D1-D2 control system for the automatic gearbox. The magazine's testers found the torque rather disappointing, which was not helped by the gearbox's reluctance to change down for acceleration. The suspension was 'much firmer – even a little harsh and pattery on rough roads – than might be expected'. The Daimler was clearly not a modern design: 'a small reminder that this basic design is now some ten years old is the need to grease ten points every 2,500 miles'. Nor was its acceleration startling, with 0–60mph taking 14.7sec, but 'it can still return fast journey times if the driver means to press on, while at any speed the smoothness and quietness of the V8 are superb.'

RIVALS

Shrewdly positioned in the market, the Daimler had very little competition. On the British market, there was nothing that could have been considered a direct equivalent of the model, at any price.

When the Daimler 2.5-litre V8 saloon was introduced in October 1962 it was priced at £1,785 15s 3d, inclusive of purchase tax. For exactly the same price, the British buyer could have a Citroën DS19 saloon, which was a quite remarkable car in its own right but was certainly not going to appeal to the person who was tempted by the Daimler. In the same price bracket were the Alfa Romeo 1600 Spider and the Humber Super Snipe estate, but these would not have interested a Daimler customer, either.

By 1965, the Daimler's price had increased to £1,599 including purchase tax, which made it more expensive than the £1,558 Jaguar Mk 2 3.8-litre. Yet the car continued to sell steadily. By the time the V8-250 arrived in October 1967 for £1,616, the Daimler still had no serious rivals except perhaps from other Browns Lane products. However, by the time of the 1968 Motor Show, the Daimler was facing competition from the recently introduced Rover Three Thousand Five V8, priced at £1,790 19s 5d as against its £1,826 15s 0d. Browns Lane did manage to undercut the Rover by pricing the new overdrive Daimler at a bargain £1,785 18s 2d, but the competition would not last for long. The basic Jaguar XJ6 2.8 was already on sale for £1,797 7s 3d, which made the V8-250 seem expensive. By summer 1969 it was all over, and the V8-250 had gone by the time of that autumn's Motor Show.

DAIMLER V8 (1962–1969)

IDENTIFICATION – DAIMLER V8

Identification numbers are stamped on a plate in the engine compartment, attached to the right-hand inner wing. These numbers are repeated elsewhere, as shown below.

Car Number
The car number, also known as the chassis number or VIN, is stamped into the bonnet-catch channel, just ahead of the radiator header tank. A typical car number might be 1A 3347 BW. The prefix identifies the model, the numerals are the car's serial number and the letters show the transmission type.

The prefix codes are:

1A	2.5-litre V8
1K	V8-250

Cars fitted with power-assisted steering have an additional P prefix, so the code becomes P1A or P1K.

The serial number sequences are:

	RHD	LHD
2.5-litre V8	1001–13377	20001–20622
V8-250	1001–5780	30001–30105

The suffixes decode as follows:

BW	Borg Warner automatic gearbox
DN	Laycock de Normanville overdrive

Engine Number
The engine number is stamped on the side of the cylinder block above the oil filter. On cars built after May 1968 it is stamped on the engine bellhousing on the left-hand side. A typical engine number might be 7A 13702. This breaks down into two elements:

7A	Engine type identifier (2.5-litre V8) The prefix for a V8-250 engine is 7K
13702	Serial number

Body Number
On cars built before 1965, the body number is stamped on a small plate attached to the right-hand side of the scuttle, under the bonnet. On cars built after 1965, the body number is stamped on a small plate attached to the right-hand side of the body behind the rear bumper. (It should not be confused with a similar plate on the left-hand side that shows the Pressed Steel reference number.)

Gearbox Number
On all manual gearboxes, the gearbox number is stamped on a small shoulder at the left-hand rear corner of the gearbox casing, and on the top cover around the rim of the core-plug aperture. On automatic gearboxes, the number is stamped on a plate attached to the left-hand side of the gearbox casing.

PERFORMANCE FIGURES – DAIMLER V8

These figures should be seen as representative rather than definitive. Note that the V8-250 figures relate to a car with the taller final drive gearing.

2.5-litre V8 automatic

0–60mph	13.5sec
Maximum speed	110mph (177km/h)
Fuel consumption	16–20mpg (14–18ltr/100km)

V8-250 overdrive

0–60mph	10.8sec
Maximum speed	112mph (180km/h)
Fuel consumption	19–25mpg (11–15ltr/100km)

SPECIFICATIONS – DAIMLER V8

Engine
Daimler overhead-valve V8, with cast-iron block and aluminium-alloy heads
2548cc (76.2 x 69.85mm)
Single central camshaft, chain-driven
Five-bearing crankshaft
Compression ratio 8.2:1
Two SU HD6 carburettors
140bhp at 5,800rpm
155lb ft at 3,600rpm

Transmission
Hydraulically operated clutch with 9in diameter (manual) or torque converter (automatic)
Three-speed Borg Warner type DG automatic (type 35 from September 1965)
Ratios 4.97:1, 3.09:1, 1.00:1
Four-speed manual gearbox (Jaguar all-synchromesh type) optional from February 1967
Ratios 3.04:1, 1.97:1, 1.33:1, 1.00:1
Optional overdrive with 0.77:1 ratio.

Axle ratio
4.55:1 to November 1964
4.27:1 from November 1964
4.55:1 with overdrive

Suspension, steering and brakes
Independent front suspension with wishbones, coil springs and anti-roll bar
Live rear axle with radius arms, Panhard rod and cantilevered semi-elliptic leaf springs
Burman recirculating-ball, worm-and-nut steering
Disc brakes with 11.125in diameter front and 11.375in rear, with servo assistance as standard

Dimensions
Overall length	180.75in (4,591mm)
Overall width	66.75in (1,695mm)
Overall height	57.75in (1,467mm)
Wheelbase	107.375in (2,727mm)
Front track	55.5in (1,410mm)
Rear track	53.875in (1,368mm)

Wheels and tyres
15in steel disc wheels standard, with 5in rims
15in wire-spoke wheels with 5in rims optional
6.40 x 15 cross-ply tyres

Kerb weight
3,046lb (1,382kg)

SO YOU WANT TO BUY A DAIMLER V8?

These two Daimler models have a character that is all their own and are delightful cars with a very different appeal from contemporary Jaguars. Structurally and inside the passenger cabin, the Daimler models are essentially the same as the Jaguar Mk 2 models, and the buying advice given in Chapter 5 applies to them as well.

The V8 engine is unique to these Daimlers. It gained a reputation for being more or less unburstable and for being very tunable. However, correct maintenance is very important for its longevity. If the engine overheats, the likelihood is that the waterways in the aluminium cylinder heads have corroded, and that water passages and possibly the radiator as well have become partially blocked with debris.

When overhauling a Daimler V8 engine, remember that if one head has to be skimmed, it will be necessary to skim the other one by the same amount – otherwise the inlet manifold will not fit properly. If only one head is skimmed, there will be slightly different compression ratios between the cylinders on each bank, and it will then be next to impossible to tune the carburettors properly.

Note that although the Daimler SP250 sports car shared the same basic engine, there were several specification differences between the two types. Parts for one version of the engine will not always fit the other.

PAINT AND TRIM COLOURS – DAIMLER V8

These cars generally had a rather smaller selection of the colours and trims available on the contemporary Jaguar Mk 2 and 240/340 ranges. The 2.5-litre V8 models were more commonly ordered with opalescent (metallic) paints than were their Jaguar contemporaries. As with the Jaguars, there were a few special-order paint and trim colours.

2.5-litre V8

October 1962 to November 1964
There were six standard paint colours, of which four were metallic finishes. Eight interior-trim colours were available.

Body	Interior
British Racing Green	Beige, Black or Green
Old English White	Black or Red
Opalescent Dark Green	Suede Green or Tan
Opalescent Gunmetal	Red or Tan
Opalescent Silver Blue	Dark Blue, Grey, Light Blue or Red
Opalescent Silver Grey	Grey, Red or Tan

Note: A few very early cars, including 1A1001 – the Earls Court Show car – were finished in Opalescent Maroon. At least one car – 1A1004, also shown at Earls Court – was finished in Cotswold Blue. Neither of these colours appears to have been standard.

December 1964 to March 1966
There were ten standard paint colours, of which five were metallic finishes. The same eight interior-trim colours remained available.

Body	Interior
British Racing Green	Beige, Black or Green
Indigo Blue	Black, Dark Blue or Red
Old English White	Black or Red
Opalescent Dark Green	Suede Green or Tan
Opalescent Golden Sand	Red or Tan
Opalescent Gunmetal	Red or Tan
Opalescent Silver Blue	Dark Blue, Grey, Light Blue or Red
Opalescent Silver Grey	Grey, Red or Tan
Pale Blue	Black, Dark Blue or Red
Warwick Grey	Black, Dark Blue, Red or Tan

April 1966 to March 1967
The ten colours available earlier were increased by one, as Black was added to the list. The interior-trim colours remained unchanged.

Body	Interior
Black	Beige, Dark Blue or Red

March 1967 to August 1967
The colour range was reduced to nine standard colours, of which just one was a metallic finish. (It appears that Black was no longer available.) The interior-trim colours remained unchanged.

Body	Interior
Beige	Light Tan, Red, Suede Green or Tan
British Racing Green	Beige, Light Tan, Suede Green or Tan
Carmen Red	Beige or Red
Cream	Dark Blue, Light Blue or Red
Dark Blue	Grey, Light Blue or Red
Opalescent Dark Green	Beige, Light Tan, Suede Green or Tan
Warwick Grey	Dark Blue, Light Blue or Tan
Willow Green	Beige, Grey, Light Tan or Suede Green

V8-250

September 1967 to July 1969
There were six standard paint colours, none of which was metallic. Four interior-trim colours were available. Upholstery was in Ambla, with leather an extra-cost option.

Body	Interior
Beige	Beige, Black, Blue or Red
Black	Beige, Black, Blue or Red
British Racing Green	Beige or Black
Cream	Beige, Black, Blue or Red
Dark Blue	Beige, Black, Blue or Red
Warwick Grey	Beige, Black, Blue or Red

CHAPTER EIGHT

DEVELOPING THE JAGUAR S-TYPE

In the late 1950s and early 1960s, Jaguar's design engineering was carried out by a very small number of people – a ridiculously small number, by modern standards – and as a result they were constantly busy. The company generally worked on an eighteen-month cycle for new models, and no sooner had a design been passed on to the development engineers than the designers would start work on the next new model. More complicated component developments would take place over several years, alongside the engineering activity devoted to specific new models, and one of the most complicated developments as the 1950s turned into the 1960s was the development of independent rear suspension (IRS).

Jaguar historian Paul Skilleter has pointed out that many of the essential ingredients of the Jaguar IRS can be traced back to the prototype of the VB, a miniature military runabout capable of being transported by air that Jaguar worked on during the Second World War. However, serious work on IRS for Jaguar cars did not begin until more than a decade later, in 1955.

By that stage, the Jaguar engineers felt that they had gone as far as they could with a conventional 'live' rear axle. Its weakness was that it compromised handling. If one rear wheel hit a bump or dropped into a pothole, its vertical movement was immediately transmitted along the axle tube to the opposite rear wheel. There were two results. One was a bumpy ride for the passengers – particularly unwelcome in a luxury saloon. The other was a change in wheel attitude, which could cause both rear wheels to lose grip briefly at the same time. This was potentially dangerous on ordinary roads, and was extremely undesirable in the sporting events (and fast road driving) that attracted Jaguar owners.

IRS would provide benefits for both Jaguar's big saloons and its high-performance sports cars, but the limited resources at Browns Lane meant that a single design would have to do both jobs. Although variations in dimensions could be accommodated, the basic layout of the system would have to be common for all the models on which it would be used. This helps to explain why it took six years for Jaguar to get their system into production, and also why it was such a complicated piece of engineering when it was introduced on the big Mk X saloons and the E-type sports cars in 1961.

DEVELOPING THE IRS

Early experimental IRS designs were tested on Mk 2 saloons, and quite possibly on Mk 1 models before that. In the beginning, the differential was rigidly mounted to the underside

Jaguar's complex independent rear suspension was perhaps the company's biggest engineering advance at the start of the 1960s. Here it is in Mk X form – the version used on the S-type would differ only in track width and spring rates.

DEVELOPING THE JAGUAR S-TYPE

of the monocoque body, but it soon became clear that this caused unacceptable transmission of noise and vibration. So the Jaguar engineers decided to mount the differential and the entire IRS assembly within its own cage (usually known as a 'bridge-piece') and to insulate this from the bodyshell with rubber bushes. In the production design, two V-shaped Metalastik rubber bushes were fitted to each outer end of the suspension cage and it was these rather than the cage itself that were bolted to the body. Additional rubber bushes between the radius arms and the body floor further ensured that there was no metal-to-metal contact anywhere in the rear suspension, thus making the Jaguar IRS exceptionally quiet.

To get the wheel control they wanted, Jaguar designed what was essentially a double-wishbone system, but a key feature was that the driveshaft on each side doubled as the upper wishbone. The tubular lower wishbone was located fore and aft by a radius arm attached to its outer leading edge, and the radius arm was in turn mounted to the underside of the body. On each side, not one but two coil springs acted on each wishbone to even out vertical movements so that the wishbone could not twist and alter the position of the wheel. Inside each coil spring was a damper, and the use of four spring-and-damper assemblies actually took up less space than two larger and heavier assemblies. The overall result was a suspension that kept the rear wheels upright at all times in order to maximize the contact patch, and thus grip, of each tyre on the road. The very small changes of track that the system did allow were insufficient to upset the car's handling.

This layout reduced the transmission of suspension movement into the body, to the benefit of ride comfort. In addition, the disc brakes were mounted at the inboard ends of the driveshafts to minimize unsprung weight. Passengers were therefore relatively unaware of the work the suspension was doing as it absorbed bumps and potholes in the road surface. The new IRS resulted in a tiny alteration to the wheelbase of the compact saloon bodyshell and a very slightly wider rear track.

From the very beginning, the Jaguar IRS was highly acclaimed. As *The Motor* of 22 March 1961 stated:

> *Before we had driven the E-type very far it became clear that the new independent rear suspension was a major step forward which had put the road manners of the car into the highest category. The springing is quite soft and provides a most comfortable ride.*

Before reactions like this had become commonplace, it must have been obvious to everybody at Jaguar that the new system's excellence was also a disadvantage. It meant that the ride and handling of the Mk 2 saloons was immediately outclassed. There would have to be a further development of the Mk 2 Jaguar with that new suspension if the car were to remain competitive in its class. And in that realization lay the genesis of the car that would become the Jaguar S-type in 1963.

DESIGNING THE S-TYPE

The next iteration of the compact Jaguar saloons was drawn up in the early 1960s with the new IRS system as its major

The Jaguar Mk X of 1961 took Jaguar engineering and styling several steps further forward, although it was in many ways a controversial model. It was inevitable that some of these advances should find their way down to the compact saloons – the S-type was the first to have them.

The rear-end design of the Mk X was a completely new departure, with twin fuel tanks in the wings in order to increase the space available for the boot. It was the key styling change adopted for the S-type.

new feature. Surviving documents make clear that the car was developed with the project name Utah Mk 3, which followed on logically from the Mk 1 compact saloon (Utah) and the Mk 2 (Utah Mk 2). However, Jaguar historian Andrew Whyte has pointed out that the car was also known to Jaguar as an XJ3 when it became one of the first models to bear the new in-house engineering code numbers.

In addition to its independent rear suspension, the 1961 Mk X saloon had introduced a distinctive new visual style for Jaguars, and it obviously made sense to incorporate elements of that into Utah Mk 3. For cost reasons, the centre section of the Mk 2 body was left well alone, but as the rear end had to be redesigned to accommodate the new IRS, there was every reason to give the car the long 'tail' of the Mk X. At the front, the basic Mk 2 structure could be retained, but new skin panels could give a distinctive appearance for relatively little cost. On this basis, design went ahead.

Body Styling

Cyril Crouch was assistant chief body engineer at Browns Lane when Utah Mk 3 was under development, and more than thirty years after the event he remembered quite clearly the work that was done to adapt the Mk 2 body-shell for its new role. On this occasion, styling did not begin from scratch in the time-honoured Lyons fashion with a full-size mock-up made of wood. Both Lyons, as stylist, and his body engineers started from the existing Mk 2 bodyshell and modified it. To all concerned, the S-type was always a facelift of an existing style rather than a completely new car. As Cyril Crouch recalled:

> Lyons was completely in charge; he was the stylist. So he decided, 'Let's make it more like the Mk X.' On a facelift like that, he wouldn't resort to a wooden block. He would go straight into panels, wheeled up in the shop – a laborious job – until he was satisfied. It would be done as a complete vehicle, taking a Mk 2, lopping off the affected panels back to the scuttle, and starting again with panel-work from there.

Photographs survive in the Jaguar archives to show the results of that process on the S-type mock-up, with very visible join lines below the rear windows and on the rear wings where new panels have been joined to the old.

At the rear, Lyons wanted an extended tail with styling features generally similar to those of the Mk X, which by this stage had only just entered production. The Mk X-style rear

■ DEVELOPING THE JAGUAR S-TYPE

This was the styling mock-up for the S-type, with the long, low rear of the Mk X and that car's slimline bumpers and flattened rear wheel arches grafted onto what was probably a Mk 2 bodyshell. On the original photogaph, prior to retouching, it is possible to see the joins where new panels have been added. The doors do not seem to fit the roofline very well, probably because Lyons had been juggling with the shape of the roof to get it right.

The lines of the Mk X's rear end were followed to the letter and even the curved styling lines on either side of the number-plate box were retained. The tail-light units were unchanged, too.

wheel arch with its flattened top replaced the Mk 2 type with its detachable spat, and the new tail brought with it elegant slimline bumpers, totally unlike those on the Mk 2 that could trace their ancestry back to the big Mk VII saloon of 1950. Of course, the front bumper would have to match. It was then only a small step to graft other elements of the Mk X onto the front end of the Utah Mk 3 mock-up, notably its wraparound turn-signal lenses and low-mounted sidelights.

Time and cost prevented the front-end restyle from being too radical, so the four-headlamp style of the Mk X was not carried over. Cyril Crouch remembered that 'it was timescale and cost; I think it was timescale as much as anything. But I don't remember doing a four-lamp mock-up before the 420. It was a case of "modify the back end, and let's get on with it".'

DEVELOPING THE JAGUAR S-TYPE

So the Mk 2's rearward-hinged bonnet and curved wings remained in the specification, even though the Mk X had introduced a flatter wing style and a forward-hinged bonnet. Lyons had the fog lights recessed more deeply into the wing fronts, gave the grille a thicker surround and centre strip, and added small peaks to the headlamps. These tended to make the car look slightly longer from the side, and so helped to balance the longer tail.

Just one other area of the external panel work was changed. The curvaceous rear roofline of the Mk 2 matched the similar styling of the rear wings, but did not work well with the flatter shape of the Mk X-style tail. So Lyons modified the roofline to look more like the Mk X's, extending it rearwards slightly to make it look flatter and adding a more upright rear window. This helped to make the car look larger, too, but perhaps its primary benefit was to give rear passengers a little bit of extra headroom – an improvement that would be further enhanced by changes to the interior furniture.

As an expedient redesign of the Mk 2, Utah Mk 3 did the job, but it has always been one of the more controversial Jaguar shapes. The short and curvaceous front end never did quite balance the extended tail, and even Cyril Crouch had considerable reservations about whether the style was totally successful:

> We ourselves appreciated what an ugly-looking car it was, and when it came out there was a 'Is that the best you can do?' sort of thing! People like myself had to take the stick for producing such an abomination! Perhaps I shouldn't call it that, but I think everyone was very pleased to see the end of the S and move on to the 420. It seemed an odd-looking vehicle.

Does it look different enough? A production Mk 2 saloon is parked next to the S-type mock-up to check. The two certainly do look different, though related – like brothers perhaps. It later became apparent that the new elongated rear end did not sit very well with the older rounded style of the front. On the original of this photograph, the flatter S-type roof panel can be clearly seen, as can the join where new rear pillars have been grafted on.

113

Bodyshell Structure

Once Sir William had pronounced himself satisfied with the modified styling, Cyril Crouch's real work began. The rear of the monocoque had to be completely re-engineered to incorporate the independent rear suspension and the new body panels, and Crouch carried out this work with input from Reg White, who was the chief engineer at Pressed Steel where the bodies would be manufactured.

Looking at the S-type monocoque, its Mk 2 ancestry shines through. The Mk 2's underbody reinforcing rails were simply extended rearwards and boxed in, to sweep over the rear axle and terminate at the tail of the car. The rear floor was double-skinned, and the boot floor was strengthened with deep ribbing. The integral well for the spare wheel was relocated centrally, instead of being offset to the left as in the Mk 2, and the fuel tank was taken out of the floor of the boot altogether to be replaced with twin tanks, one inside each rear wing, exactly as on the Mk X.

As for the front of the car, the structural changes were minimal according to Cyril Crouch:

> *It was mostly exterior panel work – new wings, new front fenders of course, the attachments, new wheel arches and also the bumper mounting because the bumpers were completely new. The longitudinal bracing struts to pick up the dash structure were unchanged. As far as I can recall, there were no changes to the inner scuttle and the windscreen.*

Steering, Suspension and Brakes

Jaguar never had any intention of changing the Mk 2 front suspension during the development of the S-type so the new car ended up with the same subframe-mounted, coil-sprung, twin-wishbone layout as its predecessor. The brakes would once again be Dunlop discs, which had proved more than adequate to cope with the performance of the most powerful 3.8-litre Mk 2. Browns Lane did not believe that the extra weight of Utah Mk 3 would prove too much for them.

Steering was a different matter, though. The major modifications to the basic design had to be paid for somehow so Utah Mk 3 would have to be a more expensive car than the existing Jaguar Mk 2. That meant it would need power-assisted steering as standard (it was an extra-cost option on the Mk 2). However, the Mk 2 set-up had come in for a fair amount of criticism because of its low gearing, so for Utah Mk 3 the Jaguar engineers chose a higher-geared system, again made by Burman, which gave 3.5 turns lock-to-lock instead of the 4.3 turns of the Mk 2's steering. In addition, this new system incorporated a torsion bar linking the input shaft and the hydraulic valve, which greatly improved the feel of the steering.

The IRS was a third version of the basic design that had been introduced on the E-type in March 1961. The Mk X version introduced a few months later had a much wider track. The Utah Mk 3 version had a track that was midway between the two existing types. In all essentials, though, it was the same system that had so impressed buyers and commentators on its announcement in 1961.

Engines

By the time Utah Mk 3 was in development, Jaguar had three different basic versions of the XK 6-cylinder engine in production, and different carburation created different power outputs to suit different models. All three sizes were already available in the Mk 2 saloons – the 2.4-litre with 120bhp, the 3.4-litre with 210bhp and the 3.8-litre with 220bhp – but the smallest engine must have been considered a non-starter for the new car. It was already something of an embarrassment to Jaguar, who were never able to get the 2.4-litre Mk 2 to perform as well as the Mk 1 car with the same engine. As Utah Mk 3 was going to be heavier than the Mk 2 – by around 3cwt (336lb/152kg) in the end – making it available with a 2.4-litre engine would simply have resulted in further embarrassment.

Besides, this was to be a more expensive car than the Mk 2, and so making it available with only the larger engine sizes would help to reinforce the differentiation between the two models. This would be necessary because it was planned that the Mk 2 would remain in production alongside the new IRS models, even if only for the short term.

So the Utah Mk 3 car was drawn up around the 3.4-litre and 3.8-litre engines. Both would have the same tune as they had in the Mk 2 saloons. The marketing plan was to make the new car available only with the larger engine at first in order to help establish its position in the Jaguar range between the Mk 2 and the big Mk X. The smaller engine would then be made available as an alternative once the model had become established.

Interior Design

Sir William Lyons had 'quite a lot' of input to the design of the new saloon's interior, according to Cyril Crouch:

> He used to like to sit in the thing. He used to have his seat very upright, and he had to ensure that he could reach the steering wheel, the radio, and be able to change gear, etcetera, etcetera, and be able to wind the windows down – without too much discomfort. Similarly with the rear; rear headroom, etcetera.

However, Lyons was not the only 'model' used to gauge the effectiveness of the interior design. Cyril Crouch again:

> I'm long in the leg and short in the back, so I could sit on the back seat with loads of room. And then somebody would come along who was the other way round. We had to keep pushing the cushion down so the tall man could get in. There was a lot of trial and error on those sort of things.

The Mk X influence on the cabin design was even stronger than it had been on the exterior. The overall effect was of a scaled-down Mk X in style, helping to give the Utah Mk 3 a closer association with the larger and more expensive Jaguar. The Mk X dashboard, with its distinctive centre panel and impressive-looking row of switches, was effectively replicated in the Utah Mk 3. As the big saloon's heating and ventilating system – a major improvement on the inadequate Mk 2 type – was also incorporated, with it came the Mk X-pattern sliding air controls and push-button switches. The full-width parcel shelf below the dash and a neat centre console also reflected Mk X practice, with everything being made a little smaller to fit the narrower bodyshell of the compact saloons.

Door trims, front and rear, were Mk 2-sized but incorporated a unique horizontal fluting. Mk X-type armrests were a feature of the front doors, while the rear doors had unique armrests that incorporated a small chromed flip-top ashtray as well as a magazine pocket.

Front and rear seats, too, followed Mk X styling cues. The front seats were less clearly individual buckets than on the Mk 2, with a squareness about their inboard edges that made them appear more like a single bench when set at equal distances from the dashboard. In this respect, they followed Mk X practice, but in size they were more like the seats seen in the 1962 Daimler V8 version of the Mk 2 Jaguar. Each seat had its own inboard armrest, like the Mk X type, and each was mounted on a unique fore-and-aft adjustment mechanism. Instead of the conventional sliding runners, this used swinging links that lowered the front of the cushion and raised the rear as the seat was moved forwards, and vice versa.

The front seats had thinner backrests than the Mk 2 type, which provided a little bit more legroom for rear passengers. As in the Daimler V8, picnic tables were dispensed with, saving a little more room (and money); it was also undeniable that picnic tables were beginning to fall out of fashion by this time, even in large luxury saloons.

Further space – this time for heads rather than legs – was created by a rear seat squab that was 2in (50mm) thinner than its Mk 2 equivalent, and by a more steeply inclined rear backrest. The altered rear roofline already mentioned made a further contribution to headroom. The gains were perhaps small, but the overall result was to give at least the impression of far greater room in the back of the car than there was in the back of a Mk 2.

Prototypes

Most of the mechanical elements of Utah Mk 3 had already been proved in existing Jaguar models, and those that had not – such as the quicker-ratio power steering – were easily built into Mk 2 development hacks at Browns Lane. Even the IRS had been partially developed on such cars, and one of them has already been mentioned in Chapter 4. So the first prototypes of Utah Mk 3 were actually 'semi-tooled' or 'off-tools' cars; that is, they were built using as much of the production tooling as had been completed at the time. They were then completed by hand and went out on test.

By this stage, Utah Mk 3 also had a new name. It was to be called the Jaguar S-type – a name on which Jaguar seem not to have commented when the cars were introduced to the press in 1963. It was probably based on earlier Jaguar practice: just as the XK150S had offered more than the plain XK150 in 1958, so too would the S-type offer more than the car on which it was still quite clearly based. As for the meaning of that letter, buyers were free to speculate, but 'super' or 'special' would certainly have caught the flavour of Jaguar's intentions.

CHAPTER NINE

JAGUAR S-TYPE (1963–1968)

Jaguar described the S-type as 'the latest development of one of the world's most successful cars' in sales literature and focused the attention of potential customers on 'greatly increased interior space with more head and leg room affording the highest degree of comfort front and rear.' There was 'increased parcel accommodation', too. Clearly, this was a luxury car rather than a sports saloon like the Mk 2.

As the previous chapter explains, Jaguar introduced the bigger-engined 3.8-litre S-type first in order to establish the model's position in the Jaguar pecking order. It was announced in October 1963, just ahead of that year's Earls Court Motor Show, although not very many cars were actually built before the end of the year. The 3.4-litre car followed after a year, but there was never any doubt which was the more attractive of the two variants. There would never be a 3.4-litre S-type on the press demonstration fleet at Browns Lane, and the initial press information included performance figures for the 3.8-litre car but not for its smaller-engined sister.

In the USA, Jaguar's most important market at the time, the 3.8-litre car was the only model made available. For US Jaguar enthusiasts, therefore, the 3.4-litre S-type might just as well not have existed.

THE S-TYPE AND THE PRESS

The leading British motoring magazines were unanimous in their enthusiasm for the S-type Jaguars when the cars were announced in October 1963. All the more surprising, then, that none of them published a full road test of the 3.8-litre car until very much later, by which time radial tyres had replaced the original cross-plies. Perhaps Jaguar had been reluctant to lend examples for evaluation until the radials were available to show off the independent rear suspension to its best advantage.

The first magazine to test a 3.8-litre S-type was *Autosport*, whose John Bolster reported on an automatic model regis-

The cowls over the headlamps and fog lamps gave a certain distinction to the front-end styling. This is a 3.8-litre model.

JAGUAR S-TYPE (1963–1968)

New JAGUAR 3·4 & 3·8 'S' models

join the famous range of Mark 2, Mark Ten, & 'E' type models which continue unchanged

The latest development of one of the world's most successful cars

The new 'S' models make available in a car of compact dimensions, the very latest refinements in Jaguar design and engineering.

The wide choice of high-performance high-quality motoring which the Jaguar range already provides, is now further extended by the introduction of these new 3.4 and 3.8 'S' models. With impeccable body styling and spacious interior proportions, these cars are powered by the world famous Jaguar XK engine of either 3.4 litre or 3.8 litre capacity. The many important features incorporated include:—

- All round independent suspension providing the utmost riding comfort under all conditions.
- Self adjusting Disc Brakes on all four wheels and self adjusting handbrake.
- Driver operated variable interior heating with on or off control for rear compartment.
- Reclining seats for driver and front passenger.
- An exceptionally large luggage boot giving an entirely unobstructed cubic capacity of no less than 19 cubic feet.
- Twin petrol tanks—one in each rear wing with change-over switch in dash panel.
- Spacious interior with generous head and leg room affording the highest degree of comfort.

See the Jaguar range including the new 'S' models on **Stand 118 Earls Court**

Although both models were announced at the same time, in practice there was a delay before the 3.4-litre models reached the showrooms.

tered 2233 KV in the magazine's issue dated 7 August 1964. Describing the car in terms of the Mk 2 saloons his readers already knew, Bolster wrote:

> As regards the performance of the S-type, this can be defined as slower than the Mk 2 in figures but faster across country. The more luxurious car is naturally heavier than its smaller brother, but its independent rear suspension allows it to corner faster. Furthermore, the rear passengers receive a much less hectic ride, which again encourages the driver to press on.

And press on he did, recording a 0–60mph time of 11.6sec and a mean maximum speed of 115.4mph (185.7km/h). 'On fast roads,' he noted, 'the S-type cruises in restful silence at over 100mph.'

Again taking the Mk 2 as his yardstick, Bolster continued:

> The extra weight is noticeable during hard acceleration, but again the better traction allows all the power to be used, particularly on wet roads. There is a wonderfully effortless feeling about the way in which the car runs, seeming to have power to spare at all times and never becoming noisy when pressed. The power of the brakes, and the freedom from locking of the independently sprung wheels, inspires the confidence of the driver. The hand brake is much better than those of previous disc-braked Jaguars, but it can be kicked off accidentally on leaving the car.

JAGUAR S-TYPE (1963–1968)

Very high marks must be given to the new power-assisted steering. Although it is light in action, it retains all the feel of a particularly good normal design. In the past, some servo arrangements have rendered steering positively unsafe at high speeds. I could find absolutely no circumstances under which the power assistance was a disadvantage.

Bolster went on to praise the heating and ventilation system, the comfort of the seats, and the standard of the interior appointments. He was less keen on the angle of the steering column, and wondered whether the twin 7-gallon tanks really carried enough fuel when it was being used up at a gallon every 13 to 18 miles. However, his overall impression of the car was very favourable indeed:

The Jaguar 3.8S is a fast car of very great refinement. Until recently, it has been argued that the virtues of independent rear suspension were not appreciable for large, heavy cars. Now Jaguars have proved that, for roadholding, safety, and riding comfort, a good independent rear end cannot be equalled. This car will cause a lot of re-thinking among the manufacturers of luxury vehicles.

The main interest of the S-type was at the rear, with that long tail and the independent rear suspension beneath. This is a 3.8-litre model, with the desirable extra of chrome wire wheels.

Although the wire-wheels option was very popular, very many S-types were delivered with the standard specification of steel disc wheels.

Again in the person of John Bolster, *Autosport* tried out an overdrive model rather less than a year later for their issue dated 14 May 1965. The car was EDU 482C, which also figured in other road tests of the time. In Bolster's hands, the car took just 10.2sec to reach 60mph from rest and went on to a maximum of 122mph (196km/h) – incidentally demonstrating just how much automatic gearboxes of the time harmed both acceleration and maximum speed. The maximum of 110mph (177km/h) achieved in direct top showed exactly how valuable that overdrive was for high-speed motoring, and Bolster commented that the car still felt 'wonderfully lively on top gear'. The gearbox – by this stage Jaguar's new all-synchromesh type – earned praise, too: 'The gears are easy to change, have crash-proof synchromesh on all four speeds, and are controlled by a delightful little lever. The ratios are very well chosen,' but the clutch was 'rather heavy to operate continually in traffic.'

Brakes and steering came in for the same praise as before, and again there was a comparison with the Mk 2. The heavier S-type 'does not feel so fierce to drive as a 3.8-litre Mk 2. On the other hand, the better roadholding and incomparably more comfortable ride render the S-type a faster car for a long day's march.' Comfort still got high marks, although Bolster must have tried rather harder with this overdrive car as he criticized the front seats for providing insufficient lateral location under cornering forces.

'Perhaps the most spectacular feature of the Jaguar is its behaviour on atrocious surfaces. Neither by bumping nor by muffled sounds does the car protest if potholes are taken at an almost ridiculous speed,' wrote Bolster, and he concluded that the car was 'a delight to drive…. As we have come to expect of any Jaguar product, the price is very much less than could be imagined and the machine represents quite remarkable value.'

JAGUAR S-TYPE (1963–1968)

The overdrive car, EDU 482C, was also tested by *Autocar* and by *Motor* during 1965. *Autocar* reported a few months earlier than its rival, in its issue dated 19 March, and summarized the 3.8S as 'an outstandingly good car in its class ... an extremely fast and safe means of transport'. The magazine's test team recorded performance figures similar to those that *Autosport* obtained, with 60mph coming up in 10.4sec and the mean maximum speed working out at 121.5mph (195.5km/h). 'During normal driving,' they wrote, 'one can leave all but the bigger sports cars behind by making very gentlemanly changes at about 2,500rpm.' However, they obviously kept the engine a lot nearer to the rev counter's 5,500rpm red line for most of the test, and managed a miserable overall fuel consumption of just 12.8mpg (22ltr/100km).

The brakes proved to be superb and the power steering inspired confidence, while 'the handling is virtually neutral right up to the limit of adhesion, with perhaps just a trace of understeer. This is indicated by the car's ability to run arrow-straight at 120mph with the driver's hands virtually off the wheel.' However, there were criticisms. Like *Autosport*, the *Autocar* team found the seats gave poor lateral support and the clutch was heavy in comparison with the other controls. The accelerator, too, was unprogressive, and the car proved susceptible to strong side winds.

Nor was that all. *Autocar* wondered whether the traditional wood-and-leather interior was perhaps a little passé for the mid-1960s. The interior may have been 'rather like ... one of London's older-established clubs', but 'the use of this amount of wood seemed to some of the test staff to be slightly excessive, and they would have preferred to see more use made of black leather or other non-reflecting material.' Their wishes would of course be met when the XJ6 was announced, some three years later.

The *Motor* road test of EDU 482C was published in that magazine's 14 October 1965 issue. Performance figures were again close to those obtained by *Autosport* and *Autocar*, and the magazine was particularly enthusiastic about the car's ride quality, describing it as 'probably unexcelled by any other European car'.

> *The car does not set out to be a four-seater E-type, and indeed it is not so fast as the lighter 3.8 Mk 2, but ... the overall feel of the car is such that it would probably lose nothing to either on any non-motorway journey and be completely untiring whatever the distance.*

That was praise indeed.

By 1966, however, the 3.8-litre S-type was old hat as far as the motoring magazines were concerned. The model was three years old and Jaguar had made no specification changes that would justify a retest; besides, it was in 1966 that Jaguar announced the new 420 and its Daimler Sovereign variant, which between them used up all the column inches that editors were prepared to spare for the mid-range Jaguar saloons.

As already noted, Jaguar did not provide any examples of the 3.4-litre S-type for road test. However, *Autocar* magazine did run performance tests on a three-year-old overdrive car in its Used Car Test series, on 19 November 1970. By this time, the XJ6 had been released, and the magazine had to admit that 'although not up to XJ6 standards, the ride is extremely good'. The car had worn very well, and delivered performance figures of 0–60mph in 13.9sec and fuel consumption of 14–17mpg (17–20ltr/100km), although no maximum speed figure was taken.

MAXIMUM INTERCHANGEABILITY

The 3.4-litre and 3.8-litre S-types shared a single design of bodyshell, which could be used on both right-hand- and left-hand-drive models. This was the most cost-effective way of building the cars as it minimized manufacturing costs. The very first 3.4-litre S-type was in fact built with a bodyshell originally earmarked as a 3.8-litre type and bearing car number 1B 50003. When that shell was fitted with a 3.4-litre engine, it was renumbered as car number 1B 1001.

Several late cars swapped identities during 1967, starting in January, peaking in May and June, then tailing off in numbers towards the end of the year. Probably around thirty cars were affected, many of them in the range from 1B 59300 to 1B 59500. At this stage, demand for the S-type was dwindling, and Jaguar probably painted shells in anticipation of demand, then renumbered them to meet orders if that was convenient. The swaps went in both directions: 3.4-litre shells were built up as 3.8-litre cars, and vice versa. The original numbers were never reused, with the result that the 'official' overall production totals (which are based on first and last car numbers) are slightly inaccurate.

JAGUAR S-TYPE (1963–1968)

THE CKD S-TYPES

Beginning in January 1966, a quantity of 3.8-litre S-types were produced in CKD form for overseas assembly. Exact figures are not available, but the late Jaguar historian Andrew Whyte estimated that there were 850 of them, all with the 3.8-litre engine.

As far as it is possible to establish, all of them went to South Africa and were shipped through Tozer, Kemsley and Milbourn Ltd, a London shipping agent. The assembly operation was taken over by Jaguar Cars South Africa Ltd on 1 September 1966. By 1968, assembly was at the former BMC plant at Blackheath in the Cape, but it is not clear if all the South African S-types were assembled there. Both overdrive and automatic types were assembled.

Certain items would undoubtedly have been locally sourced, such as paint, tyres, batteries and possibly glass, but most of the components of these cars would have originated in the UK.

PRODUCTION FIGURES – S-TYPE

The 3.4-litre S-type always sold more slowly than the 3.8-litre before 1967, when the availability of the new 420 was probably the main factor affecting sales. The 3.4-litre, reduced in price for its final season, then came into its own as a budget-priced luxury car.

Calendar year	3.4-litre	3.8-litre	Total
1963	1	42	43
1964	2,169	4,863	7,032
1965	3,825	5,916	9,741
1966	2,575	3,685	6,260
1967	646	362	1,008
1968	712	197	909
Total	9,928	15,065	24,993

The combination of the rounded front end and long tail worked well from some angles, but was not wholly successful – and Jaguar knew it.

JAGUAR S-TYPE (1963–1968)

The leaping Jaguar mascot was a standard feature on the S-type.

KEY PRODUCTION CHANGES

As a small company building a relatively small number of cars, Jaguar could not afford to make regular changes to its models. So the S-types that went out of production in 1968 were very much the same cars that had entered production five years earlier. Yet there were differences, and for the most part these differences had made the cars better ones.

1964 Season

Only minor modifications were made over the first few months of S-type production and the first major change did not occur until right at the end of the car's first year in production. That was when Dunlop SP41 radial tyres replaced the Dunlop RS5 cross-plies as original equipment – unless, however, whitewall tyres were wanted, in which case they had to be RS5s.

The change made much more difference than might at first be apparent. The stiff sidewalls of the RS5 tyres had always made the S-types prone to tyre squeal under hard cornering, and when they reached the limit of their adhesion, the RS5s tended to let go rather suddenly. The radials, by contrast, would absorb more of the cornering forces in their sidewalls, more or less eliminating squeal and giving more warning of breakaway at the limit.

1965 Season

The next changes came a few months later and coincided with the beginning of the 1965 season in October 1964 and the arrival of the 3.4-litre models. They affected the brakes and the manual gearbox.

The brakes simply gained a bigger servo (with an 8in diameter instead of the earlier 6.875in diameter) so that lower pedal pressures were needed. For the gearbox, there were the beginnings of a complete change, from the sturdy old Moss four-speeder with its unsynchronized first gear to the brand-new four-speed type designed and built by Jaguar themselves. In practice, this gearbox seems to have been in short supply for the first few months and was initially promoted as an option. Full production began in March 1965. As before, overdrive was an optional extra, and there was a new type for the 1965-model S-types, although it was supplied by the same maker who had built overdrives for the earlier cars.

As already noted, Jaguar had to proceed one step at a time and make the best use of its engineering resources. Although a replacement for the old Moss gearbox was really long overdue, the company had wisely focused on changes of greater significance, notably developing independent rear suspension (see Chapter 8) and a 4.2-litre derivative of the XK engine (see Chapter 10). However, the Moss gearbox was, frankly, old-fashioned and was not at all suitable for a car of the S-type's pretensions, let alone those of the Mk X in which it was also available. Perhaps customers who bought the S-type as a small luxury saloon usually chose the automatic option, but there was no doubting the need for that new gearbox.

Its key features were baulk-ring synchromesh on all forward gears, and provision for a pressure oil feed. This was achieved by a pump driven from the rear of the mainshaft unless the gearbox was accompanied by an overdrive, when the overdrive oil pump also fed the main gearbox. From the driver's point of view, the all-synchromesh gearbox was a very great improvement, offering a smoother shift action and quieter acceleration away from rest – although some enthusiasts must have bemoaned the loss of the vintage whine emitted by the first gear in the Moss gearbox. Revised gears in the new all-synchromesh gearbox also made a perceptible difference to acceleration in the intermediate ratios.

Despite these advances, the Jaguar gearbox still has its detractors more than fifty years after its introduction. They argue that the higher first gear takes the edge off initial acceleration; that the gear-lever travel is longer than on the Moss gearbox and so hinders quick changes; and that the newer gearbox lacks the character of the older one. So be it: Jaguar probably knew at the time that they would never be able to satisfy everybody when they introduced major new components.

From this angle, the domed roof of the passenger cabin gave away its origins in the earlier compacts, even though the roofline had been flattened.

JAGUAR S-TYPE (1963–1968)

The Jaguar name was still displayed at the rear, although now within the casting of the boot-lid handle. Illumination for reversing came from the lights on either side of it.

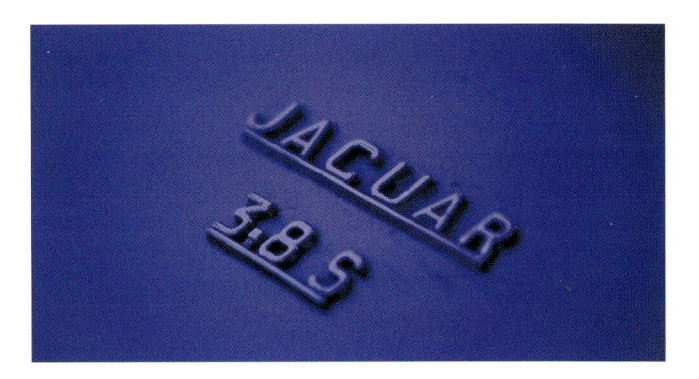

The S-types of course had their own identification on the boot lid.

The rear light clusters, borrowed from the Mk X, had a much more resolved design than those used on the Mk 2 models.

Most manual S-types came with the overdrive option, which was now a Laycock A-type, a rather smaller unit than the one it replaced and one that was often described in Jaguar service literature as the 'compact' type. However, this was one change that made no difference to the driver of an S-type. The A-type overdrive shared its 0.77:1 ratio gearing with the superseded type and was operated in exactly the same way by means of a switch on the dashboard.

Shortly after the start of the 1965 season, in December 1964, the colour range was changed. There were fewer exterior colours than before, but more upholstery colour options.

1966 Season

For 1966, automatic S-types took on the Borg Warner 35 gearbox as did their Mk 2 counterparts. Subsequently, the only change of any real note in the S-type's third season on sale came in the spring of 1966 when the optional heated rear window was given its own switch on the dashboard. Before then, it had been permanently in circuit with the ignition, and had no doubt contributed to a few problems with flat batteries. Jaguar must have recognized that they were out of step with other car manufacturers on this issue as they fitted the switch to other models at the same time.

1967 Season

Very little changed during the 1967 season, although a Borg and Beck diaphragm-spring clutch arrived at some point in

1966 and seems to have been in production by the time the 1967 cars started coming off the lines. From December, the chromed ends that had originally been part of the tailpipe assembly were made detachable. In March 1967 cars for the USA, where a hazard-warning-light system was part of the standard specification, gained a larger-capacity fuse to protect it. March 1967 also brought a reduced range of paint colours, which now no longer included any of the opalescent metallics.

1968 Season

When manufacturing cost reductions had been made on the Mk 2 saloons in autumn 1966, the specification of the S-types had remained unaltered. However, alongside the simplified 240 and 340 models announced in the autumn of 1967, Jaguar introduced simplified S-types. They would not be on sale for long because the new XJ6 models would be introduced in summer 1968 for the 1969 model year and S-type sales were in fact already declining quite sharply. As a result, many Jaguar enthusiasts are surprised to learn how extensive the S-type changes really were.

OPTIONAL EXTRAS – S-TYPE

The S-type was a well-equipped car in standard form, but Jaguar offered a number of extra-cost options.

Heated rear window
Lock for steering column and ignition switch
Overdrive (with manual gearbox)
Power-assisted steering
Radio (MW only)
Radio (MW/LW)
Radio (SW/MW)
Seat belts (front), with lap and diagonal straps
Seat belts (rear), with diagonal strap only
Sundym tinted glass
Whitewall tyres
Wing mirrors (standard equipment in some countries)
Wire wheels, chromium-plated
Wire wheels, stove-enamelled in aluminium colour
Wood-rim steering wheel

The S-type engines had the same state of tune as in contemporary Mk 2 saloons. This is a 3.8-litre type.

■ JAGUAR S-TYPE (1963–1968)

The rear quarter-light shared its shape with the Mk 2 and operated in the same way too, as this sequence shows.

On the 3.4-litre car, the Powr-Lok limited-slip differential option was dropped. On both models, the paint colour range was reduced from seven to six options. An obvious exterior change was that the fog lamps were removed and replaced by dummy horn grilles – exactly as on the revised Mk 2 saloons. The 1968 models also took on the latest type of wheel trims, which had been introduced originally on the companion-model 420 in 1966 and were now also specified for the 240 and 340. On the inside, the changes brought Ambla upholstery in place of leather and tufted carpets in place of the woven type. There were now only four colour choices for the upholstery, reduced from the nine available earlier.

One final important specification change was yet to be made. On cars with the optional power-assisted steering, from January 1968 a Variomatic system (see Chapter 10 for further details) replaced the earlier type. This had been standard on the Mk X saloons since 1964 and was also available on the 420s and Daimler Sovereigns. It provided reduced assistance close to the straight-ahead position and so gave a more positive feel to the steering.

Right at the very end of production, a new water temperature gauge with zone markings replaced the calibrated type and cars destined for Canada were fitted with a 110-volt cylinder-block heater as standard. To meet new regulations in West Germany, S-types for that country were fitted with 'pilot headlamps', which had a sidelight incorporated in the headlight bowl; on these cars, the standard sidelamps were not connected. However, few cars were built with these final changes and S-type production came to an end over the summer of 1968 to make way for the new XJ6 range. The last 3.8-litre car was built in June – and the last S-type of all was a 3.4-litre built in August.

JAGUAR S-TYPE (1963–1968)

POLICE S-TYPES

Although the 3.8-litre Jaguar Mk 2 was popular as a police fast-response car in the 1960s, it was not ideal for the job. Its biggest drawback was a lack of room in the boot and, as explained in Chapter 5, it was not uncommon for the rear seat to be removed in order to provide carrying space for the cones and emergency equipment normally carried by a motorway patrol car. So it was hardly surprising that the S-type Jaguar, with its very much larger boot, should have attracted interest from police forces. It had its own drawbacks, of course – its greater weight made it slower than a 3.8-litre Mk 2 and the car was also more expensive. As a result, the S-type seems not to have been very common in UK police service, although examples joined police fleets right through the production run.

The first 3.8-litre S-types to enter police service may have been a pair of cars (registered JNJ 274D and JNJ 275D) delivered to the East Sussex Constabulary in June 1966. London's Metropolitan Police took a further pair in January and February 1967 and one went to Fife Constabulary in March 1967.

The four known police users of S-type Jaguars were as follows:

Ayrshire Constabulary
East Sussex Constabulary
Fife Constabulary
Metropolitan Police

There may have been others, but there cannot have been many: the new XJ6 became available in 1968 and was a much better car for police patrol duties, despite its relatively high cost.

In addition to the usual means of identifying a police car, Ayrshire Police felt the need to advertise their ownership on the side of this 1968 S-type.

ABOVE: **Official police photographs regularly show cars with the equipment they carry, as in this East Sussex photograph. The car is a 1966 S-type that belonged to the traffic division.**

RIGHT: **London's Metropolitan Police was the major police user of the S-type Jaguar. This posed official photograph shows one of its 1969-season purchases.**

127

■ JAGUAR S-TYPE (1963–1968)

RIVALS

In Britain, Jaguar followed its usual policy of niche pricing, which meant that customers found very few alternatives at Jaguar prices. Those cars that offered anything like the same blend of qualities were in different price brackets and so not directly competitive.

When the S-type was announced at the 1963 Earls Court Motor Show, the basic 3.4-litre car cost £1,669 5s 5d (£1,381 plus £288 5s 5d purchase tax) and the 3.8-litre model was £1,758 13s 9d (£1,455 plus £303 13s 9d purchase tax). Realistically, however, even the 3.4-litre car was likely to cost most customers between about £1,720 and £1,800 because most would have ordered either overdrive (£54 7s 6d extra) or an automatic gearbox (£126 17s 6d extra).

Even so, there was precious little serious competition on the British market. Slightly cheaper than these Jaguars – at least, before desirable extras were added – were the big Citroëns, the Humber Super Snipe estate and the Volvo P1800S sports coupé. Slightly more expensive was the Rover 3-litre, and more expensive still were the Alfa Romeo Giulia 1600 Sprint, the Lotus Elite and some American imports. For comparison, a Jaguar Mk X cost £2,022 2s 1d (£1,673 plus £349 2s 1d purchase tax).

Frankly, the only one of these cars that might have attracted the S-type customer was the Rover, which had no sporting pretensions but was a better-looking car that offered plenty of luxury and prestige together with excellent build quality. Nothing much altered over the next few years. Newer cars in the same price range included the Mercedes-Benz 190 and the Auto Union SP 1000 sports coupé from 1964, the BMW 1800TI from 1965, and various Alfa Romeos and Lancias thereafter. However, at a time when buyers still overwhelmingly bought British and imported cars were subject to additional taxation, the S-type Jaguars remained pretty well unique.

THE S-TYPE IN THE USA

In the first two years of the 1960s, Jaguar's range of saloons in North America consisted of the entry-level 3.8-litre Mk 2 and the top-of-the-range 3.8-litre Mk X. At this stage, there was no 3.4-litre Mk 2, although a few had reached the USA as special orders. So when the S-type was announced for the USA in the spring of 1964, it was accompanied by a range realignment. The Mk 2 3.8 was discontinued and was replaced with the 3.4-litre Mk 2, which became the entry-level Jaguar saloon. Above that came the S-type, available only with the 3.8-litre engine. The Mk X remained at the top of the range with its more powerful, triple-carburettor version of the 3.8-litre engine. The hierarchy became clearer a few months later when the Mk X went over to a 4.2-litre engine.

The USA was far and away Jaguar's best overseas market and so the company took great care to provide its US dealers with the cars they wanted. The new three-tier range structure for the saloons was more or less on target, although the 3.4-litre Mk 2 was never a very strong seller because Jaguar buyers wanted as much performance as they could get.

By the mid-1960s, Jaguars had a negative-earth electrical system and the company thought it advisable to remind anybody working on the car.

A Lucas dipping rear-view mirror was standard equipment on the S-type.

JAGUAR S-TYPE (1963–1968)

Jaguar pinned a number of hopes on the 3.8-litre S-type in the USA. They had to deal with criticisms aimed at its Mk 2 predecessor, of inadequate luggage capacity, inadequate rear passenger space and inadequate fuel capacity for the long-distance motoring that was more common in the USA than in Britain. Greater boot space was certainly a benefit of the S-type and the raised rear roofline and seating modifications brought its rear passenger accommodation up to scratch. However, despite the twin rear fuel tanks that could carry a total of 2 gallons more than the Mk 2, fuel capacity was still not enough. Those two extra gallons were not enough to compensate for the new car's additional thirst, and Americans did not take kindly to making refuelling stops every 200 miles (320km) or so, regardless of the other pleasures of driving a Jaguar.

In fact, the S-type was rather less of a success across the Atlantic than Jaguar had probably hoped. It sold well enough, but disappeared from the US range as soon as the 420 arrived in 1966. Priced at around $6,000 on the West Coast (and slightly less on the East Coast because of lower shipping costs), the S-type was always an acquired taste. Not many Americans could understand the attraction of a relatively small imported saloon that cost more than all but the most expensive Cadillacs of the time and demanded specialist servicing. By contrast, any half-competent US mechanic could deal with the Cadillac's 340bhp 7-litre V8 engine – and in those figures lay part of the problem. It was difficult to maintain social prestige against a Cadillac owner with an imported car that had an engine only just over half the size and with a mere 220bhp; Americans had to drive the car to understand its merits.

Although the S-type Jaguar exported to the USA was essentially a left-hand-drive 3.8-litre model, it did have a few special features. Like the US-model Mk 2 cars, it had dummy horn grilles in the front wings instead of fog lights. From September 1965, it came with a hazard-warning light system as standard. Some cars were also fitted with an air-conditioning unit by the US importers. Typically, this would be placed in the boot above the rear suspension, nullifying the benefit of the extra luggage space that Browns Lane had carefully engineered into the car. Exact figures are not available, but it seems probable that most S-types shipped to the USA had the automatic gearbox rather than one of the manual options.

Inside, the S-type offered the usual Jaguar ambience with leather upholstery and wooden door cappings.

129

■ JAGUAR S-TYPE (1963–1968)

The front door trim of an S-type shows the horizontal lines characteristic of the model and the neat door pocket for stowing maps and other items.

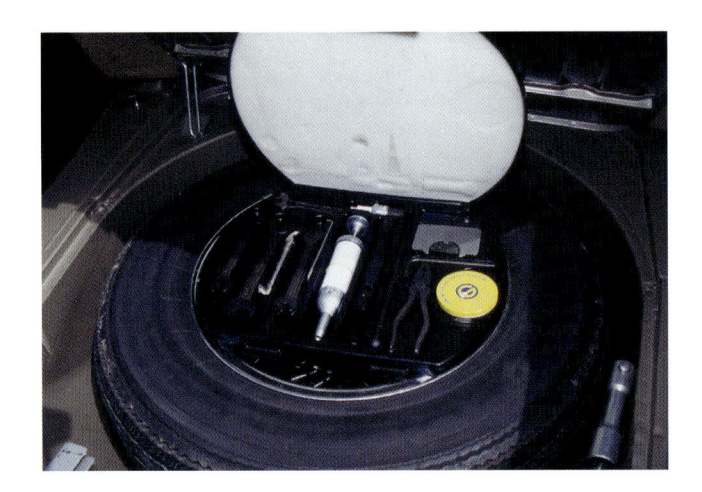

The tool kit was there once again, as always stowed in a neat tray that fitted into the spare-wheel rim.

THE S-TYPE AND THE US PRESS

A number of US journalists were invited to Britain to try the S-type in the early spring of 1964, as a promotional move to tie in with the car's US launch. Quickest off the mark with a report was *Cars Illustrated*, who published their findings in that year's April issue. The car was an overdrive model, equipped with the original RS5 tyres, and the road tester managed to find somewhere to record a mean maximum speed of 121mph (195km/h) and to clock the car at 11.2sec for the 0–60mph sprint.

Generally, the news was good. 'The car's directional stability is admirable,' and its 'long, easy stride combined with a lack of mechanical noise from engine or transmission makes it easy to cover long distances at high average speeds without fatigue for either driver or passengers'. There was oversteer at the limit, but this could be easily corrected.

Criticisms focused on the slow gear change (this was the original Moss gearbox), the weight and long travel of the clutch, and on the fuel capacity: 'The total of 14 gallons, an increase of only two gallons over the Mk 2, is not really great enough to be of worth.' (It is interesting that the writer quoted the increase in imperial gallons; in US gallons, it would have been slightly more.) The magazine also had doubts about the styling, noting that 'the comments of several owners and prospective owners of Mk 2 models were not loud in their praise.'

Car and Driver reported on their experiences with 2300 KV, another overdrive model, in their June 1964 issue. They also wondered about the styling, commenting that 'the front and rear ends seem somehow mismatched', and they too were unhappy with the slow gear change of the Moss box. Nevertheless, they did like the traditional British interior with its unspecified 'modern functional' elements. 'Directional stability, handling and braking of the S-type are all fully in keeping with its performance,' they said, which showed up as a remarkable 126mph (203km/h) maximum and 10.2sec for the 0–60mph dash. Overall, the car was 'a great step forward for what has always been a fine automobile'.

It was *Road & Track* who did the job properly in the USA, however, borrowing an automatic model from the Jaguar showrooms in San Francisco and taking it to the Cotati racetrack outside the city for performance testing. The results were published in the magazine's October 1964 issue. They loved the car:

At a selling price of around $6,000, the S-type Jaguar ... must be one of the best buys in the luxury car field – and offers assured driving pleasure to the discriminating owner.

On the drag strip at Cotati, they recorded a 0–60mph time of 11.5sec and a maximum of 116mph (187km/h).

The limited-slip differential and the independent rear suspension assure good traction under all but the most hopeless circumstances. It is difficult to fault the handling as the servo-assisted steering is precise, the suspension is superior to almost any sedan you can think of, the power is adequate and the big disc brakes are a pure delight.

If the automatic gearbox was not the best ('the torque comes in at comparatively high revs', and 'there seems to be a lot of gear shifting going on under your foot when you're driving in traffic'), they felt that S-type drivers would soon become accustomed to it. Praising the wood and leather interior, *Road & Track* were nevertheless not 'wholly convinced that the proportions of the car are improved by the longer rear end and increased overhang'. However, they did value the increased luggage space in the boot: 'Not even those used to Detroit car trunks would find the difference worth complaining about.' There was just one warning, which was that servicing would require a specialist and might be expensive: 'No-one who buys an S-type should expect it to continue running indefinitely without expert attention.'

IDENTIFICATION – S-TYPE

Identification numbers are stamped on a plate in the engine compartment, attached to the left-hand inner wing. These numbers are repeated elsewhere, as shown below.

Car Number

The car number, also known as the chassis number or VIN, is stamped into the bonnet-catch channel, just ahead of the radiator header tank. A typical car number might be 1B 1234 BW. The prefix identifies the model and is 1B for both 3.4-litre and 3.8-litre types; the numerals are the car's serial number; and the letters of the suffix show the transmission type.

The serial number sequences are:

	RHD	LHD
3.4	1001–9665	25001–26371
3.8	50001–59717	75001–80418

The suffixes decode as follows:

BW   Borg Warner automatic gearbox
DN   Laycock de Normanville overdrive

Cars fitted with power-assisted steering have a P prefix; for example, P1B 4321 BW.

Engine Number

The engine number is stamped on the right-hand side of the cylinder block above the oil filter and again at the front of the cylinder head casting, beside the front spark-plug hole. A typical engine number would be 7B 58350/8. This breaks down into three elements:

7B	Engine type identifier (used for both 3.4-litre and 3.8-litre engines)
58350	Serial number
/8	Compression ratio (/8 for 8:1 compression, /7 for 7:1, /9 for 9:1)

Serial number sequences for 3.4-litre engines begin at 1001; those for 3.8-litre engines begin at 50001.

Body Number

The body number is stamped on a small plate attached to the right-hand side of the body behind the rear bumper. (It should not be confused with a similar plate on the left-hand side that shows the Pressed Steel reference number.)

Gearbox Number

On all manual gearboxes, the gearbox number is stamped on a small shoulder at the left-hand rear corner of the gearbox casing, and on the top cover around the rim of the core-plug aperture. On automatic gearboxes, the number is stamped on a plate attached to the left-hand side of the gearbox casing.

■ JAGUAR S-TYPE (1963–1968)

SPECIFICATIONS – S-TYPE

Engines

3.4-litre
Type XK 6-cylinder, with cast-iron block and aluminium-alloy head
3442cc (83 x 106mm)
Twin overhead camshafts, chain-driven
Seven-bearing crankshaft
Compression ratio 8:1 (7:1 and 9:1 available)
Two SU HD6 carburettors with automatic choke
210bhp at 5,500rpm (with standard compression)
216lb ft at 3,000rpm

3.8-litre
Type XK 6-cylinder, with cast-iron block and aluminium-alloy head
3781cc (87 x 106mm)
Twin overhead camshafts, chain-driven
Seven-bearing crankshaft
Compression ratio 8:1 (7:1 and 9:1 available)
Two SU HD6 carburettors with automatic choke
220bhp at 5,500rpm (with standard compression)
240lb ft at 3,000rpm

Transmission
Hydraulically operated clutch with 9in diameter (manual) or torque converter (automatic)
Four-speed manual gearbox
Moss type with no first-gear synchromesh, 1963–64
Ratios 3.37:1, 1.86:1, 1.28:1, 1.00:1
Jaguar type with synchromesh on all forward gears, 1964–68
Ratios 3.04:1, 1.97:1, 1.33:1, 1.00:1
Optional overdrive with 0.77:1 ratio
Three-speed Borg Warner type DG automatic (type 35 from September 1965)
Ratios 4.97:1, 3.09:1, 1.00:1

Axle ratio
3.54:1 with non-overdrive manual and automatic gearboxes
3.77:1 with overdrive

Suspension, steering and brakes
Independent front suspension with wishbones, coil springs and anti-roll bar
Independent rear suspension with lower wishbone and upper link by driveshaft, radius arms and paired coil springs
Burman recirculating-ball, worm-and-nut steering; power assistance optional
Disc brakes with 11in diameter front and 11.4in rear, with servo assistance as standard

Dimensions

Overall length	187in (4,750mm)
Overall width	66.25in (1,683mm)
Overall height	55.75in (1,416mm)
Wheelbase	107.5in (2,730mm)
Front track	55.25in (1,403mm)
Rear track	54.25in (1,378mm)

Wheels and tyres
15in steel disc wheels standard, with 5.5in rims
15in wire-spoke wheels with 5.5in rims optional
6.40 x 15 cross-ply tyres (to June 1964); 185 x 15 radials thereafter

Kerb weights

3.4-litre	3,584lb (1,625kg)
3.8-litre	3,696lb (1,676kg

PERFORMANCE FIGURES – S-TYPE

The 3.4-litre S-type was not released to the press for road tests and no verified performance figures are available.

3.8-litre overdrive

0–60mph	10.2sec
Maximum speed	121mph (195km/h)
Fuel consumption	15mpg (19ltr/100km) approx.

3.8-litre automatic

0–60mph	11.8sec
Maximum speed	116mph (187km/h)
Fuel consumption	15mpg (19ltr/100km) approx.

PAINT AND TRIM COLOURS – S-TYPE

The same options were available on both models. Some cars were painted and trimmed to special order.

October 1963 to November 1964
There were fourteen standard paint colours, including six opalescent (metallic) finishes. Six interior-trim options were listed.

Body	Interior
British Racing Green	Champagne, Suede Green or Tan
Carmen Red	Black or Red
Cotswold Blue	Dark Blue or Grey
Dove Grey	Grey, Red or Tan
Imperial Maroon	Red
Old English White	Red or Tan
Opalescent Blue	Dark Blue, Grey, Light Blue or Red
Opalescent Bronze	Red or Tan
Opalescent Dark Green	Champagne, Suede Green or Tan
Opalescent Gunmetal	Red or Tan
Opalescent Silver Blue	Dark Blue, Grey, Light Blue or Red
Opalescent Silver Grey	Grey, Red or Tan
Pearl Grey	Dark Blue, Grey, Light Blue or Red
Sherwood Green	Suede Green or Tan

December 1964 to February 1967
There were ten standard paint colours, of which five were opalescent (metallic) finishes. White was offered on police models only, during 1966 and 1967. Nine interior-trim options were listed.

Body	Interior
Carmen Red	Beige or Red
Cream	Dark Blue, Light Blue or Red
Dark Blue	Grey, Light Blue or Red
Opalescent Dark Green	Beige, Light Tan, Suede Green or Tan
Opalescent Golden Sand	Light Tan or Red
Opalescent Maroon	Beige or Maroon
Opalescent Silver Blue	Dark Blue or Grey
Opalescent Silver Grey	Grey, Red or Tan
Sherwood Green	Light Tan, Suede Green or Tan
Warwick Grey	Red or Tan
White	Black or Dark Blue (police cars only)

March 1967 to August 1967
There were seven standard paint colours, none of which was metallic. The special-order White for police cars remained available but was not listed. The range of nine interior-trim options was unchanged.

Body	Interior
Beige	Light Tan, Red, Suede Green or Tan
British Racing Green	Beige, Light Tan, Suede Green or Tan
Carmen Red	Beige or Red
Cream	Dark Blue, Light Blue or Red
Dark Blue	Grey, Light Blue or Red
Warwick Grey	Dark Blue, Light Blue or Tan
Willow Green	Beige, Grey, Light Tan or Suede Green

September 1967 to September 1968
There were six standard paint colours, none of which was metallic. Four interior-trim options were listed. Upholstery was in Ambla, and leather was an extra-cost option.

Body	Interior
Beige	Beige, Black, Blue or Red
Black	Beige, Black, Blue or Red
British Racing Green	Beige or Black
Cream	Beige, Black, Blue or Red
Dark Blue	Beige, Black, Blue or Red
Warwick Grey	Beige, Black, Blue or Red

■ JAGUAR S-TYPE (1963–1968)

SO YOU WANT TO BUY AN S-TYPE JAGUAR?

The S-type has a very different appeal from the Mk 1 and Mk 2 models. It is less raw and less obviously sporty, being pitched at the luxury market – but it was still a high-performance car in its day. An S-type may not be as fast as the lighter Mk 2, but its independent rear suspension gives much greater ride comfort and better roadholding as well.

Like the Mk 1 and Mk 2 Jaguars, the S-type rusts badly, so a careful check of the body structure is essential. The advice given in the earlier chapters for Mk 1 and Mk 2 models holds good for these cars as well, although the rear-end structure is different and needs to be examined accordingly. In particular, check the attachment points for the rear suspension's radius arms for signs of rust. Rust around and under the fuel tanks mounted inside the rear wings is an additional problem.

The 3.4-litre and 3.8-litre engines have the same virtues and vices as in Mk 1 and Mk 2 cars. As gearboxes changed during production (for the better), the later cars are preferable with their all-synchromesh manual or Borg Warner type 35 automatic gearboxes.

The independent rear suspension is quite complex and can be expensive to overhaul. The differential can leak, and although it will probably only need new oil seals, the whole rear bridge-piece has to be dropped for the job, which adds to the cost. If the dampers are worn, remember that there are four of them to replace at the rear. At the front, worn springs may sag and allow tyres to rub against the wheel arches. Modern tyres may bring other problems, as explained in the sections about buying Mk 1 and Mk 2 models.

As for all the models covered in this book, restoring a tired or worn interior will be very expensive.

CHAPTER TEN

DEVELOPING THE JAGUAR 420 AND DAIMLER SOVEREIGN

Almost as soon as the S-type was off their hands and had entered production, the Browns Lane engineers turned their hands to a fourth iteration of the compact Jaguar saloon. The catalyst for the new model was the introduction in 1964 of a 4.2-litre version of the XK engine, which had been developed primarily for the Mk X saloons, but there were several other factors that pushed Jaguar towards this new model.

On the face of things, the Jaguar saloon range was already uncomfortably complicated. At the cheaper end of the scale (and no Jaguar was ever really cheap) were the three Mk 2 compacts, with 2.4-litre, 3.4-litre and 3.8-litre engines. Just above them came the Daimler 2½-litre V8 derivative of the Mk 2. Next up were the 3.4-litre and 3.8-litre S-types, and right at the top of the range sat the Mk X, introduced in 1961 with a 3.8-litre engine but after 1964 boasting that new 4.2-litre engine.

However, the Mk X was not selling as well as Jaguar had hoped, and the 4.2-litre engine had been developed largely to improve that situation. More power and more performance would certainly help, but the car was also widely seen as too big and too cumbersome. What was needed was a smaller Jaguar saloon with Mk X standards of luxury to pick up the sales that the big saloon was losing. Then there was the fact that the S-type had also been a disappointment, arousing the sort of mixed reactions that no Jaguar before it had ever done. Lyons and his advisers must have realized that its odd looks were costing the company sales, so it made sense to improve on its styling as soon as Jaguar had the resources to do so.

Given these circumstances, the idea of creating that fourth derivative of the original compact design made very good sense at Browns Lane. It could pick up where the S-type had left off, adding improved styling and the new 4.2-litre engine into the mix. With high standards of luxury and equipment, it was no doubt intended to capture the buyer who thought a Mk X was too big, while its better looks and performance would appeal to those who might otherwise have wanted an S-type but found the car unattractive or too slow – particularly when compared with the cheaper 3.8-litre Mk 2. So the 420 was not a model that simply complicated the top end of the Jaguar saloon range. On the contrary, its purpose was to shore up that range where it was failing.

Although the 420 could trace its lineage directly back to the original compact Jaguar of 1955, it was not developed with yet another project name in the Utah series. As Chapter 8 explains, the S-type had started out as Utah Mk 3 but had become XJ3 when Jaguar changed its system of project names. The 420 was also known internally by one of the new codes and became XJ16. It appears that XJ4 was an early iteration of the car that in 1968 was launched as XJ6, but quite why such a high number was chosen for the new compact saloon is not at all clear.

STYLING

Lyons's idea for the 420 was simple enough: he wanted to graft the four-headlamp nose of the Mk X saloon onto the S-type bodyshell. It was a change that, in the opinion of body engineer Cyril Crouch, 'transformed the car'.

A first glance at the front end of the 420 suggests that it was taken directly from the Mk X, but a closer look reveals many differences in both structure and detail. The Mk X was a much wider car than the compact saloons, so the new frontal design had to be scaled down to fit. To suit the structure of the compact saloons, the front-hinged bonnet of the Mk X gave way to a rear-hinged bonnet in the same mould as that on the Mk 2s and S-types. This allowed a

■ DEVELOPING THE JAGUAR 420 AND DAIMLER SOVEREIGN

LEFT: **This was the front end of the Mk X Jaguar, the inspiration for the new front end of the 420. The Mk X had a forward-hinged bonnet, which explains those panel lines between the headlights. The 420 would have a conventional crocodile-type bonnet. It would also be much narrower.**

BELOW: **A close look at what is claimed to be the very first 420 Jaguar reveals that the front panel below the headlights is plain. Clearly, somebody thought this was not good enough: for production a pair of dummy grilles were added to fill the space.** JDHT

DEVELOPING THE JAGUAR 420 AND DAIMLER SOVEREIGN

This was the final production design for the front end of the Jaguar 420, with horizontal grilles below the inner pair of headlamps. The essence of the Mk X design is there but the whole thing has been scaled down to fit.

full-width front panel on the 420, without the vertical panel line between each pair of headlamps that interrupted the smooth lines on the Mk X.

The headlamps themselves were arranged in much the same way on both models, with peaks above them to add definition, but the 420's front panel was more nearly vertical than that on the Mk X. A different radiator grille was designed, too, with a vertical centre bar that was not present on the Mk X (although when that car became a 420G later, such a bar was added). Sidelamps and wraparound indicators were carried over to the 420 from the Mk X, but the smaller car took on rectangular horn grilles below the inner pair of headlamps rather than the round ones of the Mk X. Surviving photographs show that the 420 was initially designed with no small grilles at the front, but that the front end looked rather bare so that the grilles were added to improve the appearance.

The rest of the 420's body remained unchanged from the Utah Mk 3 or S-type. However, there were other distinguishing features in the external design, quite apart from the badges on the boot lid. The 420s had wheel trims with out-turned central sections surrounding a black plastic disc bearing the jaguar's head emblem – infinitely more attractive than the early Mk X style used on the S-types, which would probably have served rather well as a saucepan lid. These new trims actually appeared on the larger saloon at the same time as the 420 was launched in 1966, when the Mk X was renamed 420G (in a move that emphasized how close the two ranges were, so giving the new 420 a more upmarket appeal). A year later, the new style would also appear on the 240 and 340 compact saloons.

THE 4.2-LITRE ENGINE

The original 3.4-litre XK engine had been designed with a bore of 83mm. Its capacity was raised to 3.8 litres at the end of the 1950s by increasing that bore size to 87mm. A larger bore than that could not be achieved without eating into the water passages in the cylinder block. So for the 4.2-litre engine, the cylinders were repositioned within the block to allow for a bore increase to 92.07mm. Cylinders three and four were moved closer together (as allowed by the extra-long centre main bearing between them on the original engine), while cylinders one and six were moved further apart. The crankshaft was redesigned to suit, and with the original stroke the new swept volume worked out at 4235cc.

In the Mk X saloon and the E-type sports car, the 4.2-litre engine came with three SU carburettors and 265bhp, but for

137

DEVELOPING THE JAGUAR 420 AND DAIMLER SOVEREIGN

The 4.2-litre engine had already appeared in the Mk X and the E-type. As fitted to the 420, it was slightly less powerful, with 245bhp instead of the 265bhp in the other two models. Model differentiation was one issue, but from a practical point of view there was not enough room for the triple carburettors of the other cars, so the 420 had to make do with two.

the 420 the engine was detuned slightly to 245bhp. There were two reasons for this, one being entirely practical: there was simply not room in the compact saloon's engine bay to fit a triple-carburettor manifold. The second reason must have been to protect sales of the 420G (née Mk X); after all, 265bhp in the lighter 420 body would have given the smaller car better performance than the larger and more expensive one that was supposed to be Jaguar's flagship.

The installation of the 4.2-litre engine gave Jaguar's engineers an opportunity to deal with the cooling problems that had so often afflicted Jaguars in the USA, and they replaced the S-type's radiator with a larger and more efficient cross-flow type. They also fitted an alternator in place of the older cars' dynamo – an item becoming increasingly common on luxury models with extra electrical equipment – and in place of the inertia-type starter came the latest pre-engaged variety. In addition, the 4.2-litre engine was fitted with a Holset 'Torquatrol' viscous-coupled cooling fan to reduce the power drain and noise of a heavy, engine-driven type.

TRANSMISSION AND BRAKES

With the bigger engine came changes in the transmission. Although the all-synchromesh Jaguar manual gearbox standardized on S-types during 1965 had been designed to withstand the increased torque of the 4.2-litre XK engine, the optional Borg Warner 35 automatic gearbox was not up to the job. So the Jaguar engineers turned to a more heavy-duty model from Borg Warner, the Model 8, and used this behind the new engine in the Mk X and the 420.

The new automatic gearbox brought with it new control options. The simple 'D' of the earlier selectors was replaced by 'D1' and 'D2' options. In 'D1', all three forward gears would be selected in the normal way, but 'D2' cut out bottom gear to give smoother (if rather slower) starts from rest and to prevent the gearbox from 'hunting' between gears in slow-moving traffic.

The choice of disc brakes all round for the 420 was a foregone conclusion, but Jaguar were able to specify the latest design, which reduced brake squeal. It had taken the brake manufacturers some time to discover that this irritating noise was caused by high-frequency vibrations of the disc and that it could be eliminated by adding what was in effect a vibration damper. So the new generation of discs available in time for the introduction of the 420 had a band of cast iron set into a groove on their outer periphery. To meet anticipated requirements in the USA, the 420 was also designed with twin hydraulic brake circuits.

STEERING

The 420 became the first of the compact Jaguars to have the latest Marles Variomatic Bendix power-assisted steering. The system had actually been introduced on the 4.2-litre version of the Mk X Jaguar in October 1964, and that car was the first production model in the world to have it. It was a natural choice to help distinguish the 420 from the other compact Jaguars, and in due course it would also become an option on the S-types (in January 1968) and the Mk 2 (in March 1967). The 420, however, would have it as an option from the start of production in 1966.

Variomatic was a variable-ratio, power-assisted steering system based on an original design by an Australian, Arthur Bishop, and developed by the Bendix Corporation in the USA. Its design was derived from an aircraft nose-wheel gear in the mid-1950s, and Bendix adopted it for production in 1958. The attitude of the US motor industry to such engineering innovations is well illustrated by the fact that the first customer was not found until six years later – and that this customer was not an American company!

Unlike other types of variable-ratio steering, the progression of the steering ratio in the Variomatic depended on a closely controlled and predetermined curve in which the ratio reduced rapidly from the straight-ahead position and then levelled out completely by mid-turn. The effort at the steering wheel was matched to the slip angle of the road wheels to give the Variomatic its most marked advantage – a very much greater degree of steering 'feel' (the driver's impression that he or she is in direct control of the road wheels) than earlier power-assisted types, which had tended to make the steering feel as if it was being operated by remote control.

In mechanical terms, the Variomatic was an hourglass worm-and-roller steering box, with hydraulic power assistance. Jaguar used an American-made Saginaw hydraulic pump, but the main components of the Variomatic were made under licence in the UK by Adwest in Reading.

INTERIOR

The interior design of the 420 was based on that of the S-type, but it made steps in the direction of the latest Mk X models. Safety features were becoming an issue, and so the whole dashboard took on a padded surround that was covered with matt black Rexine. The lower edge of the parcel shelf took on some light padding, with similar trim, and the deep wooden door fillets of the S-types gave way to rather ordinary-looking padded rolls with no more than a thin wooden garnish rail on their horizontal top surfaces.

The 420's dashboard was given additional distinction by a rectangular electric clock in its padded top rail, although in this case the driving factor had been necessity rather than appearance. Jaguar wanted to change from the mechanically driven rev counter of the S-type to an impulse-driven electric rev counter. On the S-type dash, the clock was embedded in the face of the rev counter, but no electric rev counter with integral clock was available. So the clock had to go somewhere else – and that necessity was turned to good account in the final design.

The new rev counter would not have been possible without another, less visible, change under the skin of the 420. Previous Jaguars had used positive-earth electrical systems. However, by the mid-1960s, the trend worldwide was towards negative-earth systems, and component manufacturers were leading the way in this. So the 420 was designed with a negative-earth system – and to remind those who maintained the cars, Browns Lane fitted a warning plate on the battery cover.

DAIMLER SOVEREIGN DERIVATIVE

Evidence suggests that Jaguar embarked on the design of the 420 model with the intention of making it purely a Jaguar. However, the impetus to produce a Daimler-badged derivative came some time around October 1965, according to *Daimler Century*, by Lord Montagu and David Burgess-Wise. James Smillie of the Daimler dealer Stratstone's complained to Sir William Lyons that the Daimler dealers needed a new model. Few customers were trading in their 2½-litre V8, and

■ DEVELOPING THE JAGUAR 420 AND DAIMLER SOVEREIGN

the dealers had nothing to offer them as a trade-up anyway, except the outmoded and rather expensive Majestic Major.

Not very long after that, Smillie and Stratstone's managing director, John Olly, were summoned to Browns Lane to view a prototype – a badge-engineered Jaguar 420. Lyons asked them what they thought the car should be called. Olly suggested Daimler Royale; Smillie suggested Daimler Sovereign. Lyons initially agreed with Olly, saying that Royale was the name Jaguar had been thinking of themselves, but later on he changed his mind and settled on Sovereign. It was a name that had no precedent in either Daimler or Jaguar history, and the only car ever called a Sovereign before had been built by a short-lived American company early in the twentieth century. However, it did have a rather grand ring to it, and that could only help sales.

To the engineers at Browns Lane, the new Daimler was known rather more prosaically by its project name XDM6. It seems to have been conceived as a 420 with all the extras as standard, so power-assisted steering was made part of the standard specification; on cars with a manual gearbox, so was overdrive. In addition, it appears that the Sovereign's seats were upholstered with a higher grade of Connolly leather than was used on the 420. The leather was certainly distinctive, as the seats featured perforated centre sections like those on the Daimler 2½-litre V8 models. The sun visors also had better quality covers, and the wood trim certainly appeared to be of a higher quality than that used on the Jaguar 420 – or perhaps that was just an impression suggested by the grandeur of the Daimler name.

In other respects, the Sovereign would be purely a rebadged 420. In fact, it became the first Daimler to contain nothing at all that was recognizably Daimler in origin; Jaguar's first badge-engineered Daimler, the 2½-litre V8 of 1962, had at least had a Daimler engine. The Daimler identity was conveyed at the front by a fluted Daimler-badged grille in place of the Jaguar type, and at the rear by a fluted number-plate housing on the boot lid. The wheel trims were given flying-D badges in their centres, and the engine rocker covers carried a Daimler logo instead of a Jaguar one.

Central to the transformation of the 420 into a Daimler Sovereign was the substitution of a fluted Daimler grille for the Jaguar type.

The Daimler's bonnet also had to carry a winged-D mascot.

CHAPTER ELEVEN

JAGUAR 420 AND DAIMLER SOVEREIGN (1966–1969)

The Jaguar 420 was introduced in October 1966 and appeared that year on Jaguar's stands at the Paris, London and Turin motor shows. Americans first got to see it at the Los Angeles show in October.

In Britain, the press release was dated 13 October 1966, and the new model was presented to the buying public for the first time on 19 October on stand 138 at the Earls Court Motor Show. As the most exciting addition to the Jaguar range that year, the 420 was given pride of place on a revolving turntable, where the Opalescent Maroon car with its Beige interior could hardly fail to attract attention. A second 420 stood on the floor of the stand, this one in Opalescent Silver Blue with a Dark Blue interior; and there was a third car on stand 169, which belonged to Pressed Steel Fisher who were responsible for the 420's bodyshell. This one was finished in Golden Sand and had a Red interior.

Production of the new car had actually started back in August to allow for dealer stocks to be built up before the public announcement. The first examples of right- and left-hand-drive 420s left the assembly lines at Browns Lane on

Wire wheels were not standard wear for the 420, though large numbers of cars had them.

141

■ JAGUAR 420 AND DAIMLER SOVEREIGN (1966–1969)

From the rear, a 420 was hard to distinguish from an S-type without a look at the badges – but from this angle the flattened top to the front wheel arch was the giveaway.

With the new grille came a new style of Jaguar emblem, still surmounted by the leaping cat.

23 August 1966; 1F 1001 BW had Warwick Grey paint and a Dark Blue interior, while P1F 25001 BMW was in Willow Green with Beige upholstery. Not surprisingly, the latter car went to Jaguar's most important overseas market, the USA, destined for California.

JAGUAR 420 ON SALE

It quickly became clear that the 420 was exactly what the market wanted. Although its short lifespan of just two seasons in production meant that the overall build total was not very great, it sold faster than any of the S-types had done. Sales of the 3.4-litre S-type averaged around 2,000 a year over five years, and those of the 3.8-litre model ran at about

The earliest cars had this style of rear badging above the number-plate box, but on later models the '420' was moved to the lower right of the boot lid.

3,000 a year for the same period; but sales of the Jaguar 420 averaged 5,000 a year over its two-year life. On top of that, its Daimler Sovereign sibling averaged another 2,000 a year.

As soon as the 420 and the Sovereign reached the market, sales of the S-types practically collapsed. With sales of the Mk 2 models and their later 240 and 340 derivatives already sliding, and the big 420G (née Mk X) a slow seller, the 420 became Jaguar's best-selling saloon of the period. However, all good things have to come to an end. The XJ6 saloon was due to be launched in October 1968 and the 420 went out of production to make way for it. The last left-hand-drive

> **OVERSEAS ASSEMBLY OF THE JAGUAR 420**
>
> By the time production of the 420 started, Jaguar's only CKD assembly operation was in South Africa. Jaguar Cars South Africa Ltd had opened for business on 1 September 1966 and had taken control of the local assembly operation as part of its remit.
>
> Jaguar statistics suggest that 840 examples of the 420 were delivered in CKD form for overseas assembly. In addition, a further 12 (or 13) cars were delivered in 'chassis only' form for special bodywork (see Chapter 12). The two figures make a total of 852 (or 853) such vehicles, which tallies nicely with the estimate of 850 CKD cars made by the late Jaguar historian Andrew Whyte.

car was built on 29 August 1968; finished in Sand, with Cinnamon upholstery, PIF 27629 DN was shipped to Jaguar's Swiss distributor, Emil Frey. Production of right-hand-drive 420s did not end quite so cleanly, though. PIF 8324 BW was completed on 30 August and was, to all intents and purposes, the last right-hand-drive car, but one more car was built at Browns Lane on 6 September. This car, PIF 8349 BW, was also finished in Sand but had Red upholstery and was supplied to PJ Evans in Birmingham.

That car was not the last 420 of all, although it was the last to be assembled at Browns Lane. All those numbered from 8325 to 8348, and then 8350 to 8595, were shipped out in CKD form for assembly in South Africa. The very last of them, PIF 8595 BW, left Browns Lane on 4 November 1968. After that, 420s continued to be built in badge-engineered Daimler Sovereign guise until July 1969.

DAIMLER SOVEREIGN ON SALE

The Daimler Sovereign was primarily a car for the British market. It could not be sold in some countries where the rights to the Daimler name were jealously guarded by Daimler-Benz, makers of rival Mercedes-Benz cars. Relatively few were sold overseas; none went to the USA, where the Daimler name meant nothing; and just 355 of the 5,824 Sovereigns built had left-hand drive – a paltry 6 per cent.

Surprisingly, the very first Sovereign built was a left-hand-drive car. Car number 1A 70001 BW was completed on 25 August 1966 and was finished in Green with a Black interior. It was followed on 30 August by the first right-hand-drive car, PIA 30001, which was finished in Silver Grey with Grey leather. Production proper got under way in the first week of September.

It seems clear that Browns Lane was aiming at the traditional Daimler buyer with this new model, and was not aiming to attract new customers. So potential buyers of the Sovereign would have been middle-aged or elderly; necessarily fairly wealthy; probably conservative in outlook; and certainly appreciative of fine luxury goods. They were more concerned with refinement than extremes of high performance – though many of the more traditional Daimlers had been capable of a surprisingly high turn of speed when called upon – so most Sovereigns were supplied with the Borg Warner automatic gearbox. The alternative was the four-speed all-synchromesh Jaguar manual gearbox with Laycock de Normanville overdrive as standard.

■ JAGUAR 420 AND DAIMLER SOVEREIGN (1966–1969)

The fluted Daimler grille arguably suited the car even better than the Jaguar alternative, although the optional wire wheels added a sporting touch that perhaps suited the Jaguar better.

BELOW LEFT: As the most expensive version of the compact Jaguars, and its final iteration, the Daimler Sovereign probably had the best of the design features as well.

BELOW RIGHT: There was no fluting on the boot-lid handle; instead, the Sovereign had the Daimler name moulded into its centre.

The Sovereign was on sale for three seasons, one season longer than the 420. This was because Daimler versions of the new XJ6 model were delayed until 1969 and Daimler dealers still needed a model to sell. Sales remained fairly constant throughout the model's production life, at around 2,000 a year. These were not perhaps big figures, but they did represent sales that Browns Lane might not have made without the Sovereign in their line-up, because many traditional Daimler customers still saw Jaguars as rather flash cars in the 1960s.

The lower-volume, left-hand-drive cars were the first to go out of production, the last one being PIA 70355 BW, a Regency Red car with Beige upholstery that was built on 23 April 1969 and went to Italy. The right-hand-drive Sovereign remained in production for about another ten weeks, the last car being PIA 35476 BW, which had Sable paintwork with a Cinnamon interior. It was completed on 9 July 1969 and, fittingly, was delivered to Stratstone – the Daimler dealer whose intervention had led to the creation of the Sovereign in the first place. From that October, Daimler customers were offered the new XJ6 saloon wearing Daimler Sovereign badges.

The final Sovereign closed an era in Browns Lane's history, because it was the last of the compact saloons with independent rear suspension to be built. It was not the last compact of all – that would be another Daimler, a V8-250 saloon completed on 5 August 1969 – but the S-types and Jaguar 420s had all ceased production during 1968. With the demise of the big 420G model in June 1970, Jaguar completed the rationalization of its saloon ranges and the XJ6 took over completely.

KEY PRODUCTION CHANGES

Although there were dozens of minor changes to the Jaguar 420 and Daimler Sovereign during their production life, few were of any major consequence. There were, however, two quite important changes.

The first of these was a change of final drive on automatic models, from the original 3.31:1 to 3.54:1. This change was made during 1967, but in January 1968 the same change took place for cars with manual gearboxes, although the old 3.31:1 final drive remained available as an option. The second change occurred in August 1967, when the Powr-Lok limited-slip differential option was discontinued. There is some indication that these changes took place at different

A further nice touch was the Daimler logo on the spinners of the wire-wheel option. Note that these spinners do not have the large 'ears' normally found on the Jaguar type. Safety regulations had already outlawed them in some countries and the Daimler version was produced to a design that would meet regulations everywhere.

times on the two models: the final drive change occurred earlier on Sovereigns but the limited-slip differential option was dropped earlier for the 420s.

That change to the final-drive gearing was perhaps not entirely for the better. The new lower gearing certainly did help acceleration, 'particularly in the 35–40mph range when Low is no longer available and Intermediate a little high', as *Autocar* commented in their 8 February 1968 issue. However, Stuart Bladon, author of that report on the magazine's long-term test Sovereign, added:

JAGUAR 420 AND DAIMLER SOVEREIGN (1966–1969)

At least for owners who drive fast, this [lower overall gearing] seems to me to be a retrograde move. Even with the 3.31 to 1 final drive used in this early Sovereign, the engine is turning at 4,450rpm at 100mph, and there is appreciably more engine noise than with the overdrive model. At maximum speed of 119mph the engine is beginning to produce quite a roar, and the rev-counter needle is well into the red segment at 5,300rpm.

With the lower final drive, the maximum speed actually dropped, and engine noise levels at speed increased. Perhaps the real reason for the change was rationalization and cost saving: the 420 and Sovereign were the only models from Browns Lane with a 3.31:1 final drive, whereas the 3.54:1 gear setting was used in several other models of the time.

One final change is worth noting. Right at the end of 420 production, the engines took on ribbed cam covers in place of the earlier plain type. Although hardly a major change, it is one that often occasions comments simply because it is so visible.

JAGUAR 420 AND THE PRESS

In Britain, Jaguar seem to have been in no hurry to get road-test examples of the 420 out to the motoring press. The car had already been on sale for nearly five months when the first British test was published. The honour fell to *Autocar*, which borrowed GKV 67D and reported on it in the issue dated 2 March 1967. The magazine enthused:

PRODUCTION FIGURES – JAGUAR 420 AND DAIMLER SOVEREIGN

Jaguar 420	Daimler Sovereign	Total
9,801	5,829	15,630

Note: Various contradictory sets of production figures have been quoted over the years. Those shown here were generally accepted to be the most accurate at the time of writing.

OPTIONAL EXTRAS – JAGUAR 420 AND DAIMLER SOVEREIGN

Jaguar 420
The 420 was a very well-equipped car, but as always Jaguar dealers had a selection of optional extras to tempt buyers.

Air conditioning (available only in the USA)
Anti-theft steering lock
Automatic gearbox
Fog lamps
Heated rear window
Laminated windscreen
Limited-slip differential (to August 1967)
Metallic paint
Overdrive (with manual gearbox)
Radial tyres (Dunlop SP41 185 x 15; these were standard in all markets except the USA, where they were an option)
Radio, with remote-control aerial
Rear seat belts
Telescopic steering column
Variomatic power-assisted steering
Whitewall tyres
Wire wheels, chromium-plated (these were standard on US cars)

Daimler Sovereign
The Sovereign was fitted as standard with some of the options available for the 420. The Variomatic power steering and heated rear window were standard on all cars, and overdrive was always supplied with a manual gearbox. So the extra-cost options were:

Limited-slip differential (to August 1967)
Metallic paint (to June 1968)
Radio
Wire wheels, chromium-plated

JAGUAR 420 AND DAIMLER SOVEREIGN (1966–1969)

The ribbed cam covers on the Sovereign engines carried Daimler identification, although the engine itself was pure Jaguar XK.

In its behaviour on the road it is undoubtedly Jaguar's finest achievement so far. ... The 420 in every way lives up to high expectations. It has an extraordinary dual character in that it can at one moment provide stately, luxurious travel for an elderly party, and behave like a high performance sports car the next. With the extra cost of Variomatic steering included, it just tops the round figure as the best £2,000's worth on the market.

In terms of performance, Autocar's overdrive 420 was not a major improvement over the 3.8-litre S-type. Its 123mph (198km/h) top speed compared with 121.5mph for the overdrive S-type, while 60mph came up in 9.9sec from rest as opposed to 10.4sec. However, the figures did not tell the whole story, as Autocar explained:

The savings ... in acceleration through the gears ... may appear trivial, but the big difference is that the greater torque enables the car to do this more effortlessly. The extra power also shows up better at the top end of the scale. Above 100mph, where the S-type's performance is beginning to tail off, the 420 still has acceleration in hand, and takes only 11 seconds to go from 100 to 110mph.

The magazine also recommended the Variomatic power steering option to every buyer of a 420, but it was clear that the car's basic design was beginning to show its age in some areas. Body roll was one problem: 'on winding roads the car seems a little too soft on its springs.' The handbrake, too, was not very effective (more recent cars with rear disc brakes had shown that the problem could be overcome), while the heating and ventilating system was in need of improvement, offering no face-level air vents and giving inadequate demisting.

The age of the design was showing even more by the time *Motor* published a test of an automatic 420 in its issue dated 6 May 1967. The heating and ventilating system was found to be complex and bettered by cheaper cars, the screen pillars were 'a bit thick by current standards', and as for the interior: 'there are those among us who look forward to the time when Jaguar abandon tradition and ... produce a really modern, ergonomic interior layout.' The elderly Borg Warner Model 8 gearbox design also came in for criticism, the testers wishing that automatic engagement of bottom gear with the selector in 'L' for hill-climbing was delayed to lower speeds, 'as it is on the Model 35'.

Yet none of these criticisms prevented the magazine from forming a very favourable impression indeed of the automatic 420. 'For a combination of speed, comfort and safety,'

■ JAGUAR 420 AND DAIMLER SOVEREIGN (1966–1969)

The 420's dashboard was different yet again, with a padded top section
and the clock set into the centre of the top rail.

the testers concluded, the car 'is as good as any in the world, regardless of cost.' Such words were high praise indeed for a car that was clearly off-song and could only manage a 115mph (185km/h) top speed, even though its 9.4sec 0–60mph time was about par for the model. And *Motor* were in no doubt at all about the 420's importance to the overall development of the Jaguar saloon, although they did not express it in quite those terms:

> *What it does – and does very effectively – is to provide 420G (ex-Mk X) appearance, prestige and performance in a smaller, cheaper car, a package we ourselves think more appealing and practical if you are prepared to sacrifice a little accommodation. The 420 gives virtually nothing else away.*

148

JAGUAR 420 AND DAIMLER SOVEREIGN (1966–1969)

built. *Autocar* summarized their impressions in one sentence, which spoke volumes for the vehicle's qualities: 'This car has proved unusually free from mechanical troubles of any kind, and has given a lot of motoring pleasure to justify its costs.'

It was, of course, an expensive car to buy and to run: fuel consumption worked out at around 15mpg (19ltr/100km). Yet the appeal of its other attributes was strong. Its 'combination of luxury, comfort and such responsive controls is what makes most drivers grow so fond of the car. It responds exactly to the driver's mood.' The report, written by Stuart Bladon, went on to enumerate the car's many virtues:

> The steering is accurate, featherlight and takes only 2.8 turns from lock to lock, and the handling and adhesion are very good indeed. The car is also particularly stable in cross winds. The suspension still seems too soft, allowing occasional float and rather too much roll, particularly through fast 'S'-curves, yet the car still feels entirely manageable and light to handle, giving a driver confidence to use all the acceleration and to cover the ground very quickly indeed. With all this goes quietness – complete absence of coachwork rattles or squeaks – and great comfort. The driving position is excellent, even if the seats are not ideally shaped for lateral support.

The brakes, too, came in for qualified praise, needing 'a firm shove on the pedal for high efficiency'. Yet they were 'very progressive and most reassuring from high speed with one exception – at speed in the wet, when there is invariably a momentary delay before they bite through the water film. In heavy rain, allowance has always to be made for this.'

Autocar found their Sovereign was good for a maximum of 119mph (191km/h) and – after a tune-up at Browns Lane – would reach 60mph from standstill in 11.1sec. Meanwhile, *Motor* had tested an overdrive model in their issue dated 4 November 1967. They persuaded JWK 811E to reach 118.5mph (190.7km/h) and to reach 60mph from rest in 9.2sec.

Motor actually saw their test as an adjunct to the one they had done of an automatic Jaguar 420 earlier in the year, and confined their comments mostly to the behaviour and effects of the overdrive transmission. This did make a difference, and one perhaps not most obviously associated with the traditional Daimler qualities:

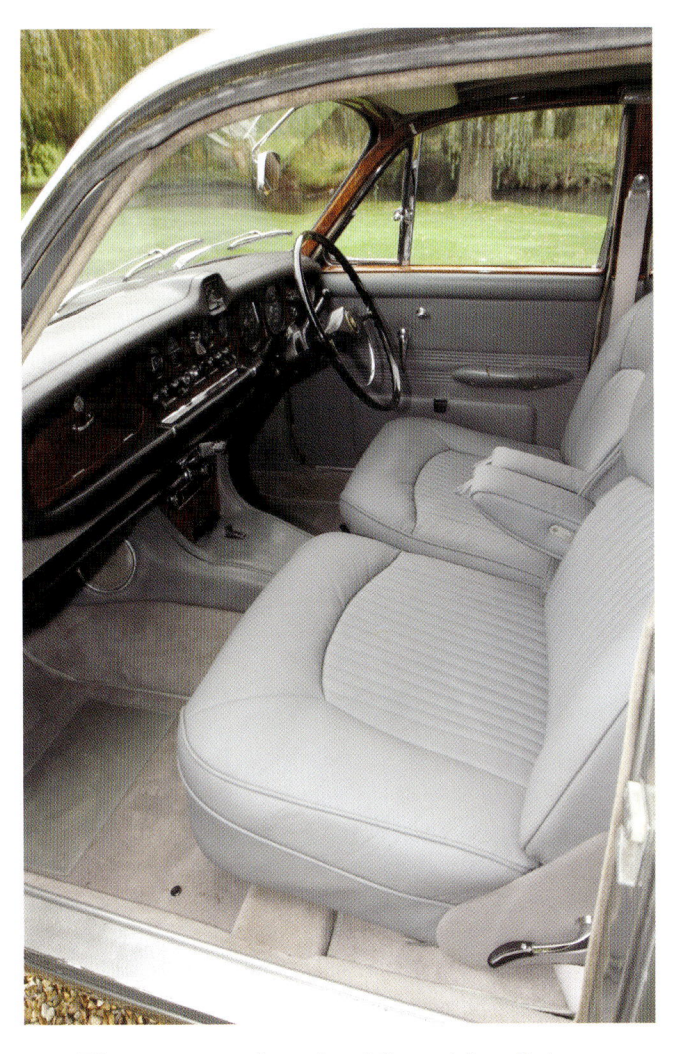

The seats were broad and flat, with pull-down armrests in the centre. The upholstery on these top models was invariably leather.

DAIMLER SOVEREIGN AND THE PRESS

The Sovereign was rightly seen very much as a 420 with different badges so few of the motoring magazines bothered to try one out once they had evaluated its Jaguar equivalent. The exception was *Autocar*. The British magazine bought one as a long-term test car in 1967 and reported very favourably on it in their 8 February 1968 issue, after it had covered 14,000 miles (22,500km).

Registered 8978 BH, the *Autocar* long-termer was an automatic model, and so typical of the majority of Sovereigns

JAGUAR 420 AND DAIMLER SOVEREIGN (1966–1969)

THE NEW 4·2 LITRE Daimler SOVEREIGN

Daimler enthusiasts everywhere will welcome this elegant and powerful new model which combines the very latest developments in modern high performance engineering and built-in safety with all the true characteristics that have made Daimler prestige motoring world famous. The new Sovereign is a car, which despite its compact dimensions, provides a spacious and luxurious 5 seater interior equipped with every refinement for the comfort of driver and passengers alike. Powered by a new 6 cylinder, twin o.h.c. 4.2 litre engine giving a flow of smooth effortless power at all speeds with remarkable acceleration and flexibility, it is equipped with either the latest Borg Warner Model 8 automatic transmission with dual drive range or new all-synchromesh gearbox with overdrive. 'Varamatic' power steering is standard. Independent suspension all-round, four wheel disc brakes with dual hydraulic systems, selective interior car temperature control, and a high efficiency cooling system are among its many outstanding features. Electrical equipment includes an alternator and pre-engaged starter, four-headlamp system, heated backlight fitted as standard, and transistorised clock mounted in padded safety screen rail. High quality leather hide upholstery, reclining front seats, centre folding arm rests front and rear, a fully lined 19 cubic feet luggage boot and twin fuel tanks with a total of 14 gallons capacity. With its most impressive appearance and the completeness of its specification, this fine new Daimler marks still another step forward for prestige motoring in the modern manner.

THE DAIMLER RANGE FOR 1967 ALSO INCLUDES
THE 2½ LITRE V8 SALOON, 4½ LITRE V8 MAJESTIC MAJOR SALOON
AND EIGHT-SEATER LIMOUSINE

Daimler dealers had called for the Sovereign, which was the first Daimler not to have any real Daimler components. This is how the cars were advertised when they were new.

BELOW LEFT: **Rear badging was simple and discreet in the way that Daimler customers no doubt expected.**

BELOW RIGHT: **Details did count – and the discreet Daimler logo on the seat-belt buckle of the Sovereign was just the sort of thing that made customers feel their car was that little bit more exclusive.**

JAGUAR 420 AND DAIMLER SOVEREIGN (1966–1969)

The Sovereign's dashboard was the same as that of the 420. This is an automatic model, with the selector quadrant just visible on the steering column above the steering wheel, which carries the Daimler logo.

BELOW LEFT: **The outboard handbrake was an anachronism on these cars but the customers suffered it to get the rest of a well-rounded package.**

BELOW RIGHT: **A capacious boot was part of the 420 and Sovereign package. This one is on a Sovereign.**

151

JAGUAR 420 AND DAIMLER SOVEREIGN (1966–1969)

The terms GT and sports occurred fairly regularly in the verbal and written comments of staff members who drove the manual car. One remarked that it was more sporting than many sports cars and certainly grander than almost any other GT proclaiming the distinction. No doubt much of this sporting flair stems from the availability of five ratios instead of three.

An increase in tyre pressures improved that sporting handling, and pumping the tyres up to 34psi instead of the recommended 30psi also reduced tyres squeal in cornering. 'A barely noticeable increase in road harshness seemed insignificant by comparison,' claimed *Motor*. Summarizing the benefits of the manual gearbox, the magazine concluded that this 'shows up to its best advantage when cruising on main roads or pressing on through minor roads and is worst in heavy traffic when the clutch ... feels appreciably heavier than on most modern designs.'

RIVALS

In Britain, the 420 was always carefully priced. The basic figures of £1,615 for the overdrive model and £1,678 for the automatic remained unchanged throughout the production run, although they could be inflated by the extra-cost options on offer.

Not many cars in Britain cost this much, and the 420 was of course even more expensive than the 3.8-litre S-type. Jaguar's strategy appears to have been to price it slightly above its natural rivals, but to justify that high price by offering just a little more performance than those rivals. Thus the Jaguar was faster and handled better than the similarly luxurious Rover 3-litre, which cost from £1,520 to just over £1,651 before purchase tax, depending on model. The same applied to the Vanden Plas 4-litre Princess R, priced at £1,650 in 1966.

Better performance than cars like these could provide came from the Alfa Romeo Giulia Sport GT Veloce at £1,585 – but that was certainly no match for a Jaguar 420 on appointments or sophistication. Likewise, the quick BMW 2000TI, at a basic price of £1,543, was perhaps tempting for some potential 420 customers, but it could not by any stretch of the imagination be considered a luxury saloon.

As for the Daimler, its target market was an even more restricted one. When announced at the 1966 Earls Court Motor Show, its UK showroom price (before purchase tax) was fixed at £1,724 for the overdrive version and £1,787 for the automatic. This made it much more expensive than the other badge-engineered Daimler – the 2½-litre V8 at £1,362 – and at the same time very much less expensive than the last of the 'real' Daimlers still on offer. These were in any case very low-volume cars, the Majestic Major costing just over £2,235 and the eight-seater Limousine variant being a massive £2,893.

Between £1,700 and £1,800 there was absolutely nothing to touch the Sovereign in Britain at that stage. In fact, the only other cars in the same price bracket were the Peugeot 404 cabriolet and coupé, at £1,750 and £1,800 respectively – and nobody would have considered them direct competitors for the Daimler. Cheaper and nearly as lavishly equipped was the Rover 3-litre Coupé at just over £1,651 in automatic form, but it had nothing like the performance of the Sovereign. Of course, there was always that very tempting proposition at a more affordable £1,678, in the shape of the new Jaguar 420 Automatic.

Browns Lane held Sovereign prices stable for 1967, not least because the car had still not come under any serious pressure from rivals. The Vanden Plas 4-litre R Touring Limousine had much of the Daimler's prestige appeal at £1,720, but it was not a well-liked car and could not offer the driving qualities associated with the Sovereign. Rover's contender was now much more serious, having acquired a powerful V8 engine and performance to match, and the 3.5-litre Coupé at £1,705 may well have tempted some potential Sovereign owners away. However, handling and roadholding were still not in the same league.

Sovereign prices went up considerably for the 1968 Motor Show. With the automatic model now priced at £1,849, the Rover still looked an attractive alternative at £1,775. Mercedes-Benz had meanwhile introduced their 220 saloon at just over £1,808, but despite impeccable build quality this was neither a luxury saloon nor a performance car. The most convincing competition once again came from Browns Lane, for the 1968 show brought with it the new Jaguar XJ6, priced at £1,810 for the 4.2-litre De Luxe model with overdrive and at £1,875 for the same car in automatic form.

At higher prices, there really was very little. The next step up was to Bentley and Rolls-Royce models, the cheapest of which cost £5,620 in 1967 – for which buyers could have had three Jaguar 420s plus a quite respectable Ford or Vauxhall family saloon! Seen in that light, the Jaguar represented quite exceptional value for money.

JAGUAR 420 IN THE USA

Once again, the arrival of a new saloon model brought about a realignment of the Jaguar catalogue in the USA. The 420 did not cross the Atlantic until 1967, when it joined the newly renamed 340 and the confusingly renamed 420G. The 420 replaced the S-type as the mid-range Jaguar saloon for the US market, and this was exactly what that market wanted; US buyers tended to want as much power, performance and equipment as they could get on cars at this price level. So Jaguar's US advertising copy for the 420 got straight to the point: 'This is the new Jaguar sports sedan,' read one 1967 advertisement. 'If you love our XK-E, this is the only sports sedan you could be happy with.'

The start of 1968 was notable for the introduction of Federal Motor Vehicle Safety Standards, with which all new cars sold in the USA had to comply. As a result, the US-model 420 had some special features. Most obvious was that the outboard headlamps had the same 5in (127mm) diameter as the inboard pair, to meet a US requirement for standardized sizes. As the wings were pressed to take 7in (178mm) lamps, a special filler piece was inserted around the outer lamps.

US buyers took some time to recognize the virtues of radial-ply tyres, and so the whitewall tyres that were standard on 420s for the USA were the Dunlop RS5 cross-ply types that had never been fitted to British 420s and had been replaced on S-types as long ago as 1964. Chromed wire wheels were standard wear on all the 976 examples of the 420 that went to the USA, and it also appears that a few of the final cars were equipped with electric windows. These must have been fitted by dealers as an incentive to buy a 420 at a time when the new XJ6 was known to be on its way.

A number of 420s sold in the USA were also fitted with an optional air-conditioning unit, which was not available on home-market cars. This was a Delaney Gallay Delanair unit, similar to the unit available as an option on the Mk X Jaguar. The system's main components were an engine-driven compressor, a radiator fitted ahead of the engine coolant radiator, and a large evaporator and drier unit that was fitted in the boot above the rear suspension. The system's controls were in a separate panel between the sliding switches for the heating and ventilating system and the panel containing the auxiliary switches and dials, and an air outlet in the rear parcel shelf brought cooled air into the passenger cabin.

JAGUAR 420 AND THE US PRESS

The first US magazine to report on a 420 in any depth was *Car and Driver*, which ran a comparison test in its July 1967 issue. The 420 was up against a Mercury Cougar XR-7. To British eyes, the comparison was outrageous: a cheap and vulgar two-door hot rod could hardly be stacked up against Jaguar's finest. However, *Car and Driver* made the point that Ford's Mercury division had carefully dissected the Jaguar's appeal and had grafted as much as possible of that appeal onto one of its own products.

More realistic was the test report in the December 1967 issue of *Road & Track*. Their overdrive 420 hit 60mph from rest in 11sec, and went on to a 120mph (193km/h) top speed. That was fast by European standards, but America was then going through the muscle-car craze, which meant that the 420 was 'no match for the medium-price American V8 with automatic transmission'. What it did offer, though, 'that the American car doesn't is the ability to cruise safely at any speed right up to maximum ... without worry about direction control, braking capability or engine damage.'

The magazine liked the 420 a lot. 'In our opinion it is the most esthetically successful of the whole series of Jaguar compact sedans, as well as looking considerably better than the 420G!' They thought its suspension offered 'as good a combination of ride and handling as you'll find in any contemporary sedan,' and observed that Jaguar were 'taking the requirements of American customers more seriously these days – with the result that the 420 seems better suited to American driving than any Jaguar sedan we've tested before.' However, they had not allowed for the average US male being rather larger than his UK equivalent; anybody over average male size was likely to find the space in the back seat inadequate, thought *Road & Track*.

Sadly, the 420 was also beginning to show the age of its design. The heating and ventilating were also not up to the latest standards and, aesthetically,

> *It is not a modern look that the 420 possesses: rather is it a classical one, and the age of the basic structure shows through in such matters as the comparatively small glass area and the layout of controls and instruments. ... The control center of the 420 is most handsome and elegant, but its engineering is of another era.*

JAGUAR 420 AND DAIMLER SOVEREIGN (1966–1969)

Nonetheless, the young *Road & Track* took on this 420 as its first-ever long-term test car, reporting on 20,000 miles (32,000km) of ownership in its July 1968 issue. There had been some minor failures – the radio aerial winder, the rev counter, a bumper bracket, which worked loose, an oil leak from the differential – and the overdrive had twice given trouble, ending with an uncharacteristic failure. Engine noise was traced to a prematurely worn tappet, but perhaps the most memorable problem was with tyres. The RS5s, worn out after little more than 11,000 miles (17,500km) of hard driving, were replaced by Goodyear radials, which seemed to be much more durable. *Road & Track* remained impressed.

The 420, steered, stopped and handled as well as when new. Its body was not as tight or as rattle-free as it originally was, but in general the car was still highly pleasurable to drive. Expensive motoring, yes – but if you can afford it, why not? There's nothing else quite like it.

IDENTIFICATION – JAGUAR 420 AND DAIMLER SOVEREIGN

Identification numbers are stamped on a plate in the engine compartment, attached to the left-hand inner wing. These numbers are repeated elsewhere, as shown below.

Car Number
The car number, also known as the chassis number or VIN, is stamped into the bonnet-catch channel, just ahead of the radiator header tank. A typical car number might be 1F 1234 DN. The prefix identifies the model, the numerals are the car's serial number, and the letters show the transmission type.

The prefix codes are:

1A	Daimler Sovereign
1F	Jaguar 420

Cars fitted with power-assisted steering have an additional P prefix; in practice, all Sovereigns came with PAS, and therefore their prefix code is always P1A.

The serial number sequences are:

	RHD	LHD
420	1001–8595	25001–27629
Sovereign	30001–35476	70001–70355

The suffixes decode as follows:

BW	Borg Warner automatic gearbox
DN	Laycock de Normanville overdrive

Engine Number
The engine number is stamped on the right-hand side of the cylinder block above the oil filter and again at the front of the cylinder head casting, beside the front spark-plug hole. A typical engine number might be 7A 12345/8. This breaks down into three elements:

7A	Engine type identifier (Daimler Sovereign) The prefix for a Jaguar 420 engine is 7F
12345	Serial number
/8	Compression ratio (/8 for 8:1 compression, /7 for 7:1, /9 for 9:1)

Serial number sequences for both Daimler and Jaguar engines begin at 1001.

Body Number
The body number is stamped on a small plate attached to the right-hand side of the body behind the rear bumper. (It should not be confused with a similar plate on the left-hand side that shows the Pressed Steel reference number.)

Gearbox Number
On all manual gearboxes, the gearbox number is stamped on a small shoulder at the left-hand rear corner of the gearbox casing, and on the top cover around the rim of the core-plug aperture. On automatic gearboxes, the number is stamped on a plate attached to the left-hand side of the gearbox casing.

SPECIFICATIONS – JAGUAR 420 AND DAIMLER SOVEREIGN

Engine
Type XK 6-cylinder, with cast-iron block and aluminium-alloy head
4235cc (92.07 x 106mm)
Twin overhead camshafts, chain-driven
Seven-bearing crankshaft
Compression ratio 8:1 (7:1 and 9:1 available)
Two SU HD8 carburettors
245bhp at 5,500rpm (with standard compression)
283lb ft at 3,750rpm

Transmission
Hydraulically operated clutch with 10in diameter (manual) or torque converter (automatic)
Four-speed manual gearbox (Jaguar type with synchromesh on all forward gears)
Ratios 3.04:1, 1.97:1, 1.33:1, 1.00:1
Optional overdrive with 0.77:1 ratio.
Three-speed Borg Warner Model 8 automatic
Ratios 2.40:1, 1.46:1, 1.00:1

Axle ratio
3.31:1 to 1967 (1968 on manual models)
3.54:1 from 1967 (automatic) or 1968 (manual)
3.77:1 with overdrive

Suspension, steering and brakes
Independent front suspension with wishbones, coil springs and anti-roll bar
Independent rear suspension with lower wishbone and upper link by driveshaft, radius arms and paired coil springs
Burman recirculating-ball, worm-and-nut steering; Variomatic power assistance optional
Disc brakes with 11.9in diameter front and 11.4in rear, with servo assistance as standard

Dimensions
Overall length   187.5in (4,762mm)
Overall width   67in (1,702mm)
Overall height   56.25in (1,429mm)
Wheelbase   107.75in (2,737mm)
Front track   55.5in (1,410mm)
Rear track   54.5in (1,384mm)

Wheels and tyres
15in steel disc wheels standard, with 5.5in rims
15in wire-spoke wheels with 5.5in rims optional (standard in USA)
6.40 x 15 cross-ply or 185 x 15 radial tyres

Kerb weight
3,696lb (1,676kg)

PERFORMANCE FIGURES – JAGUAR 420 AND DAIMLER SOVEREIGN

Road test figures for the Jaguar 420 and Daimler Sovereign showed some quite wide variations. Although some of the variation can be explained by the altered gearing that arrived in 1967, it is hard to reconcile some of the differences recorded. The figures below represent approximate averages and should therefore be seen as representative rather than definitive. Note in particular how the overdrive Daimler seems to accelerate faster than the overdrive Jaguar, but the picture is reversed with the automatic models.

420 overdrive
0–60mph   9.9sec
Maximum speed   120mph (193km/h)
Fuel consumption   15.7mpg (18ltr/100km)

420 automatic
0–60mph   9.4sec
Maximum speed   115mph (185km/h)
Fuel consumption   15.5mpg (18.3ltr/100km)

Sovereign overdrive
0–60mph   9.2sec
Maximum speed   118.5mph (191km/h)
Fuel consumption   15.6mpg (18.2ltr/100km)

Sovereign automatic
0–60mph   11.4sec
Maximum speed   119mph (191.5km/h)
Fuel consumption   17.5mpg (16.2ltr/100km)

PAINT AND TRIM COLOURS – JAGUAR 420 AND DAIMLER SOVEREIGN

The same options were available on both models. Note that the later range, introduced just before the end of 420 production, was found on relatively few 420s but was primarily for the Sovereigns, which remained in production for another year.

Some cars were painted and trimmed to special order. For example, car number PIF 26339 BW – a US-market Jaguar 420 – was ordered with a specification of Opalescent Silver Grey paint with Daimler Sovereign interior trim (with perforated leather) in Black. The car was sent from Browns Lane to the Vanden Plas works at Kingsbury for its special-order paint and trim on 23 March 1967 and returned to Jaguar to be despatched on 6 April. It finally reached the purchaser in Paterson, New Jersey, on 16 May.

October 1966 to June 1968

There were eleven standard paint colours, including three opalescent (metallic). Nine interior-trim options were listed. (NB Grey was sometimes listed as Ash Grey.)

Body	Interior
Beige	Light Tan, Red, Suede Green or Tan
Black	Grey, Light Tan, Red or Tan
British Racing Green	Beige, Light Tan, Suede Green or Tan
Cream	Dark Blue, Light Blue or Red
Dark Blue	Grey, Light Blue or Red
Golden Sand	Light Tan or Red
Opalescent Maroon	Beige or Maroon
Opalescent Silver Blue	Dark Blue or Grey
Opalescent Silver Grey	Dark Blue, Grey, Light Blue or Red
Warwick Grey	Dark Blue, Light Tan or Red
Willow Green	Beige, Grey, Light Tan or Suede Green

July 1968 to July 1969

There were ten standard paint colours. The opalescent finishes were no longer available. Seven interior-trim options were listed.

Body	Interior
Ascot Fawn	Beige, Cinnamon, Red or Suede Green
Black	Cinnamon, Grey or Red
British Racing Green	Beige, Cinnamon or Suede Green
Cream	Dark Blue, Light Blue or Red
Dark Blue	Grey, Light Blue or Red
Light Blue	Dark Blue, Grey or Light Blue
Regency Red	Beige or Grey
Sable	Beige, Cinnamon or Grey
Warwick Grey	Cinnamon, Dark Blue or Red
Willow Green	Beige, Cinnamon, Grey or Suede Green

SO YOU WANT TO BUY A JAGUAR 420 OR A DAIMLER SOVEREIGN?

Bizarrely (considering the specification and controversial looks of the S-types), 420s and Sovereigns have historically been cheaper to buy than S-types. Perhaps that partly reflects their less deliberately sporting demeanour; these are really luxury cars with the added ingredient of Jaguar performance and handling. However, their bodyshells rust just as badly as those of the S-type and their passenger cabins are subject to the same expensive wear and tear. Gearboxes and engines suffer from the same maladies, but the 4.2-litre engine was probably the very best version of the classic XK twin-cam and is ideally suited to these small luxury saloons.

For more detailed advice on buying one of these cars, see the buying panel in Chapter 9.

CHAPTER TWELVE

SPECIAL VARIANTS OF THE MK 2, S-TYPE AND 420

Browns Lane had quite enough work on its hands without producing special variants of the compact Jaguars. So it was no surprise that other companies stepped into the breach. Not only did performance enhancements become available, but so did major body transformations – an expensive thing to achieve on a monocoque shell like that used for all the compact models. However, the 're-bodied' compact Jaguars were never numerous, and are now seen as all the more exotic for that very reason.

COOMBS MK 2

The Guildford Jaguar dealers Coombs and Son had started modifying cars for racing in 1958 and had built three competition machines out of early 3.4-litre models. By 1960, they made the benefit of their experience available to customers, and over the next seven years they modified between thirty and forty Mk 2s for customers.

Most of the Coombs Jaguars were 3.8-litre models, although a handful of 3.4s were also converted. Essentially, the Coombs conversion consisted of an uprated engine matched by steering and suspension modifications, but the company offered a menu of options from which customers could choose what they wanted. Options included an additional fuel tank, a wood-rim steering wheel and a chrome-plated boot rack. Coombs would also modify the rear wheel arches, removing the spats and making up rolled edges to match the profile of the front wheel arches. The primary objective of this was to improve access for wheel changing

The Coombs Mk 2 was specially prepared to give maximum road performance but it was also suitable for competition. The neat rear wheel arch modification with its rolled edge is so much more attractive than the half-hearted spat on the standard production car. This example now belongs to the Jaguar Heritage Driving Experience and was photographed at one of their events.

157

■ SPECIAL VARIANTS OF THE MK 2, S-TYPE AND 420

The Coombs Jaguar racing legend even fuelled advertising. This August 1963 advertisement from Shell focused on racing Mk 2 BUY 12, which had been Graham Hill's mount that season.

during motor-sport events, but the modification improved the appearance of the car so much that it is surprising Jaguar themselves did not adopt the modification for production cars.

Not all the Coombs cars had the same state of tune, but the typical engine had 9:1 compression pistons, a lightened flywheel, and a different carburettor air-intake system. The whole bottom-end assembly would be balanced, and the cylinder head would be gas-flowed. A 3.8-litre saloon with a full set of Coombs modifications was claimed to be fast enough to keep pace with a 3.8-litre E-type up to 100mph (160km/h).

It may have been in response to the Coombs cars that Jaguar itself investigated building a competition derivative of the 3.8-litre Mk 2. Philip Porter's *The Jaguar Scrapbook* quotes an October 1960 memo from design chief Claude Baily to the competitions and production departments, instructing them to build a right-hand-drive 3.8-litre 'Gran Turismo' project car. The competitions department modified an unpainted bodyshell, stiffening it in several areas and reshaping the inner front wing to fit around a triple-carburettor engine.

Peter Wilson remembered this car from his time with the Jaguar competitions department for the July 1985 issue of *Thoroughbred & Classic Cars* magazine:

SPECIAL VARIANTS OF THE MK 2, S-TYPE AND 420

A single car ... was roughly assembled. The specification incorporated many features of the racing version, including revised suspension, wide offset wire wheels, increased fuel tankage (achieved by mounting the spare wheel in the boot and fitting a circular tank within the spare wheel well), high ratio steering and individual competition type bucket seats.

With three 2in SU carburettors, the engine would have developed at least 265bhp, which was the power output of the triple-carburettor 3.8-litre in the E-type at the time. However, remembered Wilson, 'it was decided at a fairly early stage not to continue with the project and the car was returned to standard.'

MK 2 COUNTY ESTATE

In the late 1950s, racing drivers Duncan Hamilton and Mike Hawthorn came up with the idea of turning a compact Jaguar into a support vehicle for racing events. Hamilton already owned two Mk VII Jaguars that had been converted to estate cars, and he approached Sir William Lyons with the idea. Lyons was not convinced that there would be sufficient demand for such a car, but Hamilton and Hawthorn decided to go ahead on their own and persuaded motor racing artist Roy Nockolds to draw up a suitable shape.

Hawthorn was tragically killed at the wheel of his 3.4-litre Jaguar in January 1959 and the project lapsed for a while. Nevertheless, Jaguar themselves revived it a few years later and had a car built during 1962 by Jones Bros (Coachbuilders) Ltd, a London company better known for commercial and taxi bodies. The car left Jaguar as a 3.8-litre overdrive saloon (chassis number 207515 DN) in January 1962 finished in British Racing Green and upholstered in Tan. It was not registered until it returned to Jaguar in September, when it became 3672 VC.

Jaguar used the car, which took on the name of County, as a support tender for various competition events in the early 1960s. It finished its days at Browns Lane as a factory hack, and was then sold on to racing driver John Pearson. It subsequently passed through the hands of a number of Jaguar enthusiasts, gaining wire wheels in place of the original steel discs and, more recently, being further modified.

The so-called County estate looks the worse for wear in most known photographs and was certainly used hard as a service back-up vehicle. The design was competent, but unspectacular.
JDHT

■ SPECIAL VARIANTS OF THE MK 2, S-TYPE AND 420

CALLUM MK 2

Ian Callum took over as design director at Jaguar in 1999 and was responsible for all the new Jaguars released after that date. However, he was not only a professional designer but also an enthusiast for customized cars and hot rods, and ever since childhood he had admired the Mk 2 Jaguar and had wanted to make his own modifications to it.

In 2012, he approached Classic Motor Cars of Bridgnorth in Shropshire, a company with a long history of working with classic Jaguars, with the idea of creating his own very special customized Mk 2. The project, which was entirely personal for Callum and was not part of his work for Jaguar, was expected to take nine months but in practice took twice as long, and the result was revealed in 2014 at the same time as CMC opened their new factory.

Callum said that his idea was to create a car that was usable every day without becoming too modern or losing its character. So the car was very recognizably a Mk 2 Jaguar on the outside, but with a large number of modernizing features under the skin. Most obvious of the changes was the replacement of the standard bumpers with new composite items that sat flush with the body contours. In addition, the wheel arches were widened to cover wider tracks and the front wings incorporated louvred air vents to improve under-bonnet airflow. Modern convenience features included modified door handles, central locking and heated front and rear screens.

This 'blueprint' from CMC shows the key dimensions of the Callum Mk 2 and highlights the main visual characteristics.

SPECIAL VARIANTS OF THE MK 2, S-TYPE AND 420

Recognizably a Mk 2, the Callum car nevertheless has cleaner, more modern lines.

Under the skin, the front subframe was repositioned to improve the anti-dive characteristics and an electric power-assisted steering system was added. CMC designed a completely new independent rear suspension, incorporating an anti-roll bar and adjustable dampers. The ride height was lowered by 1.2in (30mm) all round and the car ran on 17in split-rim polished aluminium alloy wheels, with their hubs and spokes painted to match the body. The front wheels had 6.5in rims and ran on 205/55 x 17 tyres, while the rear wheels had 7.5in rims and ran on 225/50 x 17 tyres. Braking was upgraded with 320mm ventilated front discs and 280mm solid rear discs, all with fully floating single-pot calipers.

The engine was a modified XK straight-six, with a swept volume of 4.3 litres and a power output of 260PS (256bhp); it was built to deliver torque rather than power, and had a

The Callum Mk 2 was shown at the prestigious Salon Privé when new. Its lowered stance is well illustrated in this view.

■ SPECIAL VARIANTS OF THE MK 2, S-TYPE AND 420

The reinterpretation of the dashboard on the Callum car adds modernity to the classic design.

The rear seat combines the olde-worlde feel of the Mk 2 with modern touches such as the head restraints and diamond-quilted backrest inserts.

maximum of 280lb ft at 5,000rpm with twin SU HD8 carburettors. The gearbox was a modern five-speed manual type, and the car had a 20gal (91ltr) fuel tank to improve its range.

Once the car had been announced, CMC received a number of enquiries and at the time of writing had agreed to build a dozen more, all to individual customer specification. Ian Callum had agreed to spend time with each of the customers to help them decide on the final specification of their cars. The first car to be laid down was to be a left-hand-drive model for the USA that would be finished by the end of 2015. This and others were expected to cost between £350,000 and £375,000 each – or well over four times as much as the latest 550PS (542bhp), 5-litre Jaguar XFR-S saloon.

COOMBS S-TYPE

Coombs of Guildford are best known for their work on the Mk 1 and Mk 2 compact Jaguars, but they also modified just one 3.8-litre S-type. Some time in the mid-1960s, the owner of one of their modified Mk 2s asked them to improve the performance of his S-type, and according to the Coombs Register (www.jaguarmk.2.info/coombs_register.html) this car was metallic dark green.

Unfortunately, the precise details of the modifications made to it are not known. However, it is reasonable to suppose that the engine received much the same treatment as Coombs offered for the 3.8-litre Mk 2. In those cars, the crankshaft, conrods and clutch assembly were balanced, 9:1 compression pistons were fitted, the flywheel was lightened, the cylinder head was gas-flowed and a new carburettor air intake was added. Other 'standard' modifications included a new exhaust, adjustable dampers and higher-ratio steering. No doubt the Coombs-modified 3.8-litre S-type was a little slower than the 3.8-litre Mk 2 from the same company because of its greater weight, but it would still have been a very fast car in its day.

BERTONE JAGUAR FT

The story of the Bertone Jaguar FT is one of those that will probably run and run until some clearer evidence becomes available. Most experts believe that just two cars were built, but there is a distinct possibility that there were actually more.

What is undeniable is that towards the end of 1965 Jaguar's Italian importer for northern Italy, Tarchini SVAJ, came up with the idea of creating a special grand touring coupé that would be built in small numbers and distributed through the Italian dealer network – and elsewhere, if there was interest. As Tarchini were based in Turin, it was only to be

SPECIAL VARIANTS OF THE MK 2, S-TYPE AND 420

The Bertone-designed car is seen here at the Turin Motor Show when new. Examples of the standard Jaguar product can be seen on the stand in the background.

expected that they would turn to one of the leading Turin coachbuilders for the car's special coupé bodywork and the choice fell upon Bertone.

A left-hand-drive 3.8-litre S-type (commission number 1B 78923 DN) was shipped out to Turin to become the prototype. The Jaguar records describe this as a 'drive-away chassis unit' and show that it left Browns Lane on 23 December 1965. By the time of the Geneva Motor Show in March 1966, Bertone had turned it into a two-door coupé and the car was displayed as a 'Jaguar FT Bertone', the 'FT' being in honour of Dr Ferruccio Tarchini who had founded the Italian dealership. The show car was finished in metallic grey with red seats.

The Jaguar FT was one of the first cars designed for Bertone by the company's recently appointed head of design, Marcello Gandini. Gandini would go on to create some stunning designs such as the Lamborghini Miura and Countach and the Lancia Stratos. However, he was clearly still finding his feet when he designed the Jaguar and, as Rob de la Rive Box and Richard Crump put it in their book *The Automotive Art of Bertone*, 'one gets the feeling that Bertone was not relaxed with this British-built car.' Although the large glass area was a commendable feature, there were elements of awkwardness about the design, and the overall proportions of the S-type underframe did not lend themselves well to a two-door coupé.

Gandini's design nevertheless retained a number of Jaguar elements, such as the front sidelights and wraparound turn signal lamps. The rear wheel-arch shape echoed that of the Jaguar original, and there was a recognizably Jaguar grille integrated into the front end, which otherwise bore some resemblance to Bertone's design for the Alfa Romeo 2600 Sprint. The car retained its standard S-type wheel trims and a leaping Jaguar mascot on the nose of the bonnet.

This first car was shipped over to Browns Lane at some point, probably over the summer of 1966, and among those who examined it was body engineer Cyril Crouch, who still retained fond memories of it nearly thirty years later:

■ SPECIAL VARIANTS OF THE MK 2, S-TYPE AND 420

These three photographs of the Bertone S-type when new show the car's very Italianate lines. It was certainly more Bertone than Jaguar, although perhaps not one of the styling house's more successful designs. The deep windows look wrong from some angles and the wheelbase looks too short.

SPECIAL VARIANTS OF THE MK 2, S-TYPE AND 420

I thought that was an excellent job they made of that; a beautiful paint finish, I remember, a greyish finish … metallic grey. This metallic was rather different to the metallics we know now. I immediately associated it with these rather wonderful marble gravestones that you see; it was a sort of marble effect rather than the spatter of a metallic. It was quite intriguing! The seats were red. It was a very elegant-looking car. I took it out on the road, and was very pleased with it. I was very sorry that we weren't going to continue with it. It was a one-off and I think we were a little unfair when we said it wasn't particularly good … that could have been overcome. I personally liked the car very much. I think they did an excellent job on it and their coachbuilding was really excellent – which they are renowned for, of course.

Just one other car is thought to have been built with the Bertone coupé design, this time based on a 420 and commissioned by a private customer. The car resurfaced after many years in storage and was sold at auction. When first rediscovered, it was on wire wheels.

165

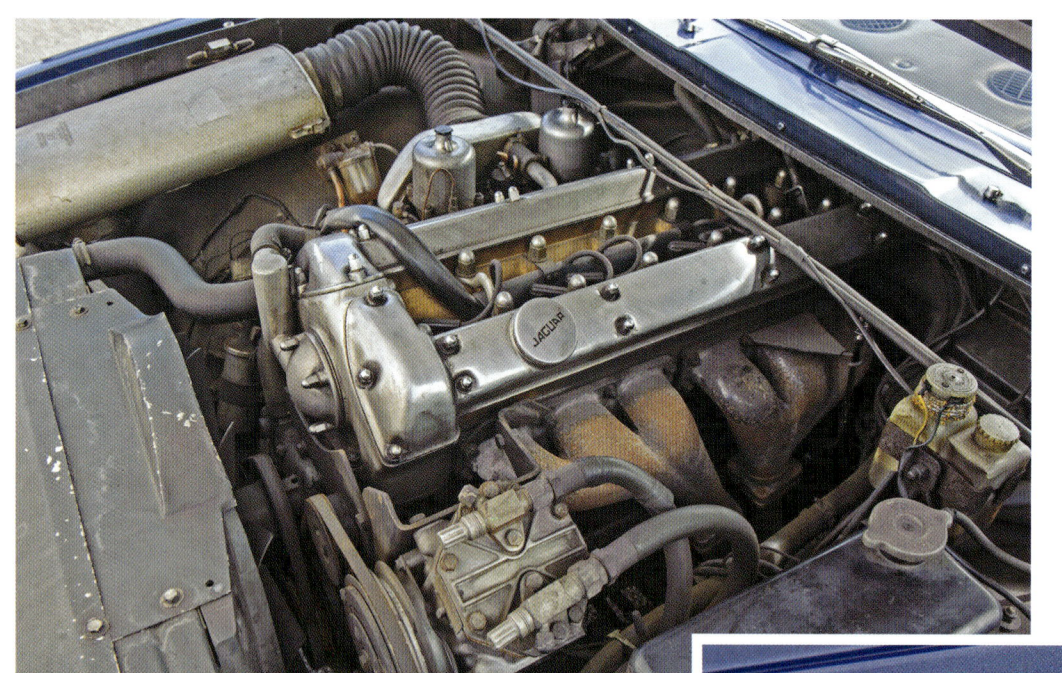

■ SPECIAL VARIANTS OF THE MK 2, S-TYPE AND 420

Engine bay accessibility in the Bertone cars was much better than in Jaguar's standard production models. This is the 4.2-litre car.

BELOW: **Bertone 'signed' both Jaguar coupés with this logo.**

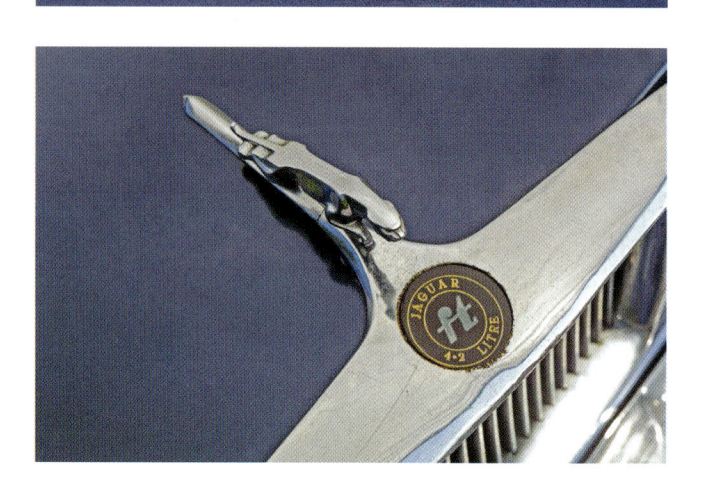

This was the bonnet badge on the 4.2-litre Bertone car when it was rediscovered. Whether it was original is open to question; the car had also been fitted with a chrome 'Coupé' badge on the boot lid, but that badge had come from a Rover!

Tarchini subsequently ordered a further twelve 'rolling chassis' for bodying in Italy and these left Browns Lane between November 1966 and February 1967. However, by this time the 420 model had become available so those rolling chassis were all supplied with the larger engine and were numbered as 420 types. They probably represented the number of cars that the Tarchini dealership believed it could sell. As orders came in, the rolling chassis would presumably have been sent on to Bertone to be bodied.

Those dozen were delivered in two batches: the first six left Browns Lane on 6 December 1966, the second six on 17 February 1967. Their commission numbers were PIF 25417 DN to PIF 25422 DN and 1A/1F 26066 to 26071 respectively and the Jaguar records describe them as 'CKD'. The commission numbers for the second batch are reproduced as they appear in the Jaguar build records. Probably the person compiling those records hedged his bets about what the rolling chassis would eventually turn into: if they had been built up as Daimler Sovereigns they would have used the 1A prefix; if they had become Jaguar 420s, they would have used the 1F prefix.

It is at this point that the real mystery begins. Only one of those dozen rolling chassis is known for sure to have been built up as a Bertone FT coupé, and this carried the first of

166

SPECIAL VARIANTS OF THE MK 2, S-TYPE AND 420

The interior of the FT cars – this is the 4.2-litre again – was typical of the mid-1960s Italian GT style and very different from Jaguar's own passenger cabins.

those commission numbers, PIF 25417 DN. The completed car was bought by a Spanish aristocrat, but much of its history remains obscure before it was rediscovered in 2012 and sold at auction. At that time, the car had wire wheels, black paint and black vinyl upholstery.

The confusion comes about to some extent because photography in the 1960s was more commonly in black and white than in colour, so the identities of cars in surviving photographs are sometimes hard to pin down. The story of the first, 3.8-litre, car is clearest because it remained in the Tarchini family and retained its steel wheels with S-type trims. Originally metallic grey with a red interior, the car reappeared in 2014 in dark-blue metallic with tan seats. Those colour changes may well have been made before it was displayed at the November 1966 Turin Motor Show. It had certainly been modified in minor details by that stage, having lost the circular horn grilles originally fitted between the inner headlamps and the main radiator grille. By the time of its sale in 2012, it had acquired rubber-faced over-riders front and rear, side repeater indicators on the front wings, and a driver's door mirror. The boot lid also carried a chromed 'Coupé' script (borrowed from a Rover of the period) alongside the special 'FT Tarchini' badge.

The known 420 was all-black by 2012, although it could have been repainted at some time in its life. However, photographs mentioned in a March 2012 *Classic Cars* article about it show 'a dark green-bluish car' and a 'light green' one, apparently with a light-coloured interior. Old colour photographs can fade, and the suggested identification of the 'dark green-bluish car' with the 3.8-litre prototype, which

SPECIAL VARIANTS OF THE MK 2, S-TYPE AND 420

later became blue, is plausible. However, the identity of the light green car with a light-coloured interior is less easy to establish. That then raises the possibility of at least a third car, now missing.

Finally, what happened to the rest of the dozen rolling chassis delivered to Tarchini in 1966–67? If one of the dozen became the Spanish car and another became the possible light green car, that still leaves ten 420 rolling chassis unaccounted for. Nobody knows for certain, but it is hard to believe that they were simply left to rot somewhere in Italy and ultimately scrapped.

FRUA COUPÉ

Bertone was not the only Italian coachbuilder to rebody the S-type Jaguar. The car's controversial looks also attracted the Torinese coachbuilder Pietro Frua, who probably reasoned that this was a potentially great car in need of a more attractive body.

Photographs of the Frua-bodied car are rare. These two show that it was very much in the contemporary Italian GT mould – and even less Jaguar-like than the Bertone coupé.

Despite establishing a solid relationship with Maserati after 1963, the Frua coachworks tried their hand at several British and German chassis in the 1960s, with notable designs for the AC 428 and for Glas in Germany. A contract with Jaguar for special bodywork would have been a valuable addition to the company's portfolio, but it was not to be. The single Frua-bodied S-type displayed at the 1966 Geneva Motor Show remained unique.

The car was built on a left-hand-drive 3.8-litre underframe and featured wire wheels. Like Bertone, Frua thought the car would work well as a three-door fastback coupé, but unlike Bertone believed that a Jaguar grille at the front would be an encumbrance. So the car was built with a wide horizontal grille that incorporated its fog lights, and was distinctly reminiscent of the 1964 Bristol 408. However, the light-blue car ended up looking distinctively (and attractively) Frua and not very Jaguar, and Browns Lane seems not to have shown any real interest in it.

The car passed into the hands of Jaguar's dealer in Rome, Fattori & Montani, who displayed it on the international show circuit during 1967. It was eventually sold to an Italian gentleman called Francesco Respino, and much later reached the UK, where it was registered with the number FNN 714C.

RADFORD 420 CONVERTIBLE

The London-based Radford coachbuilding company is perhaps best remembered for its conversions of Rolls-Royce and Bentley cars in the 1950s, notably the Countryman adaptations with their picnic equipment and folding rear seats. The original company was sold on in 1961, but the new owners retained its name and in the 1960s carried out some luxury conversions on Minis. In 1967, they also turned a right-hand-drive Jaguar 420 into an elegant convertible.

Radford converted the car from a fully built 420 saloon with wire wheels, modifying the body with two long doors instead of four, and reinforcing the lower shell to compensate for the loss of a fixed roof. The car was finished in silver with a blue convertible top and seats, and had been completed by September 1967.

The car was rebuilt to original condition in 2013 by Classic Restorations (Scotland). It was displayed at that year's Classic Car Show at the NEC wearing the registration number JTS 500 and remains a fine and inspiring example of what might have been.

SPECIAL VARIANTS OF THE MK 2, S-TYPE AND 420

The Radford convertible was a complete success and arguably looked even better with its top up than with it down – a rare design achievement. It remained unique.
JDHT

169

CHAPTER THIRTEEN

THE LEGACY OF THE COMPACT JAGUARS

After the last of the compact saloons left the assembly lines at Browns Lane in 1969, Jaguar vanished from the market it had so successfully created. The new XJ6 model, introduced in 1968, became the sole Jaguar saloon available, as the result of deliberate planning by Sir William Lyons. The compact range had grown up piecemeal over the previous decade or so, with the result that that by the middle of the 1960s there were too many different varieties of the type. Lyons wanted to streamline the Jaguar range to reduce manufacturing complication and increase profits.

So it was that the compacts disappeared. Whether Sir William might have introduced another saloon range below the XJ6 a few years down the line is something that cannot be known, although it would have been only natural to look again at a second model range once XJ sales had settled down.

It did not happen because during 1968 Jaguar had become part of the British Leyland Motor Corporation, which also owned most of the other important players in the British motor industry. From quite early on, British Leyland management tried to develop a corporate strategy for the makes it owned, and although the process took some years and was never wholly successful it did have some effect. For Jaguar, it cut off whatever ambition the company might have had to extend its saloon range downwards. That market slot was more than filled by Rover (with their V8-engined 3500 model) and Triumph (with their six-cylinder 2.5 PI and its later derivatives), and there was no room for a smaller Jaguar saloon.

So under British Leyland, Jaguar was kept in its place as the maker of the company's flagship saloons (some of them badged as Daimlers, although this was really no more than badge-engineering). Even when the company became independent once again after it was floated on the stock market in 1984, there were more important things to do than to worry about a new smaller saloon. The most important task facing chairman John Egan in the later 1980s was to ensure Jaguar's long-term survival by making it profitable and stable.

As a result, there was no second Jaguar saloon range alongside the multiple generations of the flagship XJ series until 1998 – almost thirty years after the last of the compacts had been built. In the meantime, Jaguar had changed hands yet again, having been bought by Ford in 1989.

Ford management decided there should be a second Jaguar saloon range once again, and so keen was the company for this to be seen as the spiritual successor to the much-loved compacts of the 1960s that the new car was marketed under the name of one of them: it was called the S-type. However, this was far from being an echo of the Jaguar sales strategy of the 1950s and 1960s, because public expectations had changed quite fundamentally in the intervening years.

Looking back at the heyday of the compact Jaguars, they stood out with such distinction because they really had no direct rivals. No other manufacturer offered anything quite like them, and certainly not at the price. Their combination of luxury and performance was simply unequalled.

Inevitably, some of the compact Jaguar formula rubbed off on the products of other manufacturers. In the thirty years between the last compact Jaguars and the new S-type, many car makers had combined luxury with performance in a car that was usable as an everyday family saloon. Therefore, by the late 1990s many cars reflected the long-term influence of the compacts.

The saloon car market had also stratified, particularly under the influence of the ultra-successful BMW brand. In BMW's terms, that stratification was expressed by its three saloon ranges: the 7 Series (a large luxury saloon that rivalled the big Jaguars), the 5 Series (a medium saloon

THE LEGACY OF THE COMPACT JAGUARS

approximately equivalent to the compact Jaguars but with a far wider spread of models), and the 3 Series (a small saloon pitched both at younger buyers and at older buyers who wanted to downsize).

Ford's plan was to turn Jaguar into a direct competitor for BMW, but the British marque had only one saloon range: the XJ, which competed with the BMW 7 Series. To be a credible competitor, it needed two more, to rival the 5 Series and the 3 Series. Ford did not want Jaguar to compete with the cheaper versions of the BMW ranges because those were too close to its own ranges; instead, it wanted to maintain Jaguar as a purely premium brand.

So the new S-type Jaguar was conceived as a competitor for the high-end models of the BMW 5 Series range. Two years later, there would be a Jaguar X-type that was to rival the high-end 3 Series. Neither was quite the same thing as the compact Jaguars of earlier times, whatever Jaguar publicity suggested. They were quite simply cars created to turn Jaguar into a credible competitor for the major European luxury makes – none of which stopped them from being rather interesting in their own right.

The S-types, X-types and their more modern successors will all deserve books of their own some day, but it is worth a brief look here at these spiritual successors to the compact Jaguars of the 1960s.

Never the most attractive of Jaguars, the 1998 S-type reached back into Jaguar's past for its name.

The 'new' S-type's cabin matched the wood-and-leather tradition of Jaguar saloons with swoopy shapes.

THE S-TYPE (1998–2008)

Work began on the new S-type Jaguar (or X200 project) in 1995, and there was a high degree of Ford input. The X200 was based on the Ford DEW platform, which was shared with the Lincoln LS from another of Ford's many divisions. There would be engine sharing, too. At launch in 1998, the top engine was the 4.0-litre Jaguar AJ-V8 type, which became the basis of engines for Ford, Lincoln, Aston Martin and (later) Land Rover models. Below this, the 2.5-litre petrol V6 was a Jaguar development of the Ford Duratec engine. When the market demanded a diesel engine, the S-type became available with a 2.7-litre twin-turbocharged V6 diesel developed by Ford in conjunction with PSA (Peugeot-Citroën) in France. This, too, would be used in a number of other models from the Ford empire.

The S-type shape was drawn up by Jaguar's chief stylist, Geoff Lawson, and was deliberately less curvaceous than the then-current XJ model although it retained some Jaguar family cues. Its almost deliberate brutality was claimed at the time to reflect the controversial shape of the 1960s S-type. However, it was not as great a success as Ford had probably hoped, and most commentators agree that its shape had a lot to do with that. Therefore, the car was given several facelifts, becoming an X202 model for the 2002 model-year, an X204 for 2004, and an X206 for 2006.

Determined to tackle BMW head-on, Jaguar released the S-type R model in 2002, a high-performance derivative developed as a direct competitor for BMW's M5 and the Mercedes-Benz E55 AMG. With its 400PS supercharged 4.2-litre AJ-V8 engine, the car could reach 60mph from rest in 5.3 seconds, although its top speed was electronically limited to 155mph (250km/h) because Jaguar respected the voluntary 250km/h maximum speed restriction established by German car makers.

■ THE LEGACY OF THE COMPACT JAGUARS

The S-type remained in production until 2008, and was immediately followed by a model called the XF. This had been designed under Ford ownership, although by the time it reached the showrooms Jaguar had been sold on to the Indian Tata Motors group. By this time, too, Jaguar was closely integrated with Land Rover – and Tata's subsequent stewardship of Jaguar Land Rover (as the company is now called) has been an exemplary success.

THE X-TYPE (2001–2009)

The 3 Series competitor arrived in 2001 as the X-type Jaguar. It became the first production Jaguar to have an estate variant, because it had to compete with the BMW and its C-Class equivalent from Mercedes-Benz. This time, there was even more design input from Ford. Although the car's shape was by design director Geoff Lawson, and picked

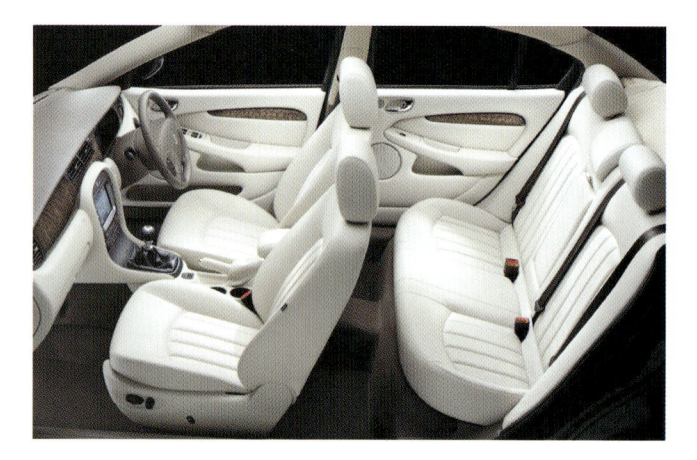

This was the four-wheel-drive layout of the X-type Jaguars, designed to give them an edge in the marketplace.

Wood and leather again added appeal to the cabin of the X-type models, as seen here.

The X-type shape drew heavily on the shape and style of the larger XJ saloons.

172

THE LEGACY OF THE COMPACT JAGUARS

With the XF, Ian Callum finally created a new 'design language' for Jaguar saloons.

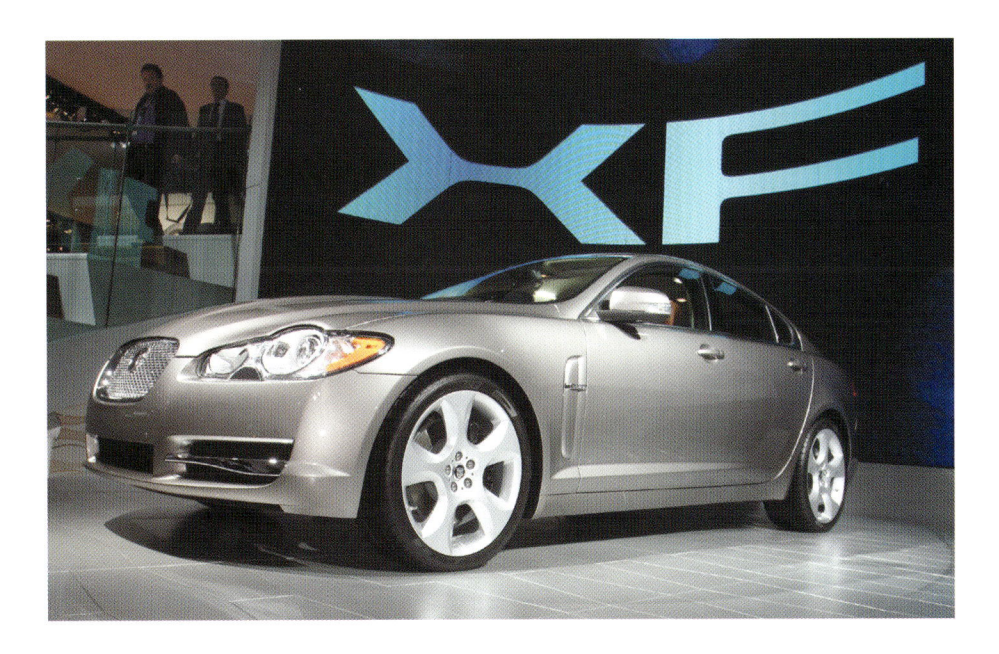

up familiar Jaguar design themes, the X-type was famously derided by his successor Ian Callum in the *Financial Times* for 28 January 2008 as having been 'essentially designed in Detroit and presented as close as a 'fait accompli' to reluctant designers and engineers at Jaguar'.

The new small Jaguar was developed as the X400 range and again drew on hardware from elsewhere in the Ford empire. It was based on a modified version of the Ford CD132 platform used in the Ford Mondeo and later (in further modified form, from 2006) for the Land Rover Freelander 2. This platform-sharing enabled the X-type and Freelander to be built at the same Halewood factory on Merseyside. Jaguar purists grumbled that the X-type was not built at the marque's traditional home, but the reality was that Browns Lane did not have enough space.

The first X-types had four-wheel drive as standard, which Jaguar thought would give their model an edge. In the beginning, there were 2.5-litre and 3.0-litre V6 petrol engines, and in 2002 a 2.1-litre derivative was added. These engines were Ford designs which had been extensively re-engineered for their Jaguar applications, and now carried the name of Jaguar AJ-V6. Among their unique features was variable valve timing.

The X-type range was developed through the addition of four-cylinder diesel models (with an engine derived from the Ford Mondeo's Duratorq type), plus entry-level models with front-wheel-drive only. Facelifted models became available in early 2008, although the range of engines was reduced, and X-type production finished towards the end of 2009.

Although more than 350,000 cars had been built – a figure that puts those for the compact Jaguars of the 1960s into the shade – the X-type had again not been the success its makers had wanted. At launch, the company had aimed for annual sales of 100,000, and although the X-type did become Jaguar's best-seller during its nine-year production run, it never exceeded around 50,000 sales a year. Sales in the vital US market slid badly after 2003, and it would be some time before Jaguar would try its hand again at the market still dominated by German manufacturers.

THE XF (2007–2015)

Although early models for the S-type's successor simply updated the earlier car, design director Ian Callum realised that the Jaguar marque really needed a totally new design language; it could no longer rely on the traditional saloon shapes originally created by William Lyons. With a high tail and rounded features, the design he developed has been described as a 'saloon within a coupé', a shape that looks like a coupé but provides the interior space of a saloon.

First revealed as the C-XF concept at the Detroit Motor Show in January 2007, project X250 entered production with little alteration as the XF later that year and was greeted with critical acclaim. The shape was new, but the engineering was still reliant on Ford designs. The XF used much of the old S-type's underpinnings, with the same suspension and

■ THE LEGACY OF THE COMPACT JAGUARS

mountings, and a broadly similar range of engines. At launch these were a V6 diesel, a 4.2-litre petrol V8 and a supercharged 4.2-litre petrol V8. However, new engines were not far off, and for 2009 the supercharged V8 was increased to 5.0 litres. At the same time came a new XF-R derivative to rival the BMW M5.

A facelift followed for the 2012 model-year, as did a 2.2-litre four-cylinder diesel option. For 2013, a Sportbrake estate was added to give the XF a competitor for the BMW 5 Series Touring and the Mercedes-Benz CLS Shooting Brake. Confirming the high-performance orientation of the XF, a supercharged 3.0-litre V6 engine arrived for 2013, along with an even more powerful supercharged V8 engine option that created the XFR-S, capable of 0–60mph in 4.4 seconds and a maximum speed of 186mph (300km/h).

As this book went to press, a replacement XF range, coded X260, was beginning to reach showrooms.

THE XE (2015 ON)

Project X760 took time to mature into the XE model, and became the first Jaguar to use the company's new modular aluminium architecture, a lightweight monocoque structure of its own conception that allowed it to abandon the Ford-derived platforms of previous models. As the aluminium architecture was shared with Land Rover, the new small Jaguar was built at that company's Solihull plant, which had become the centre of excellence for this type of construction within Jaguar Land Rover. It was yet another Jaguar that would not be built at the company's traditional home.

Although the move to aluminium construction was a key element of the XE's specification, Jaguar were determined to make the car as good as possible and so used steel for the boot floor and boot lid in order to get a perfect 50-50 front-to-rear weight distribution. Aluminium was also used for the major suspension components, with a double wishbone system at the front and a multi-link rear suspension (called Integral Link) mounted on a sub-frame.

Unlike its X-type predecessor, the XE was introduced as a rear-wheel-drive car, although Jaguar did not rule out four-wheel drive versions for later. The launch engines were headed by a 3.0-litre petrol V6, but there were also new 2.0-litre four-cylinder petrol and diesel types, developed by Jaguar Land Rover for use across both marques and known as Ingenium types.

EPILOGUE

It is often said that you can never go back – and Jaguar discovered that the hard way during the late 1990s and the first decade of the 21st century. Yet the latest small Jaguars, the XE and XF, successfully embody the spirit of the great compact saloons of the 1960s while taking Jaguar into a new and promising future. The wheel has in many ways come full circle as Jaguar now returns to the fray against brands that became successful by drawing inspiration from its products in the first place.

The new Jaguar shape matured further for 2015's XE model, which promises to give Jaguar a strong contender in a market once dominated by the company's compact saloons.

INDEX

1960 season changes 60
1961 season changes 61
1962 season changes 61
1963 season changes 62
1964 season changes, Mk 2 62
1964 season changes, S-type 122
1965 season changes, Mk 2 63
1965 season changes, S-type 122
1966 season changes, Mk 2 64
1966 season changes, S-type 124
1967 season changes, Mk 2 65
1967 season changes, S-type 124
1968 season changes, S-type 125
3.8-litre 340 89

AJ-V6 engine 173
AJ-V8 engine 171
Aston Martin DB2 24
automatic gearbox, 420 138
automatic Mk I 36

Baillie, Sir Gawaine 74
Bertone Jaguar FT 162
BMW 171
body structure, Mk I 25
body structure, S-type 113
bodyshell interchangeability, S-type 120
brakes, 420 138
brakes, Mk 2 52
brakes, Mk I 26
brakes, S-type 114
British Leyland 170
buying advice, 240 and 340 94
buying advice, 420 156
buying advice, Daimler Sovereign 156
buying advice, Daimler V8 models 107
buying advice, Mk 2 79
buying advice, Mk I 50
buying advice, S-type 134

Callum, Ian 173
Callum Mk 2 160
CKD see Overseas assembly
compact Jaguar, the need for 20
convertible 3.4-litre prototype 55
Coombs Mk 2 157
Coombs S-type 162
Coombs, John 73
County estate (Mk 2) 159
coupé proposal, 1956 34
cylinder block heater 126

Daimler V8 engine 95
Daimler, background 95
Daimler, origins of 2.5-litre V8 model 98
Defining the nature of the Mk I 22
Dewis, Norman 17

Egan, John 170
endurance racing, Mk 2s 74
engine, 3.8-litre 52
engine, 4.2-litre 137
engines, S-type 114
Equipe Endeavour 72
experimental XK engines 22

Ford 170
Frua coupé (S-type) 168

gearbox, 420 138
gearbox, Jaguar 64, 123
gearbox, Mk I 23

Halewood factory 173

identification, 240 and 340 93
identification, 420 154
identification, Daimler Sovereign 154

identification, Daimler V8 models 106
identification, Mk 2 77
identification, Mk I 47
identification, S-type 131
independent rear suspension, 109
Ingenium engine 174
Inspector Morse Mk 2 69
interior, 240 and 340 83
interior, 420 139
interior, Daimler Sovereign 140
interior, Daimler V8-250 101
interior, Mk 2 53
interior, Mk I 28
interior, S-type 115
introduction of 420 model 141
introduction of Mk 2 models 57
introduction of Mk I 2.4-litre 29
introduction of Mk I 3.4-litre 34

late 1940s, Jaguar in 15
Lawson, Geoff 171
Lyons, Sir William 170

mechanical changes for 240 and 340 83
mechanical changes for Mk 2 51
Mk V saloon 17
Mk VII introduction 18
Mk X, slow sales 135
modular aluminium architecture 174
Monza records Mk 2 75
motor sport, Mk 2 in 69
motor sport, Mk I in 43

narrow track, Mk I 27

optional extras, 240 and 340 85
optional extras, 420 146
optional extras, Daimler Sovereign 146
optional extras, Daimler V8 100

175

INDEX

optional extras, Mk 2 65
optional extras, Mk I 40
optional extras, S-type 125
origins of Jaguar 9
overseas assembly, 420 143, 166
overseas assembly, Mk 2 66
overseas assembly, Mk I 42
overseas assembly, S-type 121

paint and trim colours, 240 and 340 94
paint and trim colours, 420 156
paint and trim colours, Daimler V8 models 108
paint and trim colours, Daimler 56
paint and trim colours, Mk 2 80
paint and trim colours, Mk I 49
paint and trim colours, S-type 133
performance figures, 240 and 340 93
performance figures, 420 155
performance figures, Daimler Sovereign 155
performance figures, Daimler V8 models 106
performance figures, Mk 2 79
performance figures, Mk I 48
performance figures, S-type 132
police 240 and 340 90
police Mk 2 70
police Mk I 43
police S-type 127
power assisted steering 52
powertrain of Mk I 22
press views of the 2.4-litre Mk I 30
press views of the 240 and 340 87
press views of the 3.4-litre Mk I 37
press views of the 420 in USA 153
press views of the 420 146
press views of the Daimler Sovereign 149
press views of the Daimler V8s 105
press views of the Mk 2 57
press views of the S-type in USA 130
press views of the S-type 116
pricing, 240 and 340 84
privateer racing Mk Is 44
privateer rallying Mk Is 46

production changes, 240 and 340 85
production changes, 420 145
production changes, Daimler 2.5-litre V8 100
production changes, Daimler Sovereign 145
production changes, Daimler V8-250 103
production changes, Mk 2 59
production changes, Mk I 1955–1957 31
production changes, Mk I 1957–1959 38
production changes, S-type 122
production figures, 240 and 340 85
production figures, 420 146
production figures, Daimler Sovereign 146
production figures, Daimler V8 100
production figures, Mk 2 58
production figures, Mk I 41
production figures, S-type 121
production, end, 240 and 340 92
prototypes, Mk 2 55
prototypes, Mk I 28
prototypes, S-type 115

Radford 420 convertible 168
rallying Mk 2s 76
rivals, 240 and 340 89
rivals, 420 152
rivals, Daimler Sovereign 152
rivals, Daimler V8 models 105
rivals, Mk 2 65
rivals, Mk I 42
rivals, S-type 128

sales, 240 and 340 85
sales, 420 142
sales, Daimler 2.5-litre V8 99
sales, Daimler Sovereign 143
sales, Mk 2 58
sales, Mk I 41
Solihull plant 174
Sovereign name 140
specifications, 240 and 340 94

specifications, 420 155
specifications, Daimler Sovereign 155
specifications, Daimler V8 models 107
specifications, Mk 2 78
specifications, Mk I 48
specifications, S-type 132
Sportbrake 174
SS Jaguars 12
SS models, first 11
steering, 420 139
steering, Mk I 26
steering, S-type 114
styling, 240 and 340 82
styling, 420 135
styling, Daimler Sovereign 140
styling, Daimler V8-250 101
styling, Mk 2 52
styling, Mk I 23
styling, S-type 111
S-type 171
suspension, Mk I 26
suspension, S-type 114

Tata Motors 172
timeline 7
tuning kits, Mk I 32

USA, 340 in 92
USA, 420 in 153
USA, Mk 2 in 67
USA, MK I in 31, 34
USA, S-type in 128
Utah code name 22

wartime, Jaguar in 14
wide track axle 52
'works' Mk Is 43

X200 project 171
X260 range 174
X400 range 173
X760 174
XE 174
XF 174
XK engine development 16
XK120 17